My P
of Great Price

Autobiography – Books 2 and 3

Beyond Uganda

Stewart & Val

Best Wishes

from

Edie

Thornton 2007

Edie Garvie

My Pearl of Great Price: Autobiography – Books 2 and 3

Copyright © Edie Garvie 2007

ISBN: 978 1903607 79 4 (1903607 79 5)

Typeset and published by:

Able Publishing
13 Station Road
Knebworth
Hertfordshire SG3 6AP

Tel: 01438 812320 Fax: 01438 815232

Web: www.ablepublishing.co.uk
Email: books@ablepublishing.co.uk

Contents

Foreword

All who have read Book 1 of Edie Garvie's autobiography, with its marvellous account of how she was captivated by Uganda and the people she got to know there, will be looking forward to this sequel. Sadly the political turmoil in that country in the late 1960s and 1970s meant that Edie could not return to teach there, but she has turned that disappointment into the discovery of opportunities which might otherwise never have arisen.

Her work in the Education Department of Makerere College at the university in Kampala made it clear that she should study for a degree, but it is characteristic of her that she should choose a research degree rather than something more prosaic. Moreover, she chose to work for the degree and be employed in innovative teaching at the same time. Discussions in Bradford and Leeds were concerned with how to teach English as a second language to teenage children of Asian immigrants. This led to a detailed study of how language is learnt. There were two different schools of thought: was language learnt by imitation or by the application of rules? The second volume of Edie's autobiography describes the research and the battles she had in establishing the best way forward. Before long she became an authority in this field and was asked to contribute to many conferences.

Edie has quite clearly been an inspiring team leader, where the originality of her thought and her quick response to new situations was a great encouragement to her colleagues. Working in a subordinate position gave rise to some problems: it was difficult to keep to the straight and narrow and not to take time to follow intriguing side-lines. Often the job to which she had been appointed was in a new field and it was important to discover what was needed to be done. She made a good choice because it led on to important assignments in different parts of the world, where her capacity for making friends quickly and for going straight to the heart of a problem has been a great asset.

Edie has a very clear sense of vocation, which has been sustained by prayer. Her pearl of great price is a constant awareness of God's presence and power. Her autobiography is her spiritual journey and we are grateful that she has shared it with us.

Could someone with so much energy and drive retire? Not so: as she approaches her eightieth year, there are still challenges to be met. We are fortunate that Edie has found the time to record the story of her life in such a vivid way.

Ioan Thomas
November 2006

Preface

" ...the Kingdom of Heaven is like unto a merchant man seeking goodly pearls.
Who, when he had found one pearl of great price, went and sold all that he had, and bought it."

St Matthew 13:45 and 46

It is over three years since Book 1 of my story was published and longer than that of course since the project was visualised. As a Quaker, reflecting in the stillness beside my Quiet Time drawer (see Introduction to Book 1), the scenes of my life seemed to come up on screen. In sharing my stories with others, I was persuaded eventually to write, the more easily when I thought of donating any possible profits to an AIDS charity (see Appendix).

I decided to put Books 2 and 3 into one volume, and to make the whole about as long as Book 1. In this way I hoped to have the autobiography written before I became eighty and so could perhaps enjoy a bit of life after Book! Also, the message of my life-story had virtually been given in Book 1. It remained to demonstrate this through the many journeys and adventures which were to follow, that message of God's love and empowerment brought to me through the challenge of my life and work in Uganda, my spiritual home, and the richness of multiculturalism I found there. But it raised many troubling questions. Why was it, for instance, that about two thirds of the world could not be 'saved' and needed Christian missionaries to bring them to that state? Who appointed the British and other powers to show the 'right' way of living to these benighted souls? Did Christ, whose name is Love, come only to the West? I still seek and chase the Truth, but in a long life and now reflecting, it seems to me that my spiritual journey has brought me a little closer.

I have a concept which I call 'Universals and Particulars'. I believe that there are universal truths amongst the particular mores of all cultures, and that the more of the latter we encounter and try to understand, the nearer we get to the God of all Truth. I agree with Pope that *"the proper* study of mankind is man" (An essay on Man, Epistle 2, 1733) and that this is true in both a secular and a spiritual sense. Does this detract from my Britishness or my Christian faith? I don't think so. The conviction has brought me peace of mind and contributes to that pearl for which I gave up what might be considered much treasured 'furniture'. I was groping towards the notion in my early years as I tried to show in Book 1. I hope it becomes plainer in the present volume, when I move forward, taking the 'Uganda factor' with me.

I have called the present work, 'Beyond Uganda'. I nearly called it 'Furth of Uganda', the word 'furth' being very Scottish and requiring explanation, so it would have been unwise to put it in the title. It does mean 'beyond' in the physical sense, but there is also an element of rounding out. For me, the seminal Uganda experience (1960 - 1965) brought a special dimension of which I have remained conscious in all my subsequent travels. During my professional journey, I wrote a book for teachers of English called *Story as Vehicle*, where my aim was to show how language could be helped in its development by means of narrative. The story carries the learner along. In a sense, a life story does the same job, sometimes more covertly than overtly. I hope that mine is the vehicle for expressing my pearl of great price.

Another concept born in my teaching years is something I call 'Field and Focus'. It is introduced briefly in Chapter 12 of Book 1 and is properly launched and developed in the present volume where there is a diagram to illustrate it after the Preface. 'Field and Focus' is my understanding of the process of learning, carrying with it certain implications for teachers and for those who train them. As one teacher said, it is common sense written down, and for me it is a useful general blueprint to be interpreted in particular circumstances. I spent much of my professional life helping teachers and their trainers in many parts of the world to do just that. Again, I find an analogy in my life-story. Hence the reflection of the 'Field and Focus' diagram on the cover of this book. It should really have appeared on that of Book 1 also if I had thought about it earlier. The contents of that book, including my years in Uganda with all their significance, represent the initial 'field'. The time of study now described in Book 2 is the 'focus', and the ventures of Book 3 are the wider and more challenging 'field', at the end of which, as I enter into a kind of retirement, reflecting and researching for this book, I may be said to be 'focusing' again.

One of the problems of writing over time is that things which were true at the particular time of recording may not seem so to the reader coming to them later. I have probably touched on issues of this nature without realising it. It would be impossible to keep up with the changes in present-day instant and constant communication and new information. Even the use of certain words can cause problems; 'immigrant' and 'multicultural' for example, words which seem to be uncomplicated, but which, over the years, may have acquired new political overtones, and present a different picture to the reader from that intended by the writer. Another instance of the problem has to do with names of places, as in South Africa which has recently been going through a controversial time of name-changing. I can only hope that I have not caused any misunderstanding or offence.

On the whole my story is chronological, but sometimes, particularly in Book 3, a more thematic approach is used, as chapters give way to parts. It would obviously be better if the reader went first to Book 1, but 'Beyond Uganda' stands on its own, helped by the linking chapter 'Fast Forward' which tells of my return visit to Uganda at Christmas 2002. I was to find then, to my great joy, that my 'Uganda factor' was shared and was still very much alive. But I must leave the further writing to speak for itself. It attempts to be the vehicle for the deeper message, while at the same time it offers the general interest of adventure. It reaches into the present time and points to a possible future which I think I feel equipped to face, if I'm spared.

Edie Garvie
January 2007

Field and Focus

Philosophy of Learning	Analogy with life story
INITIAL FIELD Clues to 'pick up'	MY EARLY YEARS IN SCOTLAND AND UGANDA (Book 1)
FOCUS Clues confirmed Skills gained	YEARS OF STUDY AND RESEARCH (Book 2)
WIDENING FIELD Skills used in more challenging situations	WORLDWIDE WORK – VARIED AND STRETCHING (Book 3)

Initial Field

Focus

Widening Field

Book 2

Milestones of the 'Focusing' Period

1965 – 1970

"Where there is no vision the people perish…"
Proverbs 29 : 18

Contents

CHAPTER 1

Fast Forward

Uganda Revisited 2002

THE GRAND PEARL HOTEL, KAMPALA

"Forty years on I returned to meet my ex-students and their families and I stayed in this small hotel on Tank Hill. Charles Kabuga, Paul Mugumbwa and David Kiyaga Mulindwa received me into their fellowship as though the turbulent Uganda years between had never been. We had all travelled far in more ways than one, to many corners of the globe. And in *their* case, they had gone from the depths of national tragedy and depression to an ethos of recovery and hope, in spite of the AIDS scourge which is still rampant but now better contained. It was a long time since we had shared that something special at Shimoni Teacher Training College. The college still exists and still functions. It is known today affectionately and proudly as 'the mother of all colleges'.

Thank you to my 'boys' for their love and care of an old lady, steeped in nostalgia, and thank you for confirming the conviction, grown through the years, that the Uganda and especially the Shimoni 'factor' has influenced everything which followed for me and has still never left me. In the light of the message of this life-story, the name of the hotel where Charles arranged for me to stay is very significant. As we gathered and talked within its beautiful garden, we all had a feeling of having come home. My thanks not only to the 'boys' but to their wives and children. They have given me a further treasure-trove of memories. May God continue to bless them and their lovely country."

Thus I brought the first book of my autobiography to an end. Now as I turn to the middle years of my story, I feel that I should first unpack for the reader this brief account of my return to Uganda, as some may come to this volume without having read the first. It is my aim to emphasise still more the influence that the 'Uganda/Shimoni factor' had on my life, that factor which so strongly helped me to find my pearl of great price.

I had left Uganda in 1965, a colonial civil servant who had seen

5

the British protectorate give way to an independent country. I was going home for further qualification, intending to return, in spite of the growing political unease. I had heard the palms whispering "You'll be back", but it was not until the year 2002, a whole lifetime later, that this came about. And what a very different country it seemed to be. There were few Europeans and, since Amin's purge, hardly any Asians. The three-layered social structure of the protectorate days no longer existed and the scene was predominantly African. It would be all too easy to make judgmental comparisons, to speak of a wobbly infrastructure, of amenities not working, of appalling roads and horrendous traffic with its accompanying pollution, of the terrors of AIDS, the rumblings of rebel violence and the evidence of earlier wars still not dealt with. It would have been all too easy for me to bemoan the absence of familiar comforts and to remember with regret the 'false' setup of the 'raj' and its servants.

Instead, my over-arching impression was one of joy to be back. I revelled once more in the sights and sounds of African nature. I marvelled at the huge storks still flying above the city as though scorning humans in their traffic jams and urging flight to freedom. I revelled too in the creatures of the garden, the many coloured lizards and the song-birds, and the variety of insects, even the strange round fellow with large antennae and protruding eyes who tried to share my bed. I loved him even as I put him out. But above all I revelled in the gentle courtesy of the people I met, my students and their families, the hotel staff and my fellow guests, and those I met as I went out and about. My old Uganda came to life in a new context. How I agreed with Alphonse Karr who said in 1949 *"Plus ça change, plus c'est la même chose"* (the more things change, the more they remain the same). As my visit progressed, I became increasingly aware of people with resource, who had faith and hope. It seemed as though Churchill's 'pearl of Africa' was beginning to sparkle once more.

VERANDAH TALK

And I discovered to my delight that so was mine, within it. I had been given a cottage in the lovely garden of the hotel. The verandah of this cottage became a very special place. Here I met Charles, Paul and David who brought their wives and young ones to meet me. I learned more of the ways in which they personally had coped in the face of danger and great privation. Stories of family care and rescue, of frightening escapes in the night, of families growing up outside Uganda and then returning eventually as a new leader promised better things, covered a multitude of traumatic experiences for adults and children alike. I shared with them something of my years between and somehow for my 'boys' and myself those years fell away and we were back in the Shimoni of the 60s, reliving that amazing short time when Europeans, Asians and Africans seemed to realise their common humanity and the potential for a new kind of Uganda 'Jerusalem'. On that peaceful verandah I was conscious of a very wonderful thing. My pearl of great price was shared. It was then that I truly understood the significance of the name of the hotel which Charles had found for me, though he had not at that time known the title of my book.

My own story will be further unfolded in the rest of this volume. It behoves me however to say something more now of the life journeys of Charles, Paul and David. They were amongst the first generation of Africans to leave the 'village' and take advantage of the new opportunities that Uganda's independence offered. They were admitted to Shimoni, a training-college which had been exclusively Asian, where they trained as teachers and where we all met. The input added to the richness of the diverse community which Shimoni already was, even in its Asian separateness. All these African 'boys' qualified well and went on to teach and to become head teachers. David and Charles attended university later and took good degrees, David gaining a doctorate in archaeology and museum studies and eventually becoming a professor and Principal of a college, not bad for one whose father had seen him as a sweeper or porter! Charles was for a time a Senior Lecturer in the university after which he widened his interest in Adult Education and worked for the Co-operative movement, representing his country and then Africa at large, in international circles, with a base in Paris. Paul left education altogether and became a coffee-farmer, serving one of Uganda's most important industries. He too worked internationally and at this time of meeting was still doing so. He was much involved with China, trying to persuade them to drink more coffee, and preferably of course, Uganda coffee!

These were wonderful success stories, especially when set against the years of madness in the country and the efforts needed to protect their families. I had known something of all this as I had been able to keep in touch spasmodically by letter, and had even managed to meet David in Britain before the troubles, and Charles after. I had also learnt something first-hand of the Asian problems when many of my students fled to the UK at the time of Idi Amin. Sadly I had lost touch with most of them. What I had not fully understood was the cost in human terms to Africans and Asians alike, and the extent of opportunities lost in the battle to find alternative routes, as the gates of political upheaval clanged against them. In our verandah talk, a new depth of communication was reached, and on that same verandah, especially in the early morning, I had my own times of reflection and prayer. I remembered the many questions I had asked in those far off colonial days. I asked more now. Whose fault was it that Uganda had descended into anarchy and disaster? And where lay the credit for a fair degree of recovery?

TWO IMPORTANT CONCEPTS

For me, one of the greatest achievements of my 'boys' and no doubt of many other Africans, is their ability to live in parallel worlds. I spoke of this in Book 1 when I described my visit to Charles' home in Kigezi. I was impressed by the ease with which he had slipped from the culture of European education to the world of his tradition, giving them equal place with the additional transition in his case, from Asian culture, as he was lodging at that time in the home of Shimoni College's Asian Principal. As human beings we are all capable of this kind of role-play and frequently indulge in it. Some are better at it than others. But in Africa somehow, probably because of the speed and suddenness historically speaking with which cultures met, the ability in the individual to cope and maintain an integrated personality seems more marked. This was a learning situation for me in the 60s, and now on my return to Uganda I learned more. I learned that the home village was still very important. The 'village' is much more than a place. Geographically it does exist, somewhere in the hinterland. For Charles, for instance, it is in the far southwest of the country near the Congo border. Its beautiful remoteness haunts me still. From his fine large house in Kampala, Charles and his immediate family return frequently to their roots. In the garden of this house I sat with Charles under his favour-ite mango tree and heard more of the 'village' as I looked through the cherished family albums in one of which there was a photograph of myself when I visited. I was amused to hear the story of some naughty village children who had been in the habit of scrumping plantains from Charles' shamba (plantation), and that they ceased to do so after I had been there, 'in case the white woman would get them'!

The word 'village' it seems to me, embodies in a new and intensified way all that the family stands for, family in all its extensions and ramifications, drawing forth from its members a deep sense of love, duty and loyalty. Charles could speak in the same breath of his going to the 'village' to kill a cow for the family feast and to his 'dining with kings', to return to the point about living in more than one culture. He had been invited during his international work to meet Prince Charles and there is a photograph of this meeting on the wall of his living-room in Kampala. Maintaining the balance was not always easy. Difficult choices had sometimes to be made, prestigious and lucrative positions perhaps given up if family needs seemed greater, as when towards the end of his career Charles left his apartment in Paris to return home and work from there. At least he was given the necessary office equipment.

I pondered these matters as I reflected on my verandah. What was it that was supporting the best of the old amongst the new? What was helping the birth of an insurgent drive to improve the environment, exemplified by Paul planting trees on his land? Why was David so excited by a notion he referred to as 'IK' (indigenous knowledge)? He was spreading this amongst his students. 'IK', like 'village', expresses an important idea. There was a new awareness that matters of traditional Ugandan lore were of value today and should never have been lost in the days of European conquest. Much had been gained and learnt in protectorate times, but a lot of this had been known already at a deeper level. Was it a bit like the discovery of many Christian missionaries who found that Christ had got there before them? There seems to be something here of what I see as universals and particulars, a huge topic which David and I would have liked more time to explore. It needs thinking about. Both of these concepts do. The 'village' and 'IK' have much to offer to the world whatever the race or country. Now that the internet, with its bland communication, is rapidly homogenising diversity, we need to find ways of maintaining the richness of this diversity. And now that the demands of modern living are depleting the world's natural resources, we need to replant within the context of our native lands.

SPIRITUALITY

Thére was something spiritual here, I felt, as though God were pointing the way, and there seemed to be a strong spiritual element in the lives of most Ugandans. Even the taxi drivers carried a copy of the Bible or the Koran in the cab. They were happy to talk of their beliefs as they drove, though how they could take their minds off the traffic around them I just don't know. They very much needed their faith! Sunday in Kampala was a remarkable time. Everywhere there was the sound of prayer and singing of hymns, broadcast to the world at large with the help of modern-day means of amplification. Although now a Quaker, I went to church on each Sunday of my stay, carried in the cars of my 'boys' and reflecting joyfully on the days when I carried them there in mine. But to be in Kampala at Christmas was a special bonus. Over the three services on Christmas Sunday in the All Saints cathedral, there were eight thousand worshippers. Can I ever forget how I felt when the drums introduced the African carols? This was a poignant time for me as I thought back to All Saints as it used to be in the protectorate days, an expatriate Anglican church, sparsely attended by Europeans and a sprinkling of Africans. There is a sense in which the changes here seemed to symbolise the changes generally. I was made more aware of the hope that was in the land and some of the questions posed above seemed to be answered.

The 'boys' had learnt that I was a retired Reader (lay-preacher) in the church and I was asked to preach as I still am in England occasionally. I did so now in two churches, and both times I based my sermon on 1st Corinthians 13, the well known chapter on faith, hope and love. It seemed appropriate. One of these churches was in Katwe, a poor area of the city where Paul and his family had lived out the difficult years of war, and where the needs of the people had prompted them to help establish a church and centre of the community. I felt very honoured to be asked to take part in a service. The words of my sermon had to be interpreted. This happened in more ways than one. First Paul repeated in Luganda what I said in English and then the choir sang my message in true African manner with spontaneous question and answer. As the choir members danced their way back to their seats, the congregation applauded and I continued with my sermon. It was a wonderful experience, culminating in my being asked to shake hands with everyone at the door, and repeating the Luganda blessing which Paul whispered into my ear.

But the sense of spirituality was not something confined to Sunday and church as I had noticed with the taxi drivers. It seemed to be never far from the surface in all matters of everyday; for instance at the end of an evening of talk on the verandah, when there were moves towards departure, someone would offer a prayer of thanks for the richness of the fellowship. I was impressed that it was very often one of the young ones who did so, quite spontaneously and without embarrassment. And there was always grace before meals. It was assumed that I was in tune with all this and I was quietly included. Even the hotel staff spoke often and easily of God and how important their beliefs were to them. The other church I preached in was attended by Edith, my namesake, the waitress who had been particularly assigned to care for me.

In this context of spirituality, I was struck one day by the motto on a Barclay's Bank T-shirt I saw a lad wearing. It said "Making it possible", referring of course to the business of the bank, but could it be, I wondered, that this power of the Spirit which I sensed so strongly, was the real force which was making the country's recovery possible?

PLACES OLD AND NEW

I did not stray too far from base during my visit. I think my 'boys' would have been a little worried if I had gone wandering off into the hinterland as I had done so easily in my young days. But I was able to return to several of my old haunts within Kampala and its environs and to visit one or two new places. The former brought a mixture of renewed joy with some sadness and nostalgia, the latter interest and stimulation but also a few thoughtful questions. Charles took me to Shimoni College. Amongst the somewhat dilapidated buildings I was greeted by an elderly maintenance man who, to my astonishment, remembered my name after forty years. This was a high-light, both the years and the dereliction falling away and taking me back to the heyday of my thirties when I was full of life and energy. I went also by taxi, accompanied by Edith from the hotel, to the university, Makerere College on its hill above the city. I had moved there from Shimoni when the Faculty of Education needed someone with primary teacher-training experience. Now I saw an institution bulging at the seams, badly in need of a huge investment of money. The over-subscribed lectures found overflows of students in the corridors, and as one student put it to me, the only books they could get hold of were those brought in by their teachers. The library could not afford to acquire any. But there was still the ethos of a beautiful campus, one of the loveliest I have seen anywhere in the world. The taxi took me on to Mulago Hospital and I glimpsed the building where I had run my little school for the children with polio. Sadly George Sebagala had passed away. He was the young man who had progressed from an iron lung to a wheelchair. He had eventually helped me in the school.

On another occasion, Paul took me to Mengo where I visited the Kabaka's palace and seat of government, the Lukiko. The Kabaka, traditional monarch of the Baganda, has had a rough ride over the years. The present one has been allowed to come back, and his palace was being made ready for him when I was there. I was given special permission to see round it. What impressed me most was the place near the gates where the 'eternal flame' has been lit. Long may it stay alight. On that same outing I visited a beacon of a different kind, again on a hill overlooking the city, the famous Namirembe Cathedral. This large Protestant establishment, along with Rubaga, its Catholic equivalent, is steeped in Uganda's story, much of it fierce and gory. I paused thoughtfully at the graves of the martyrs and also at the little thatched building housing the drums which used to call the people to worship. It is still preserved, another poignant part of history.

Still with churches, I have referred already to All Saints, the former expatriate church, now a cathedral. I had visited it and had met the vicar, the lovely Canon Monica, before I went to worship there and I was amazed to see how it had been changed and extended. Another old haunt was the National Theatre which had been something of a second home to me, on both sides of the footlights. It seemed smaller and darker and now stood amid a vortex of stalls and trading, the noisy, busy and somewhat grubby centre of downtown Kampala. I had known it as the newly-opened place of culture, pristine white amongst the greenery, and very European and colonial! To my delight it was still a place of culture. I watched a musical act rehearsing.

For places new, I went to see the imposing Sheraton Hotel, all very glitzy and modern. It had its own money exchange and I found this useful. What I did not enjoy was the non-stop and ubiquitous American television with all its frenzy concerning the impending Iraqi war. It was interesting that the Africans seemed not to be all that excited. I had noticed that even in church Iraq was not mentioned specifically in the intercessory prayers. Africans have their own '9/11s' which change *their* world. I felt that things were put in perspective for me.

Another new place, only recently opened, was the shopping-mall, built on part of the old golf course and right opposite Shimoni. For many, the escalators were a novelty, the young folks riding up and down with great glee. I thought back to the time when there was one small supermarket in Kampala Road. In this new mall I was taken by Paul and his family to a pleasant Indian restaurant. This was after the church service where I had preached and I remember that the discussion at table, whilst ranging over many things, analysed the sermon and really kept me on my toes. In a French bistro-type restaurant in another part of town I enjoyed a meal with Charles and his family, and here I was put on the spot on a different subject. "What kind of student *was* my Dad?" asked Kamara, one of Charles' sons. Fortunately I could say quite truthfully that he was a 'born' teacher. The entire group enjoyed the story of his teaching a class of Asian children a French song. David and his wife took me to yet another Asian restaurant, again a new establishment, very tasteful and culturally evocative. I shall never forget this lavish hospitality both in homes and outside eateries. The fellowship of the verandah was deepened and extended to other family members and friends. We became true companions in reminiscence and there was much fun and laughter.

THE BOXING DAY PARTY

How could I show my gratitude? I decided to give my three special families a little party in the garden of The Grand Pearl. The hotel staff cooperated magnificently and organised a barbecue. The event put to rest a certain fear which had been present from the time of my decision to visit. We all had our memories of a very special time when we shared the 'Shangri-la' of the Shimoni years. Would we be able to stand the dissolving of an idyll, the knocking-down of icons? I suppose this danger exists in all 'going back', but here in Uganda which had emerged from such a crucible of horror and disaster, the danger was writ large. To our great relief, we found that the regrets were not insurmountable, the reflections on how things had changed not too painful. We began to realise that the business of getting old, the awareness of which is always enhanced by meeting companions of younger days, did not necessarily invite morbid preoccupation. During this happy party we laughed a great deal as we recalled and reenacted old ventures.

It was David, I think, who brought the Central Youth Club back to life.

This had been a multiracial project in which Asian, African and European young people had enjoyed fellowship together. We had met in the hall at All Saints. My students from Shimoni and later Makerere had helped me to run the club, David being one of the first African members before becoming a student at Shimoni. He reminded us of the closing evening ceremony when we had all stood in a circle and had sung the Girl Guide song:

"Make new friends, but keep the old.
One is silver, the other gold."

While we sang we had our hands crossed as for 'Auld Lang Syne'. Any new members stood in the middle of the circle and as the song progressed, the linked hands would open and admit the newcomers. We sang this song now and the symbolic magic of forty years ago was still there. For me, the 'boys' were my old friends, their friends and acquaintances the new. It seemed fitting that Canon Monica should close the proceedings with prayer, reflecting that of Margaret, Charles' wife who had said, very fervently, "God is good". The hotel staff who were serving us and who had served me so splendidly during the whole of my stay, began to understand, I believe, why

Charles, Paul and David reminisce

this strange 'mzungu mzee' (Swahili for 'old European') had returned. I had made new friends, including them, but I had kept the old and everything seemed to be coming together. The 'Uganda/Shimoni factor' had remained and seemed to be felt, inherited perhaps, by the young ones, as they realised who that strange white woman was in the family album!

Last Minute Thoughts

As I sat on my verandah on my last morning and was greeted as always by the gardener asking "How was the night?" I thought of Uganda's long night of trouble and how the darkness seemed to be clearing to a new dawn. I remembered the many times during my visit when the electricity had failed and how dark it had suddenly become again until a member of the hotel staff had appeared with his torch to reach the generator and flick the switch, whereupon all was light. There were, and would continue to be, moments of darkness once more in Uganda but I left with the feeling that this resourceful people with their faith, hope and love, were able to flick the switch of the generator to give them light. The reunion had made me aware of the durability of what really matters.

Make new friends but keep the old

CHAPTER 2

Homeward Bound

Exciting Prospects

TOWARDS MOMBASA

I had left Uganda in June 1965. My little cat had flown out a few weeks earlier, to go to a place in Sussex which specialised in looking after animals from the Tropics, and the rest of my belongings in ten crates had been shipped to Southampton, a further crate containing last-minute presents in another ship which would dock in the Clyde. I myself was to travel once again with the Union Castle line. I had a cabin booked on the *Braemar Castle* which would take me from Mombassa to Durban, and another on the *Pretoria Castle* plying from Cape Town to Southampton. For the bit between Durban and Cape Town, I would be on a coach, travelling the famous Garden Route of South Africa. I would reach Britain mid-August, having virtually circumnavigated Africa, as my voyage out nearly five years previously had taken me by the Mediterranean, approaching Mombasa from the north. These six weeks would be my holiday, a wonderful opportunity to relax. It began as soon as the train left Kampala, with the farewells of my friends ringing in my ears and the music and excitements of *Belinda Fair*, the musical I had directed just before I left, swirling round in my head. In the train I sank in an exhausted heap, only coming to in order to greet people en route, folks who had known of my journey and who had come to a station to wave or chat at the window. In Nairobi there was even time for me to get off the train and join a friend for a cup of tea.

MOMBASA

So I progressed to Mombasa, the port of departure where the *Braemar Castle* was already berthed. The work of unloading and reloading cargo was in full swing but the time of leaving would be delayed, I learned, and I would have ten days here instead of the expected week. After a restful two and a half days on the train, I was really able to enjoy this hiatus, savouring and digesting the events of the past weeks, while at the same time I enjoyed exploring Mombasa, its Moorish remains, its beautiful coast and its night-life, in the company of friends old and new, some of whom would be travelling on with me. An old friend I met here was Savita, an excellent Makerere student whose home this was. It was while I was here too that I had a reassuring letter from the quarantine home in Sussex to say that Puss had arrived safely and all was well.

A new friend was Ted. He worked for the Harbours Department and was based in Mombasa. He was an excellent guide on all its aspects, and great fun to be with. Together we wandered through the old town, explored Fort Jesus and the sad remains of the place where slaves were held prior to embarking on the 'middle passage'. The site brought sombre reflection. On a happier note we enjoyed the lovely beaches, lingered in cafes and joined the after-dark revellers. Ted was a fount of knowledge on the 'in' night-spots.

It was a glorious time of unwinding for me except that I caught a most virulent cold, as a result of sitting too long and too late in the roof-garden of the Hotel Splendid where I was staying. I spent quite a lot of time on the roof, fascinated by the activities on the neighbouring roofs, such as women hanging out their washing and children playing round the plant pots. At the appointed hour, five times a day, the muezzin sounded from the nearby mosque. Sights and sounds became an ever-changing kaleidoscope. But I paid for this malingering and was quite fevered for a couple of days. Perhaps being so tired had also something to do with it and maybe the cold was 'sent' so that I would be forced to slow down. Ted and the hotel manager looked after me and nursed me back to health. I was packed off to bed with a pile of 'who-dunnits' to keep me company while the hotel staff kept tempting my appetite with tasty titbits. As the cold took its course I made a new friend in this caring manager. He was German with lots of languages at his command. He tried to persuade me to go to Germany rather then Britain, assuring me that he could find me work in the hotel trade!

Still sniffing and suffering with sinus trouble, I had to go aboard the ship which was now ready to sail. I discovered that Ted would be coming too! He had some work to do in Durban and then would be returning to Mombasa. By some mysterious magic wrought by him I found myself in a very fine outer cabin on the main deck, far more luxurious than the one appointed for me. Though this ship did not have first and tourist classes, it did have a kind of hierarchy of accommodation. Like the *Kenya Castle* which had taken me to Africa it was known as a cabin-class ship. On this latter I had been in a very lowly cabin somewhere in the bowels of the vessel. Now I had one of the top cabins, with all the appointments and service that went with it. I rejoiced in my temporary greatness which brought much teasing from my friends, especially Tinker Bell of my Kampala theatre company and the McMullen family, Jim and Marjory and their two children. Jim was a high-ranking officer in the Uganda police and Marjory had been a colleague in educational circles. At the end of the day we would part, I going off to my 'palace' and they returning to the 'slums'. We managed not to have a class war!

Towards Durban

How different this experience was for me from the voyage out in 1960! Then, as I faced the unknown and exciting future, I had looked to my fellow travellers, the hardened colonialists, for guidance and support. Now I was one of them. It seemed that most of the present passengers were old hands, either going home temporarily, as I thought I was at that time, or leaving for good. There was a general feeling of 'end-of-term'. The atmosphere was one of collective relief, the usual ship-board 'letting go', where what is done is finished and what is to come has to wait. At the same time for many of us from Uganda, I believe there was a special kind of apprehension. We had left the three-year-old independent Uganda with its growing political and security problems. Those of us who would be returning had mixed feelings about doing so. Just what would we be going back to? Also with those not returning we shared the expatriate fear of leaving the 'cocoon'. With all its difficulties Uganda had still been this, a kind of shelter from the 'real world' of the West. Soon we would be back there with all its paranoia and media frenzy. How would we cope? And for me personally, how was I to react to being an undergraduate when for nearly two years I had *taught* in the university and been a member of the senior common room? There *were* moments of panic. Had I done the wrong thing? Should I have listened to those who said I had 'got there' without the degree? As things were to transpire, I believe the degree *was* meant to happen, as I hope to show in this story. Suffice it for now to say that at that time I had my own particular sense of insecurity, as no doubt did many others on the ship, all of which added up to a general mood of quietness, almost jadedness at times. In the suspension of reality, the days at sea were peaceful and lacked the action-packed programme of my outward voyage. The nights under the stars lent themselves to lounging but also to a little dancing and socialising, sometimes into the small hours.

DAR-ES-SALAAM

The journey from Mombasa to Durban took a week, during which the hour and the weather changed as we left the equatorial zone. Our first port of call was Dar-es-Salaam, the capital of Tanzania. It was then one of the prettiest harbours in the world, particularly after dark when the lights extended north and south round the curving shore-line like the jewels of a necklace. We were able to enjoy this scene from both ship and land as, once again, work on the cargo meant a delayed departure. It was fun exploring yet another African city. I had been once before and had managed to visit the home of one of my Edinburgh pupils, Roshan Daya. Her father was an Indian doctor and her mother a bonny red-haired lass from Glasgow. I had been made very welcome in their home and was taken for what turned out to be a candle-lit dinner, as the city lights had failed, a frequent occurrence it seemed.

My special memory of the present occasion had a more sinister note. We were berthed near a Chinese ship, and our Chief Officer, at whose table I sat, informed us that this ship was probably up to no good. It was the height of the cold war which was fought on many battlefields, including Africa. He suspected that the port of Dar-es-Salaam was the hub of the arms trade and the centre of a spy ring. It was just possible from our top-deck to see over the stockade which the Chinese had built on their ship. I recall an altercation, the import of which was quite clear even if the words were not, as a few cameras on our ship clicked. We were assured of the presence of a British submarine which lived permanently in the harbour 'in case of emergency'.

As the *Braemar Castle* ploughed on towards Beira in Mozambique, life continued in its somnolent pattern. There were few official times of fun and games though certain sports were available. We all seemed to succumb to a glorious lethargy, reading, sleeping and, cat-like, emerging at intervals to eat! I did, however, manage to make some of my reading focus on the linguistic studies that lay ahead at York. I thought it was a strange way to be launched on my university life, curled up in a deck-chair with the shipboard noises for accompaniment and the waves for most of the time gently rocking. I slipped in and out of high-powered academia and peaceful doze and daydream. In fact it was a wonderful introduction to the next stage in my career as it gave me time and space to think before the 'focusing' was upon me.

BEIRA

At Beira we moored off-shore. The weather was much cooler as we had entered an area where winter of a kind was experienced. A few of us went by small boat to see something of the place, very Portuguese and European. I was reminded of holidays on 'the continent' in my earlier days. We roamed in the city centre and had coffee at a pavement cafe amongst the modern high-rise buildings. I recognised sadly that I had said goodbye to 'my' Africa, though it would be another couple of weeks or so before in Cape Town I actually left the African continent.

And so on to Durban which for me and the McMullen family would be where we left this ship and continued our journey by road to Cape Town. We had arranged a coach trip which was to leave Durban in three days' time. We took just enough luggage for the South African sojourn, the rest being left on the ship, to be conveyed to the *Pretoria Castle* in Cape Town.

DURBAN

In Durban I thought I had gone back fifty years or more. It was so Edwardian British in a strange kind of way, with its white uniformed nannies pushing babies in large perambulators along tree-lined roads in leafy suburbs. Shop names familiar in Britain in former days graced the city centre stores where I shopped in leisurely fashion. This was South African winter and I needed warmer clothes. I also needed some respectable footwear. In the white society of Durban I could no longer slop about in open sandals, and no stockings. I had been met and welcomed in Durban by friends of my Makerere colleague, Verona Harries, and I stayed in their home. They willingly acted as guides to the city and its many beauty spots, its shops and other amenities. They also introduced me, whether or not they realised it, to the prevailing Zeitgeist, as I heard the radio and absorbed the gist of conversation. This was the land of apartheid or separate development which I had known of in theory. Here in Durban its impact in the three days I spent in the city came as a bewildering shock.

I had to read the numerous signs for help. Was I using the correct door for whites, sitting on the proper bench? Was I in the section of the bus reserved for my superior race? Had there ever been such a wicked, nonsensical system? It hit me at every turn. The police and the bus drivers were white, I noticed. Could black people not be trusted to look after matters of law or drive white people around? What exactly did the black people do? I could not believe my ears when I heard one white woman refer to her servant as her 'slave'. Even some of my new white South African friends were horrified by this.

My enjoyment of a wonderful performance of *Carmen* in one of the theatres was completely marred when I realised the political scenario. The actors were from Cape Town. They were coloured, the technical term in this regime for people of mixed race. The totally white audience gave them a standing ovation which was richly deserved, and then left the theatre by their own door. They could not talk to the players or sit next to them on the bus. And I temporarily was part of this white group. Just how would I be able to last the rest of my stay in the country without exploding? And then I thought, there was a colour bar in Uganda too, exemplified in the layered society. We were not so innocent of prejudice as we might like to think. But at least it was not institutionalised and we never had to make technicians from Japan 'honorary whites' as happened in South Africa.

My experience in these ten days here made me stop in my tracks. I was meeting racism and the colour bar in an extreme form, ensconced in the regime of the country. I was shocked and repulsed that anything so vile could be an accepted way of life. But I was to discover more and more that racism was very much rife throughout the world. It just wasn't official. What had been my experience in Uganda? I remembered the joy I had had in the racial diversity of my students and the young people in my youth club and how all this had contributed to 'my pearl of great price'. But I remembered also that not all of my compatriots had shared my view. Little did I realise that my joy in inter-racial contacts would continue to influence me in years to come, even as I encountered prejudice in many countries, including the UK.

Towards Cape Town

The coach trip to Cape Town was a memorable experience both socially and scenically. Our small party, which could have been the participants in an Agatha Christie novel, included a high-ranking British diplomat and an American couple who were spending their late middle age, and no doubt considerable wealth, constantly travelling. The McMullens and I had as much enjoyment analysing the relationships and behaviour of our fellow passengers as we had from the world about us, varied and beautiful even in the less colourful winter. From the foothills of the Drakensbergs, where we really knew winter and needed hot water bottles in our beds, to the wide golden beaches of the southern coast, there was a wealth of new scenic experience every few minutes. We even visited a primeval forest.

There were two or three stopping-places. We stayed in 'good' hotels, again Edwardian and 'solid' where the laundry list included combinations, a garment I had worn in my childhood. We went on excursions including a visit to a homeland, a so-called independent state to which black people had been 'sent back' so that they could 'rule themselves' and cater for their own needs, though of course being 'helped' by the magnanimous South African government. We were shown the spotlessly clean and beautifully thatched round houses as an example of this. Methought the guide protested too much! In Pietermaritzberg we went to a shop run by a witch doctor. There he stood behind the counter, measuring out the potions of his native medicines and dressed in all his finery complete with vast feathered head-dress. My mind went back to Uganda. A conference had been planned to take place about then. This was to be a medical convention of witch-doctors and western medics, something I should have loved to attend. I never did hear the outcome but I am sure that much would be learnt on both sides.

CAPE TOWN

My prevailing memory on reaching Cape Town was the cold. I was told that winter was so short it was not worth installing central heating; just as in Britain at that time the summers were short and it was not worth putting in air conditioning. For my three days here I stayed in a hotel on a corner site. It seemed to me that the wind blew from all directions. To find some warmth as I fondly hoped, I went to a cinema and sat through the programme in chilled misery. There was no heating there either. But my soul was warmed considerably by my meeting with Mary Miller, a friend from my Edinburgh church days. She was coming to South Africa on a visit to her brother who lived in Johannesburg.

I was at the docks to meet her ship, the *Windsor Castle*, which was the largest vessel of the line. I hovered by the 'M' stance for luggage and it seemed as though I was frozen to the spot. I had gone into a kind of trance while the arrival noises flowed over me and the whirl of activity surrounded my lonely figure. Suddenly I heard a shriek - "*Edith*" - my Sunday name that few people called me any more, and I jumped into life. There was Mary, waving madly over a dozen heads. She would have to be 'cleared'. When the official wasn't looking we somehow managed between us to find 'Miller' and to put her papers on the top. In no time we picked up the luggage, found a taxi and were off. We had one day together. Mary's *Blue Train* for Johannesburg left in the evening.

This was a strange but joyful twelve hours, mainly cafe crawling. How well I remember the wind and the crashing waves as we struggled arm-in-arm along the promenade at Seapoint! Our tongues never stopped and the outer cold, for me at least, was forgotten in the inner warmth of our reunion and friendship. We were singing again in the choir of Edinburgh's College Church. What joy there can be in memory shared! The day was a mixture of fighting the elements and sitting at numerous tables, cold still but at least out of the wind, while we talked endlessly of our Scottish background.

All too soon Mary had to be at the station. I saw her off and walked back to my hotel, suddenly bereft. My spirits were not raised by my encounter with a coloured girl who asked me the way to Seapoint. So often in my life I have been asked the way when I myself was a stranger and unable to help. On this occasion I *could* assist. I even knew what bus to take and I saw the girl on to it. She was obviously in great distress, muttering something about having lost her pass and being late. I was conscious of some funny looks from white people who passed as I talked to the girl. So preoccupied had I been with my Edinburgh memories, I had forgotten I was still in apartheid country and that this girl was one of its victims. She had approached me in desperation, assuming that I was South African white, something that was totally against the law. My instinctive and I hope kindly help had astonished her and disgusted the whites around us. I took great pleasure in seeing her safely on to the bus and waving in friendly fashion as the vehicle went off. I was a lonely island in a sea of apartheid and I shuddered once again at yet another example of the depths to which humanity can sink.

I had three days in Cape Town, one of which had gone. My memories of the place at this time are strangely vague, as though muted by my growing horror of the regime. I was conscious of the 'Dutchness' of the place and of the beauty of the coastline and botanic gardens. And of course I could not fail to be aware of Table Mountain as an impressive backdrop. Its flat top was wreathed in haze all the time I was there and although the weather generally had warmed up a bit and I tried several times to climb the mountain, its top remained grey and misty. As if to cock a snook at me, it only became clear, revealing its rearing facade out of a cloudless blue sky, as I sailed away.

The next firm memory is of standing on the deck of the *Pretoria Castle* as we drew out from the wharf amid the clamour of farewell songs and the casting of streamers. At that time Cape Town was an important taking-off point for southern Africa and beyond. On this occasion there were many coloured people leaving for work on the American base of Ascension Island. Bands played and the crowds sang and shouted. Though not part of this community I felt somehow that the tumult of parting was also for me. I was saying my own particular goodbye, a realisation that it was a departure not only from Africa but from a very special period of my life. The 'initial field' had ended and I was going home to 'focus' so that the 'field' could be widened (see illustration after Preface), though I would not have expressed it that way then. I was, nevertheless, conscious of a significant milestone. I was touched when I found a huge bouquet of flowers in my cabin, sent by friends who had moved from Kampala to Johannesburg. They had been very sensitive to how I would be feeling. Sadly I was not able to enjoy the flowers as they deserved, as no vase could stand up against the storm we were now to face.

TOWARDS SOUTHAMPTON

Our luggage had been transferred from the *Braemar Castle* as arranged. The McMullens and I were now reunited with other Uganda friends who had stayed with that ship to Cape Town. The *Pretoria Castle* was the flagship of the line and our dapper little captain rejoiced in the rank of Commodore and wore a monocle as badge of office! The ship had very clear divisions of first class and tourist, and for some reason I was in tourist and all my friends, including the McMullens, were in first, a complete reversal of the situation on the *Braemar Castle*. More friendly banter and

24

teasing as it was my turn to descend to the slums! But for the first two or three days of this voyage we had other things to think about. We met the 'Cape Rollers' with a vengeance. It was the mother of all storms, caused we were told by gales known as the 'roaring forties', around Tristan da Cunha. By this time I had had enough seafaring experience to recognise the metal clips known as fiddles, which appeared, to keep the table-cloths in place. These plus the warnings and advice from the captain in his broadcasts, told of the impending storm. In fact the ship was rocking ominously before we had left harbour. We were advised not to wander about but to lie down as much as possible with extra pillows to hold us firmly in our bunks. The ship both pitched and tossed, not a very pleasant feeling, and there were times when one wondered if she would ever come upright again. There was one mealtime when I was the only passenger in the dining room! My sea-legs upheld me, as they had done so many times, and I found it all very exciting and exhilarating. But life aboard in general, for about forty-eight hours, was a nightmare of swaying and crashing. Furniture scudded from one end of a lounge to the other, dishes and glasses in the bars fell from their hooks and tables and the deserted decks were awash with enormous waves. There was no social life when the Cape Rollers came to visit.

Some people did manage to struggle to one of the lounges and to have a cup of tea mid-afternoon. I also enjoyed the sandwiches and cakes! It was during the first of these tea-times that an elderly lady fell and broke her femur. In taking her hand off the rail in a passage in order to grab the next rail on a stairway, she had slipped as the ship lurched. There followed what must have been some big decision-making and planning of procedure. We were not far out from Cape Town and it was deemed wise to turn the ship and go back into the harbour so that the lady could have her operation in a shore hospital. It must have called for skilled seamanship to do this turn in these storm conditions and then to manage the transfer of the patient to the small pinnace which brought a doctor from Cape Town. In the middle of the night I watched the poor lady, no doubt heavily sedated, being secured into a life-boat and the boat then lowered as gently as possible. The ship's doctor went with his patient and the two small boats met. The doctors exchanged words and papers after the tricky transfer of the stretcher was completed, and the pinnace disappeared into the night, while our doctor came back to the ship. We turned and headed out once again, this time with stabilisers removed in order to make up time. So we suffered the full rage of the storm a second time, only worse. The happy outcome was, as we learned in Southampton, that the lady's operation had gone well and she had been returned to her relatives in South Africa.

Gradually the storm abated and the places in the dining room filled up. A German couple at my table never appeared until we had been sailing for five days. They had just been too sick to leave their cabin. I felt disgustingly healthy and had continued to eat normally. Life aboard became more relaxed and sociable and the captain's daily spiel during breakfast took on a blander tone. We learned all about sea birds and nautical terms and then, as we approached ports of call, something of these places. Most of us appreciated our 'lessons' and found them interesting, but Leslie at my table did not. He used to leave the table as soon as he could, saying he was off "before Father starts"! He had found a spot on the topmost deck where the loudspeakers did not reach. Leslie, a typical old colonial, became quite a pal during the voyage. I found him staring hard at me across the table one day, and then he said in his very 'far-back' voice, "I'm trying to remember my dear whom you remind me of". It turned out to be Barbara Mullen in the T.V. series, *Dr. Findlay's Casebook*. "Typical Scottish face." I didn't like to inform Leslie that Barbara Mullen was Irish!

On this ship I enjoyed a visit to the bridge. I also joined in some deck games and attended the Buccaneers Ball, but at least I had nothing to do with the organising of these things, as I had on the voyage out. I preferred now to keep a low profile and to spend most of my time reading and studying. But there was one highlight. Along with Marjory McMullen and my German table-mate I won a prize in the fancy-dress competition as a Cape Roller! We had made crepe paper capes and put our hair in rollers.

St Helena

Our first stop was the island of St Helena, still British and the place of Napoleon's final exile, where he died. It lies in the South Atlantic, a tiny island which I believe can still only be reached by boat. There is no air-strip. The nearest country is over a thousand miles away. At the time of my going in 1965 there was no television and ships called once in three months. To me at that stage of my life, there was something very attractive about all this, and when an islander, on discovering that I was a teacher, asked me to consider going to live and work there I was sorely tempted. In its misty greyness the island brought to mind the mythical Scottish Brig O'Doon, which would disappear for a hundred years and then emerge again. This appealed to my imagination and my sense of the romantic. How blissful to get lost from the world for a spell! Needless to say, I did not succumb to the temptation, but I sometimes wonder, like those on a recent radio programme called *What If?*, how my life would have gone had I done so.

Our arrival in the small port was a gala occasion. It seemed as though the total population of the island was there to meet us, but we discovered isolated groups of ladies at different points along the narrow, winding roads, offering tea and cakes from trestle tables. They also sold some beautiful lace-work. We travelled all over the island in open-backed taxis, enjoying the moist, dank air and the thick vegetation which is a haven for nature-lovers. Of course we visited the tomb of Napoleon and his house which had been left just as it was when he lived there. The McMullen children rode on the back of a large amiable tortoise, said to have been alive in the time of Napoleon. We also visited (the outside of it at least) the Governor's house to which our captain was later to go for dinner, so that the two men could help to sort out the empire!

The people of St Helena lived mostly in the capital, Jamestown. My memory of this place is of a community squeezed into a fairly narrow cleft with steep, rocky hills on both sides and a huge flight of steps to climb up

Napoleon's house on St Helena

27

and out of the town. There must have been a motor road and an easier way to walk, but I decided to accept the challenge of the steps. It was days before my legs truly recovered. But my feelings towards St Helena were very warm and my memories still are, capped by an amusing incident which was the cause of our late departure from the island. I had stayed up to watch this leaving procedure, something I always loved to do, wondering why on this occasion we seemed to be late in going. I was soon to find out. I witnessed, with a delicious sense of mischief, our usually punctual and punctilious captain being piped aboard in true naval manner, a little the worse for wear! No doubt the weighty affairs of state had been discussed in an atmosphere of increasing conviviality, if the captain's gait indicated correctly! This was, I am sure, one of his favourite ports. I was to use the event later in my ship's song but more of this anon.

Ascension Island and Madeira

And so we proceeded to Ascension Island. We stayed here only long enough for the disembarkation of those going to work on the base. Some people from St Helena had joined the ones from Cape Town. It seemed that the Americans found a useful source of recruitment in these places. The island was discovered by the Portuguese on Ascension Day, 1501, and had been uninhabited until a British garrison was placed there in 1815 when the island became a dependency of St Helena and a convenient spot no doubt to keep an eye on any more antics that Napoleon might get up to. Now in 1965, it had become an American airbase, closely guarded and somewhat secretive. There was no landing-party for sightseeing. A pity! I should have enjoyed seeing more tortoises, for which the place was noted.

Soon we were ploughing northwards again, parallel with the African coast. We headed towards the Canary Islands and passed between two of them and so on to our next landfall which was Madeira, a place which even in these days was becoming something of a tourist paradise. It lies about four hundred miles from Morocco and was part of the Portuguese empire. Hilly and lush, the island has great beauty, with an attractive coastline and a pleasant, warm climate. It is vine-growing country and we greatly enjoyed some of its products as once again we toured by taxi. I shared one with my table-friend, Lesley, and I remember singing at the top of my voice, not, I hasten to add, because I had over-indulged in the lovely wine, but simply because there was so much to be happy about. Like the people in St Helena, those here were extremely welcoming and friendly as they displayed their famous basket-work and embroidery. No doubt they did well when ships came to call.

But my happy day was tinged with sadness. When I returned to the ship and picked up my mail there was a letter to say that my cat had died in her Sussex quarantine home. And I had very nearly bought her a basket in Madeira. I remember standing at the ship's rail as we left, watching our curving wake through a mist of tears. Puss had given me great joy and I blamed myself for selfishness. I should have left her in Africa where she belonged. My friends aboard were very understanding and tolerant of my unaccustomed silence at dinner that evening. I went off on my own later and 'got lost' in one of the lounges where a game of some kind was in progress. I remembered warmly the short time of happy companionship Puss had shared with me and then I began to wonder what I would have done with her at the end of the then required six months quarantine. As it turned out, I could not have kept her. It is strange how things happen. I said a fond farewell and got on with my life.

I had about a week to get over my loss before we were to land in Southampton. Although it was August and summer in Britain, there was a distinct damp chill in these European waters. But we were cheered by the big end-of-voyage party which the ship laid on. I had spent most of the previous night into the small hours concocting a song to a well-known tune, all about events during the journey, and of course including the time when the captain had returned late to the ship at St Helena. Both the words and the tune are now forgotten but it was fun and had everyone singing. The first mate said I would be up before the captain in the morning! Later I was asked if they could publish the song in the company magazine. At least I had a claim to fame in the annals of the Union Castle Line, now extinct.

SOUTHAMPTON

After the party on our last night aboard, I found myself on a high. I led a conga all over the ship, more and more of the passengers, the younger ones at least, joining our ranks. It was by this time well into the morning, and seamen were attempting to swab the decks. We leapt over the hose-pipes as we wove in and out. All the old ebullience of my voyage out seemed to return and one man asked where I had been during this voyage.

He would have found it hard to believe that I had been studying linguistics most of the time. Looking back now, I wonder if this last burst of activity on the ship was not a kind of 'farewell to arms'. The thoughts I had had on leaving Africa came back. I was very conscious of departing from the 'field' and facing a period when the walls would close in as I 'focused' on many of the things I had learnt as it were by osmosis. I would learn to 'earth' these things in greater understanding. It was a necessary move if I were to acquire that coveted university degree which would lead to a much wider 'field'. All this was to take much longer than I had anticipated, and I was to discover that it would stretch me not only academically but also professionally and spiritually, as one door closed and another one opened. Meanwhile on this ship, the last bastion of my present life, I was perhaps delaying the moving on. Then suddenly, in what is now a blur of memory, we had docked in Southampton and the next phase had begun.

CHAPTER 3

Towards 'York'

On the Brink

SETTLING IN

In early October I was to start as an undergraduate at the new University of York. I had therefore about seven weeks to settle in to British life again and to gear myself for the way ahead. This was a strange kind of vacuum. My journal records the facts, the events of everyday, but little about how I felt, and of the trepidation there must have been; nothing also of how friends and family felt to have the wanderer returned, even if parting would come again very soon. At least this time I was not to leave the country, though for many Scots, my family included, going 'down to England' *was* leaving the country!

These few weeks were a mixture of 'seeing to things' as I'd had to do on my leaves; eyes, teeth etc. and finances, the latter helped by Dad the businessman who was a tower of strength, and preparation for 'York', buying books, doing preliminary reading and collecting things to take. The packing was complicated by the fact that my crates from Africa had yet to be unpacked. The ten at Southampton and the one in the Clyde were to converge in Sheffield. Andrew and Mary Stokes, friends of my brother Alex, had agreed to receive and store them. They lived in an enormous vicarage. Andrew was an industrial chaplain for the Church of England. These arrangements had been made by the family before I left Africa. My 'base' in Sheffield was to become a godsend, a kind of axis from which the spokes of my early Yorkshire life were to radiate. But I jump ahead.

Also in the mixture of these weeks was the happy catching-up with relatives and friends. I enjoyed again my walks with Alex and Mairi, my school friend of longstanding, and I visited aunts, uncles and cousins. Edinburgh life went on around me. It was the time of the International Festival. I went to the Festival Club as the guest of Mrs Burge, an old family contact. Here I experienced a real sense of 'Edinburghness' amid the exciting world atmosphere. And I enjoyed one or two of the shows.

I was particularly impressed by *Macbeth* and by *There Was a Man*, a one-person performance depicting the life story of Robert Burns. All this was a wonderful way for me to recapture the sense of my Scottish roots which had been somewhat Africanised.

HOLIDAY IN THE HIGHLANDS AND ISLANDS

And as though to enhance this, Mother and Dad and Alex and I went on a holiday north and west. We travelled in Alex's Morris Minor, he and I sharing the driving. I could drive for a year on my Uganda licence. I remember the family being amused by my constant looking out for wild animals! The habits of my East African safaris took some time to leave me. Sadly I don't recall seeing even a stag, the monarch of the glen. We spent some time in Glasgow, Alex's home now. I had business to do in connection with the Clan shipping-line so that my crate could be directed to Sheffield via British Road Services. How the business of the other ten crates coming in to Southampton was conducted, I cannot now remember, but all was well in the end. Meanwhile our little family group proceeded in leisurely fashion by Loch Lomond and the Ballachulish ferry to Skye and the islands beyond.

It was a typical Scottish summer, damp and hazy, with reluctant sunshine attempting to break through from time to time. The sea crossings were a little rough but none of us succumbed to sea-sickness. For me, coming so soon after my experience of the Cape Rollers, this was a gentle romp. We so much enjoyed being together. As with all good holidays we relished being away from it all, and in this particular case, the opportunity it gave to reconnect and to share. We celebrated Mother's sixty-fifth birthday while we were away and at the end of each happy day we digested its events and played scrabble, a game to which the family introduced me. Alex and I walked and climbed while the old folks rested in the car or hotel. I heard all about Alex's recent holiday in Greece with university friends, one of whom was Jane, soon to become my sister-in-law. They had become engaged on Jane's birthday and were to be married the following year, just before my sister Joan and her fiancé Gavin. It was an exciting family time.

Alex was now launched on his university teaching career. He had been for five years in post as a Lecturer in Greek at the University of Glasgow. This had followed a distinguished sojourn as student in Edinburgh and

Cambridge where he gained a 'first' at both universities. His two years of military service had come between them. In his final student year Alex was engaged in research which was to be the basis of his life's work. In his teaching and writing he was to become a scholar of renown in the classical field, gaining finally a Personal Chair in Glasgow where he was to remain for the rest of his teaching career. He was much supported by Jane, who truly understood his classical interests, herself becoming a school-teacher of Latin and Greek. Later he was also ably supported by his daughter, Margaret, who gained a first in Classics at Oxford.

So I shared at this time Alex's achievements and dreams, and on my part, offered him the story of my journey home from Africa and the traumatic events of my last months there. There were also my plans for leaving the 'field' temporarily to 'focus' on further study and become an undergraduate. In this respect my little brother became my teacher and adviser, a reversal from our early years. I shall always be grateful for our very special empathy. In this blessed time out we all drew breath, reminisced and contemplated future goals, while at the same time we rejoiced in the Scotland we loved and explored new places, particularly in Harris and Lewis.

And we laughed a lot. I shall never forget the expression on Dad's face when he discovered that he had packed a dressing-table mat with his shaving kit, from a hotel in Skye! Luckily we were to come back that way and stay in the same hotel, so a shame-faced Dad was able to confess and return the mat. Then there was lunchtime at the Butt of Lewis, when our hunger was faced with a long village street resting in the rain with no-one in sight and no sign of the restaurant promised on the hotel notice-board in Stornoway. Desperation lent sharpness to my eyes and I shrieked "There it is." A very closed-up cottage had the word 'Restaurant' set in stone above the door. Leaving our parents sitting in the car, Alex and I ventured out to investigate. A lady eventually opened the door in response to our knocking. In her soft island accent she informed us that she could manage soup for four, mince for two and sausages for two, with pudding and tea to follow. We were soon clustered round the blazing fire, glad to be out of the greyness and the rain. It was a long, comfortable lunchtime, ending as it began. We enjoyed our tea by the fire. With solemn face our lady accepted Alex's suggestion that a sign saying 'Open' or 'Shut', might be a "ferry coot itea"!

KIRK WEEK

Another highlight of this settling-in time for me was Kirk Week in Perth. I went with Mairi and her stepmother. This was an ecumenical gathering of the churches, patterned on the Kirchentag which had been established in the centre of industrial Germany just after World War II. I understand that the aim had been to bring to an area which had been so involved in the war machine and destruction, a new and constructive effort by gathering the Christian churches together in a large convention.

By comparison, our Scottish affair was a modest event but the same concept prevailed, the notion that by prayer and collective action, people of God could make a difference for good in the world. I was greatly excited by it all but my recent experience in Africa with exposure to several faiths now prompted a vision where Islam spoke to Hinduism, to Judaism, to Christianity etc. in the context of the world's needs. Alas, I fear I was too far ahead. I had to be content with a concept of ecumenicism which concerned only the denominations of the Christian faith. It was disappointing but it was a start, I suppose. Maybe in the not too distant future, an enlightened Church of Scotland *would* bring together representatives of all the faiths. The words of that Muslim girl in my multicultural youth club in Kampala still rang in my head. She had requested that we have prayer in our meetings, and when I had doubted the propriety of this she had replied, "But, Madam, same God!" I fear that Scottish Kirk Week in 1965 had a long way to go, and now as I write in 2006, though ecumenicism and interfaith have a kind of tacit acceptance and are the 'in' thing in some areas, there is still a great reluctance to be inclusive, and a tendency in many quarters to link 'exotic' faiths with terrorists and asylum-seekers.

Meanwhile in 1965 I played a small part in ecumenicism by lodging with a family who belonged to the Scottish Episcopal tradition, the Piscies as we Presbyterians called them. They were lovely and I learned a lot about Scottish church history and how these Piscies related to that 'foreign' Anglican Church of England south of the border! It was a stimulating conference even if I did feel somewhat frustrated. Besides the serious content of the meetings, I enjoyed time out with old friends and made use of the central position of Perth to visit in the area. My good friends, the Mortons, had farms nearby and my mother's sister, my Auntie Gladys, lived in Tullibody. I was able to go there on my way back to Edinburgh.

34

SHEFFIELD

Came the time of departure for Sheffield where I was to spend a few days sorting out the contents of my crates before going to York. I had a special send-off at the station. We were very sensitive to 'milestones' and there was an unspoken agreement about what these were. 'Towards York via Sheffield' was one for me and my people recognised this. I was warmly grateful.

Large as the vicarage in Sheffield was, it seemed to me that Andrew and Mary were smothered in crates, one even lying along the passage to a bathroom! I had a vision of us all doing a frequent mountaineering act! Fortunately there was another bathroom upstairs. For two days Andrew gave up most of his working time to prising open the crates, helped by a visiting Lutheran pastor who was asked to volunteer! It was no easy task as the Ugandan work-team had packed with exceeding care and sealed the lids well. Only one plate was broken of all my belongings. As Andrew and the pastor opened each crate, I checked and listed the contents and took them down to the cellar. The men followed with the empty crates which were then repacked and numbered so that eventually I had an inventory of everything and could find things quickly. While I worked closely with the two men, Mary kept us all going with frequent cuppas and delicious meals. Even the two Jack Russells took part in the operation. As each crate revealed its contents, the excited dogs jumped in to investigate, their back ends and wagging tails quivering as they dived into the crate I was endeavouring to empty.

The rest of my time in Sheffield at this stage is dominated by two special memories. The first is exploration of the Yorkshire Dales and the Derbyshire Peak District. In the gentle autumn weather, Andrew and Mary took me to beautiful parts of this spectacular area. I was particularly impressed by a Son et Lumière performance at Fountains Abbey, made specially real as 'monks' chanted in the background or emerged from the shadows of the ruins. We picnicked and truly relaxed after all our hard work and I was filled with gratitude for the help and companionship I was receiving.

The other particular memory of this time was something I was able to do in a small way to help Andrew. My 'Uganda factor' came to the fore as I accompanied him into 'English Steel', one of his work-places. There had been some instances of racism when the workforce was joined by immigrants. Andrew had been drawn in and was trying to share his Christian view. He asked me to help, coming so recently as I had from my life in Africa and the richness I had discovered in multiculturalism. How far I was really able to assist I will never know but the whole experience was memorable and another 'first' for me.

This was in the days before the clinical blandness of modern-day technology. I seemed to be following Andrew through the gates of hell as he strode into an enormous work-place between blazing furnaces, dodging large, mobile pincers which clutched ingots of molten steel. It was quite terrifying. I was glad to reach the haven of an office where a foreman had gathered a group of 'blue-collar' workers to meet me. Against the slightly muted roar of work in progress, the men fired questions at me in a mostly good-humoured way and there was some useful discussion. From there Andrew took me to an upper floor where the office or 'white-collar' workers were having their lunch-break. I was amused at the hasty pushing of cards out of sight and the feet taken off chairs so that we could sit down. There was a general forced politeness here. I much preferred the rough honesty of the workers on the shop-floor.

I spent three very full and interesting days with Andrew and Mary, not only clearing my crates and exploring the countryside as they took time off on my behalf, but also sharing for a short time something of the life of an industrial chaplaincy. We became very close and I found them good listeners and helpful counsellors as my new life in York drew ever nearer. I also discussed with them my more distant goals. Eventually they took me to York and introduced me to the sights of this historic city, finally bringing me to Mrs Hodgson, the lady with whom the university lodgings office had arranged for me to stay. I took my farewell of these good folks, assuring them that one of my first jobs would be to insure separately my belongings in their home. It was wonderful to have found such a convenient base for them. It was also a good feeling that Sheffield was not far away and my friends were offering a bolt-hole. I came to value this more and more.

So I had arrived in York, so long something on my horizon, a symbol as well as a place. It was the start of a much postponed academic career, something I now knew I could have done in earlier years but was 'directed' otherwise. For this I still have no regrets. The road I had taken served me well but I was now ready for this new stage, which was to take an unexpected turn.

CHAPTER 4

University Student Part 1

York at last

FIRST IMPRESSIONS

I was fortunate to be in one of England's loveliest cities. My feet ached with all my wanderings. I had found my bearings at the two parts of the university where I would be operating, and was most impressed with the old-world beauty of Heslington Hall and King's Manor, incorporated into the new university. 'York' had been opened a year and at that time there were only two colleges. I was a member of Derwent. King's Manor, where I would be doing my language work, reminded me of a Cambridge college, with courts surrounded by stone buildings and pillared walks. The windows were latticed in small panes and the rooms contained still the ancient fire-places of the old house, though there was now central heating. The junior common-room was well-appointed with fitted carpet and armchairs to sink

Heslington Hall

into. Inevitably there was a ghost which was not difficult to conjure up as autumn days shortened and the old pillars were swathed in shadow at the end of a day. Now at the start of my York sojourn and before I was pressed by commitments, I took time to absorb my environment before the summer faded. I had lunch in the Heslington Hall dining room which must have been a banqueting-hall at one time. The woodwork is beautiful and the whole place gives an air of gracious living. I felt excited and on the brink of a vast new experience, as indeed I was.

There was also time in those early days to explore the city. Map in hand I wandered through the various 'gates' and strolled round the walls. It was a useful time of orientation which included finding bank, food shops and library etc., places I would need quickly. Other amenities and centres of interest became gradually familiar as I was much helped by Mrs Hodgson, my delightful landlady, and the minister and members of the Presbyterian church which I soon discovered. Before long I was to be singing in the church choir, doing Scottish country dancing and enjoying the theatre when time permitted. But it behoves me now to say something about the real purpose of my being in the city. What of my studies?

Course of Study

I was heading for a B.A. degree in the combined subjects of English and Linguistics; English which I had always loved in my earlier student days and would have pursued had I gone to university at that time, and Linguistics, a new subject which I believe 'York' pioneered and which interested me in particular in light of my Uganda teaching experience. Put very simply, linguistics is the study of the structure of language. It was possible in this new university to do lots of new things and there was great flexibility in the combinations of subjects. My friend Beatrice, who had worked with me on the radio teacher training project in Uganda, was also here and her combination of subjects was Philosophy and Linguistics. We shared much, not least that we were both mature students and also that, because we had been out of the country for too long, we were unable to acquire a grant. So life at York was somewhat impecunious and we had to be ingenious at finding ways and means.

I have much to thank 'York' for because of its flexibility. It was not long before I found that in English I was virtually out of my depth. The young A-level students who were my fellows were fresh off the 'conveyer belt'. It had been many years since I had done that kind of reading. Much as I would have enjoyed doing it now, time and energy were at a premium. The new subject, linguistics, was to take up most of both. In addition to the study of language structure, I found that I had to offer two languages. I opted for French and Swahili, the first like my English literature, somewhat rusty, and the second, in my case more of a 'kitchen' variety which had served me adequately in Uganda as a lingua franca, but now needed formal study. I was to find out how complicated was the grammar of this twelfth most important world language. Had I bitten off more than I could chew?

'YORK' TO THE RESCUE

I then learned just how accommodating 'York' could be. For me in my dilemma they brought forward a plan which had been only in the pipeline and which allowed me to replace my 'dodgy' English literature with a subject fresh in my experience and which I really knew something about. This was Education. I was offered a new combination of Linguistics and Education. I could relax a little in the latter as I had been teaching in the Education Department at Makerere and had gained much in the process. So I could afford to concentrate more on Linguistics. I was grateful.

For a time all went well and I got to grips with the life of an under-graduate, studying, writing essays for which I got reasonable marks, and being concerned about world affairs. I joined the young voices protest-ing about the Vietnam War. I worried about Southern Rhodesia and UDI and the subject of a current film, *H-Bomb or Sanity*. I became one of the student body putting the world to rights, with in my case a special eye to Uganda where restlessness increased and Idi Amin was waiting in the wings. Messages continued to reach me and at that stage I was still going back.

I now met Professor Harry Rée, Head of the Education Department, a man very much after my own heart. He was, I believe, half French, and had been dropped behind the enemy lines during World War II. With his gimlet blue eyes and incisive manner in tutorials, I could well imagine his confronting and dealing with 'the enemy'. Harry Rée, more than anyone, seemed to understand what I was going through. He said to me quietly one day, "What you want is simply recognition for what you have already achieved." He could see that I was not really in need of Education classes or prowess in French, though Swahili might still be useful. In all fairness

I had enjoyed the 'excursions' to the various educational establishments which I was asked to visit and then write reports about. I fear that these reports must have been more like those of a school inspector than of a student! And I was in great danger of being arrogant in my demeanour, particularly about the university teaching I was subjected to. I remember saying to Harry Rée that some teacher-training here would not go amiss. Then I was consumed with a huge guilt feeling when everyone had seemed to fall over backwards to accommodate me. The two professors, Harry Rée and Robert Le Page of Linguistics, must have got together. Towards the end of the academic year yet another plan was put to me. It was Harry Rée who dropped the bombshell.

A CHANGE OF DIRECTION

I was told that if I continued at York I would probably take a good degree. My essays and work generally had passed muster. But, it was suggested, perhaps I should now bypass the B.A. or first degree and proceed direct to a higher or Master's. In certain circumstances, it seemed, this was permitted if the student's experience could be seen to be an equivalent of the first degree. It was reckoned that I fitted this category, and in a whirl of activity, mainly on the part of Harry Rée, I found myself in an interview with Professor Musgrove of the new University of Bradford, who offered me a place on his M.Sc. in Education course. He had had four hundred applicants, had selected thirty two and was persuaded by Harry Rée that I could possibly make a thirty third.

This M.Sc., I was warned, was a more exacting course than the normal M.Ed. and would involve more stress on Research Methods and Statistics. It was hoped that students would produce research that could be replicated and contribute more to the body academic. I have to admit that the mathematical content gave me some grounds for hesitation. That had never been an interest or talent though I remembered doing better than I expected in what was called 'Mental Testing' in my teacher training course. This was because, I believe, for the first time in my education, I saw a purpose for the mathematics. Perhaps the same could happen again. But I was faced with a further and possibly more daunting dilemma. The course would take four years, two a taught period of study in the Behavioural Sciences, leading to a Post Graduate Diploma, and two further years of research if the Diploma examination results were high enough, culminating by dissertation, in the M.Sc. degree. With the year I was just completing at York, I would now have five years of study instead of the expected three, and I risked ending up with no degree at all after all I had gone through to get to York. What to do?

I told Harry Rée about my brother, Alex. He chased me to Glasgow so that I could talk it over with my faithful 'adviser' and I did, sitting in Alex's car under the dripping trees in Balloch Park on the bonny banks of Loch Lomond. We decided it was worth the risk. I would leave York and start at Bradford in October 1966. As I have said so many times in my life, "Phew!"

My York 'Legacy'

I just touch on this here, but as the Bradford years unveil I hope it becomes clearer. Amongst lots of useful experience that 'York' gave me were two things in particular. The first was a basis in linguistics and aspects of linguistic behaviour, for which I shall always be grateful to Robert Le Page and his team. The second was something other and quite unexpected, something not yet mentioned at all. In the course of my Education studies I was brought into contact with Professor Eric Hawkins, Head of the Department of Language Methods. Somehow we gravitated towards each other and I learned of a teaching experiment he was about to launch in a Huddersfield school where there was a high proportion of children who came from non-English-speaking homes. This was the period when many immigrants were arriving from Pakistan and India. To cut a long and very happy story short, I found myself leading a team of my fellow students in a project of my own designing and which Eric Hawkins approved. It was an exciting venture which had repercussions of a positive nature for my life in the near future. In addition to the professional pointer which 'Huddersfield' was, there was another one. During a residential period, I stayed with a lovely Quaker family, an important step, I think, in my spiritual journey.

So, although at times I now saw 'York' as a mistake and a wasted year, after all the build-up and eager looking forward, I soon realised it had been a necessary and valuable part of my life's journeys. What I gained there was a legacy which now made 'Bradford' possible and much more besides.

CHAPTER 5

Between the Acts

Adventure in France

FURTHER 'GIFT' FROM 'YORK'

I had not yet finished with 'York'. There was still another part of the 'legacy'. I had planned to take a summer job in France as one of the best means of improving my French. Although now I was leaving the York course and this was no longer necessary, I decided to go, for the fun of it. It would be yet another challenging adventure.

The catering officer of the last schoolgirl camp I had run before going to Uganda was a Parisian with whom I had kept in touch. Cécile belonged to a Protestant organisation which looked after displaced persons, victims of World War II, and helped with other charities. One of the latter was the running of a students' hostel in Massy, twelve miles south of Paris. During the summer vacation when the students, except those from distant countries, went home, the place was open to paying guests, mostly tourists. It was then that Madame Margot, the housekeeper, needed help, and a series of assistant housekeepers was employed. With Cécile's connections, she was able to have me join this band of workers, which, for anyone who knew me well, was somewhat hilarious. Housekeeping was not exactly my forte!

In addition to this work, Cécile arranged for me to do a course of study with the Alliance Française. I would attend class every afternoon in Paris. My friend, now sadly passed on, was a most helpful agent and catalyst. Though I never met her till near the end of my time in Paris as she was away from home, I was conscious of her sure hand at the tiller of all the arrangements.

ARRIVAL IN FRANCE

Consequently I found myself in a taxi quite late one evening, in the centre of Paris, nosing in and out of the tall buildings which in this area were mainly business premises. They were sheathed in darkness at that hour and it was difficult to find the court where Cécile's office was situated.

She had planned that I should stay for one night in the sleeping apartment there before going off to Massy the next day. The taxi driver was extremely helpful and friendly. He eventually found the courtyard and waited with me until I was settled. It was not clear which side of the court I had to be on. I went into a very dark stairway which seemed to contain some residential flats, heard talking behind one door and knocked. How the lady who came understood my painful French, I don't know, and how I understood what I took in my tired state to be a fast stream of foreign words, but somehow I gleaned that I should be in the block at right angles to this one. Somehow I conveyed this to my driver and he took over. There was much shouting between him and a head which had emerged from a window on the fifth floor. At last a lady caretaker appeared at the door, I thanked and paid off my driver, and proceeded to climb the stairs accompanied by the caretaker who regaled me with a flow of convivial French. The tone if not the words told me it was.

I was shown the small bedroom with its divan and kettle, and given a large key admitting me to the dark and mysterious business department in which was hidden a 'cabinet' containing toilet and wash-basin. I had some trouble with both light switches and key, all of which were strange to me and not very negotiable. I wondered if I might find myself in difficulties during the night, but all was well. After the travelling and excitement I had no difficulty sleeping. I was wakened in the morning by the lady of the night before, who had come to give me my instructions for the day. Concentrating hard in my sleepy state, I was able to make out that I was expected early at the Alliance Française where I would be given an examination so that I could be placed in the right level of class. After this I was to journey on to the students' hostel at Massy. The caretaker delivered this information and probably a lot more, in a quick fire manner, thrust some croissants at me and bid me farewell.

The rest of that day is now very dim in my memory. Somehow I reached the Alliance Française and endeavoured to do my test with people coming and going all the while. I would have been placed in the fourth class if my use of the subjunctive had been better. As it was, I found myself in the third level which turned out to be difficult enough for me. Then I managed to get myself to Massy where I was pleasantly welcomed by Madame Margot, the housekeeper, who would be my immediate boss, and Madame Evdokimov, a Japanese lady and wife to the White Russian gentleman who had overall charge of the hostel. Madame Evdokimov was a linguist with several languages at her command. She was an interpreter for the World Council of Churches in Geneva. I was meeting some interesting people.

MASSY

Madame Margot, who had no English, conducted me to my little room which looked over the inner courtyard and explained the ritual of the bell. This building had been a monastery, and although a large and new structure was being built behind, the ancient ecclesiastical atmosphere remained and I was glad that my apartment was part of it. The old monastery bell was used now to summon everyone to meals. At one time the rope reached down to the courtyard but it had been shortened and in order for it to be rung now, it was necessary for the ringer to be in my room and to reach out of the oriel window. Most of the time, I was there to do the ringing. I enjoyed this little enactment. I would wait at the open window until Madame Margot called for me to ring. There was then a five-minute break and the summons came to ring again. It was a scattered campus and time had to be given for people to reach the dining room, but if anyone missed the second ringing it was just too bad! I joined the people coming from all directions and then took my place at table opposite Madame Margot from where I helped her to dish out from the various pots placed by the cooks. This job became easier gradually as my French improved. The diners called to us with what they wanted, some of this or none of that. It was hard enough for me to understand but when all this was happening in the context of a noisy French dining room, I was really flummoxed at times. It took me a very long while, for instance, to decipher "Pas d'épignes" (no spinach), and I continued to send plates with spinach on to those who had asked for none. I dread to think what other mistakes I made.

FUN AND GAMES

Talk about in at the deep end! During the first few days when I overlapped with my American predecessor whose French was fluent, I had someone to lean on, but when she left after a farewell party at which she made an excellent speech and I sat thinking with consternation that I would have to do the same when my turn came, Madame Margot had to give me her instructions for the day without any helpful interpreter. I pleaded with her to speak more slowly and she did for a while and then forgot. I had fun also trying to explain to her that if she found me hanging from a door I had not taken leave of my senses. The people in the hospital in York had advised this. My back had been playing up and I had had treatment, which was cut short when I had to leave for France. And I had further fun and games working with the Spanish cooks. They had no English, I had no Spanish, and their French was worse than mine! It was just as well that I was in charge of the kitchen only once a week when Madame Margot had her day off. I became alarmed every time the chief cook stirred the soup in the large pot that stood on the floor. He was a little man and had to stand on his tiptoes. I was afraid that his beret would fall off into the soup. I don't think it ever did.

Multicultural Delights

It was my task to supervise the students in their domestic duties. Many were Africans from various French-speaking countries. They had to set tables and dry dishes. First I myself had to learn the ways of French table-setting and the names and correct positions of the numerous condiments. I also had to supervise the use of the wicked looking guillotine, which chopped up the long bread loaves. We enjoyed struggling together. But most of the time my dealings with the students were more of a social nature. On many an evening one or more would appear at my door with a bottle of cheap wine and we would have an impromptu party, or I would be invited to join them on a night out in Paris. I have strong memories of running across the Place de la Concorde and other places in the centre of the city, at some late hour, in a hectic attempt to catch the last train home. I enjoyed it all so much. It recalled the happy times I had had with the international student body at the university in Uganda. I learned yet again that there is only one race, the human race.

I quote from a letter I sent home at the time.

"I had to settle in a newcomer, an African girl from Kampala, find a towel for her, help to telephone KLM - and this afternoon I have to take a Nigerian to the Alliance Française. This evening I am going yet again on the Seine with an American who is alone. Last night I brought one of my class home to dinner. He is from North Vietnam. We have one of his countrymen dining here regularly so I brought them

together, two lost souls with their people in the middle of a horrible war. To crown the evening I invited the American to join us. Whatever their respective countries were doing, they, the representatives, were soon engaged in happy conversation and lots of fun."

All the time in work and play I was learning not only French, but sociology and psychology and other people's cultures and ideas on matters ranging from etiquette to religion and world affairs. I was a student in a school where the curriculum covered the life-views of the world.

And from these transcendent thoughts to the more immanent and practical, I was learning also some very useful everyday jobs. There was the window cleaning in the new building after the dust of the builders had settled. I discovered a wonderful red powder which was remarkably adept at clearing marks and providing the windows with a lovely shine. I took great pride in my windows. There was also the organising of the laundry. I had never realised before just how much is involved in the care of institutional linen. We take so much for granted. And how useful it is to learn these universal matters through the particulars of a different culture, a tremendous aid to the learning of the language that goes with it. Fortunately the household linen was in drawers which were carefully labelled. This helped my list-making and enriched my vocabulary. But one week, I had to include in my list the pyjamas of an American guest who had left them under his pillow. There was no drawer containing pyjamas and I did not realise that the word was the same in French except for the spelling. The English 'y' becomes 'a'. Being Saturday afternoon when the laundry van called, there were few people around to help. Then I spotted M. Bernard, the gardener, hard at work. I went out, waving the pyjamas, and asking what they were (I meant in French). I laugh when I recall his puzzled face as he pushed his beret back and scratched his head. "Pajamas", he said, his tone suggesting that there was no end to the ignorance of these foreigners!

The practical demands in this place meant that I had to become a jack-of-all-trades. Proper hotel-style bed making was one of these. Most of our guests were students and young and when they arrived they were given sleeping-bags and asked to make up their own beds. But occasionally we had guests of the V.I.P. variety and in their case the beds were made up for them. This task fell to me. One of the most interesting groups of V.I.Ps consisted of three Coptic priests from Egypt who had no French and about three words of English amongst them. They had black robes, high hats and very long beards. I wondered as I made their beds, if they slept with the beards inside or outside the bedclothes! When one of the priests needed his suitcase repairing and I was able to have this done satisfactorily, the French-speaking lay secretary who was with them expressed their gratitude by inviting me to their house in Cairo, the next time I was passing!

PUSHED TO THE LIMIT

I think perhaps that my greatest challenges, which came luckily after I had been at Massy for some time and had gained more confidence in the language, were first, serving lunch to the workmen who were mending the road outside our premises. I had to charge them each day, and the combination of money and language problems was not easy. The men enjoyed my discomfiture and teased me unmercifully in the manner of workmen everywhere, using the local slang. But it was all great fun. The second challenge came when M. Evdokimov asked me to act as a tour guide to a party of French guests round the Palace of Versailles. My heart sank. I had been to Versailles myself only twice. A frantic study of guidebooks and a huge amount of prayer and faith pulled me through, even to answering the awkward question, but my French for "Sorry, I don't know that one" must have been well used.

CHALLENGE OF A DIFFERENT KIND

Before I finish this tale of my French adventure, I must describe something of my afternoon class at the Alliance Française. I was now the proud possessor of a weekly rail ticket which I used to take me into the centre of Paris. As many times before, I enjoyed the role-play. Every afternoon I became a Parisian and found myself acting like one. My French improved with the body-language. What a wonderful way to learn! From the daily whirl of my job and often deep misunderstandings of the language that accompanied it, I went to the studious quiet of my classroom and the soft-spoken French of my elderly teacher who was a Sorbonne lecturer. I gradually adjusted and began to benefit from this 'direct' teaching though it was extremely difficult at first to learn in the language I was learning. I couldn't ask my classmates to help as the one on my right might be Japanese and the one on my left Hungarian. We were a very international group. I was fortunate in that I could have my homework vetted by my student friends in Massy. I even managed the subjunctive eventually.

But blunders inevitably occurred and one that still makes me chuckle took place in the metro. I cannot recall where I was going, but I had become confused and had to ask an official for guidance. I thought I had said to the lady "I have made a mistake" and couldn't understand why she looked at me somewhat strangely. I *had* said that in a sense, but had used the idiom for "I am a fallen woman"! The lady's expression seemed to say "What do you expect me to do about it?" Then she realised I was a foreigner, laughed and gave me the right direction. I had fallen victim right enough but to a hazard of language learning, where a phrase which seems straightforward cannot be taken literally as it has been set aside by the native speakers to have a special meaning. Only later, and now going where I wanted to go, did I realise what I had said and I bubbled with laughter amongst my startled fellow passengers.

A SATISFACTORY ENDING

My French had improved enormously in the six weeks I was in Massy and I was told I had a good Parisian accent. I had turned the corner when the language to express what I wanted to say came easily and when I could readily take part in the cut and thrust of fast-flowing conversation, especially where humour was involved. So much of humour in any language is a play on words, and if you don't have these words you are lost. Prior to this stage it was hard for me to discuss, and in order to speak at all, it was almost necessary for me to find the ideas which matched such language as I *could* use. My crowning success was that I *did* make a speech at my farewell party and that it incorporated a few funny stories at which I felt the audience were not just laughing politely. Perhaps I had been encouraged by an experience earlier in the day. We had a party of youngsters from London staying. Their teacher sat next to me at table, thought I was French and struggled to speak to me in the language. He was surprised when I suggested that he try English. He would have been more surprised if I had told him that I understood French better than the cockney English of his party!

It was the combination of the practical in Massy and the focused study of my class which had brought about my miraculous and rapid fluency in French, and I would recommend this procedure to any wannabee linguist.

It was an achievement I cherished, whatever I did with it. My thanks to both 'Massy' and the Alliance Française, to Cécile who made the whole operation possible, and to York University where the idea was born. I should have liked to stay in France longer but Scotland was calling. My brother's wedding was in August and my sister Joan's in September. I went home in time for both, but I could have returned to work for the certificate for teaching French as a Foreign Language, and that would have been a whole new story. As it was, the time had come for the curtain to go up on the second act of my university student days, and I moved from York to Bradford.

In class at the Alliance Française

CHAPTER 6

University Student Part 2

Move to Bradford

A New Beginning

For the first two years of my new life I would be studying part-time, attending the university on two evenings a week. This was to pursue the Diploma in the Behavioural Sciences, which, if passed highly enough, would be the passport to research leading to the M.Sc. in Education. My fellow students were all teachers or head teachers, continuing to work in their schools whilst they embarked on this new course of study. They had already obtained their first degrees. It seemed to me that the whole environment would suit me well and I hastened to find a teaching job so that I would be to some extent on the same footing as my companions, and also so that I could be earning again.

But first I had to find somewhere to live. After a few weeks in a grotty YWCA hostel, which was about to be pulled down, I moved into what was called a luxury flat with under-floor heating! This had just come to the attention of the university lodgings officer while I was making enquiries in her office. The flat belonged to Liz Denby, the Personal Assistant to Alan Whicker, traveller and broadcaster. She had to be away for a year and wanted it lived in. How on earth could I cope, in my present circumstances, with the rent of a luxury flat? Nothing daunted I went to see this Liz, fell in love with the place, and negotiated a wonderfully relaxed deal. Liz was guardian to a young sister who was at boarding-school. She needed a base and would be coming to the flat in vacations. Liz herself would be popping in from time to time. So one bedroom had to be available. The rent, which was not mentioned till the last minute, was phenomenally small. I was left a whole larder of food which I was just to use and replace. With very little ado, this whole gentleman's, or should I say lady's, agreement was clinched and Liz floated off, telling me about the local Beagling Club and other luxury country pursuits which

I might like to join! The arrangement was to be for a year in the first instance.

It was incredible. Quite suddenly I was established in Petersgarth, a three-sided complex of flats, mine being on the top floor overlooking Moorhead Lane at the front and the lovely enclosed garden at the back. I was in Shipley, the Saltaire part of it, on the outskirts of Bradford with easy access to the countryside and the Yorkshire Moors. Saltaire was named after Titus Salt, a nineteenth century philanthropist and mill owner, who developed virtually a whole village round his mill, establishing a hospital and other amenities and ruling his little empire with benign hegemony. I found the place immensely interesting and had reason to be grateful to the hospital where I had excellent treatment after a fall.

I soon got to know my neighbours, particularly the two ladies who lived below. We became very good friends. Now that I was able to spread myself a bit I could bring more of my belongings, some of which were in Scotland but most in Sheffield. I gradually collected what I needed. My change of address yet again brought a puzzled phone call from the Yorkshire Insurance Company. "Just checking", the voice said. "You have moved from York to Bradford, your permanent address is in Edinburgh, and the things we are insuring are in Sheffield." As I confirmed all this I realised that it must have seemed rather odd. Yes, I did see my real home as still being in Edinburgh. In fact it was not until both my parents had passed on that this changed, even though by that time I had a home of my own. Meantime my good friends in Sheffield continued to house my diminishing cache of possessions, our frequent contacts strengthening our friendship. They followed my fortunes with great understanding and we had a very special relationship.

TEACHING AND STUDY

A roof over my head, I could now turn to the business of work and study. In the Bradford Education Office I met a gentleman called Jim Rouse. He was the local Adviser for Immigrant Education and he was looking for teachers to staff a centre for teaching English as a Second Language to children of secondary age. Bradford, like Huddersfield, and many other industrial towns, had had a recent influx of people from India and Pakistan. These were the first generation of immigrants from the Indian sub-continent. The men and older boys came first, finding lodgings together and acquiring work in the woollen mills. Once established, they would send for the women, girls and younger boys. Bradford was used to immigrants, mostly Irish and West Indian. These people had been absorbed happily into the community, the children attending the same schools as the English children, and, rightly or wrongly, no special arrangements had been made. This new wave of in-comers was different. They had no or very little English. Teachers were finding it hard to cope with pupils with whom they had no means of communication. It was decided that something more might have to be done than simply dropping these children into an ordinary British classroom and expecting them to pick up the language along with all the other things they were supposed to be learning.

There were different approaches to the problem across the country, as I was to discover, but this is not the place to discuss them or to record the sometimes fiery debates which went on at conferences and in the media. Suffice it to say that the city of Bradford was in the forefront, as was exemplified by their having a special adviser for immigrant education. Jim Rouse was to receive an award in the Honours List for his untiring efforts to find solutions to the many problems which arose. As was Shirley Sutcliffe, the gifted and intrepid Head Teacher of St Michael's, the first special language centre to be opened. Bradford had opted for a withdrawal system. The children would spend two years in the centre, undergoing an intensive English teaching programme, and then rejoin their age-group in the mainstream secondary school. I think in the end there were four secondary language centres. As time went on and the families arrived, there was a need for centres, it was decided, at primary school level but in 1966 this was still to come.

My experience in Uganda, my work with the student team in Huddersfield and my study of linguistics at York University, were strong points in my favour and I was appointed to St Michael's straight away. Mr Rouse and the Bradford Education Authority were very understanding of my position and allowed me to teach part-time in the beginning, the other part of my working life to be devoted to my studies. September saw me launched at St Michael's in a practical, professional capacity, and the following month my university classes began, where the accent was on the academic. To some extent the pattern was not unlike that of my brief spell in France, where work and study complemented each other. It turned out to be a beneficial partnership which seemed to help others besides myself. I had more time to experiment with teaching methods and to share my findings with colleagues both in the authority and the university. At the same time I was working steadily towards my goal, the M.Sc. in Education.

THE TWO STRANDS

The two strands of my new life continued to run in parallel for the years leading to my Diploma examinations. It was a wonderful coming together of past experience and learning, the recent year at York where I had been introduced to the mysteries and excitements of language, its acquisition and behaviour, followed by my 'in at the deep end' time of learning French *in* French, and the short but telling work in Huddersfield, leading a student team in the teaching of immigrant children. Then, less recently but still with prevailing effect, were my teacher-training years in Uganda and even my experience in Edinburgh, teaching children with particular needs. I seemed to be in the right place at the right time, and I was part of yet another close-knit team, in the forefront of interesting and challenging work. Bradford was virtually leading with its initiations and innovations. The eye of the country was upon us. We had many visitors to our language centre, local, national and even international as other countries had similar problems at this time of much movement of peoples. St Michael's, in its experimental searchings, seemed to be a hub of interest and virtually a base for teacher training.

To me personally, the opportunities for experiment set against my studies, became a joyous and thoroughly motivating experience. It seemed as though all my previous work suddenly made sense. Another element in all this was the cross-cultural one. Yet once more I was fascinated by what I saw as the universals and particulars of the human race and the wonderful richness of diversity. I was more and more conscious of my 'pearl of great price'. In the years at Bradford, I was to work harder than at any other time in my life, but the rewards were enormous. This period, to use my 'field and focus' idea, was the real focus of my life. It was to lead to an ever widening field.

THE TWO VENUES

Before highlighting some of the milestones of the time, I must say a little more about my two working venues and the nature of the work. First, the university. This had been, until recently, a college of technology or CAT. Like others all over the country, it had been upgraded, as part of the then government's aim to expand university provision. The technological ethos still clung to it. It was a fitting alma mater for industrial Bradford, and it hoped to cater well for its own sons and daughters as well as attracting students from elsewhere by its specialities such as a Department of Peace Studies. The Education Department, in which I had been enrolled, was a new venture. It was housed not in the main college but in a high-rise building in the centre of town, which it shared with a number of other offices and commercial concerns. The building was known as the 'ice rink' because of one of these. I hoped this would not have a chilly effect on my studies!

Bradford University was a very masculine conclave. Its technological history made this so. But even the Education Department bore out the tradition. Of the thirty-two students in my group (one had withdrawn), only six of us were women, and all our tutors were men. I suppose that schoolgirls joining boys' schools in the co-educational thrust of later years, must have felt a little as we did then. We were determined to hold up our heads, especially in such topics as Research Methods and Statistics. I even joined voluntarily for a time the very new class in Computer Studies where I learned about a 'language' called ALGOL, and I trod with reverence the floor of the room filled by one computer which we nicknamed John Willy. This was 1966.

I went to the 'ice rink' two evenings a week, climbed in the lift to the thirteenth floor and attended the lectures in the Psychology and Sociology of Education and Social Science, hedged about with Research Methods and Statistics. It was a vast new enlightenment and an onerous load, especially as I also faced the challenges of the language teaching centre.

St Michael's had been a Victorian primary school, due for demolition as it was long past its sell-by date, but in a strange kind of way, with its large hall, one or two classrooms and separate yards for boys and girls, it served our purposes well as a centre for teaching English intensively to our pupils aged 12 to 15. The children were almost entirely from the sub-continent of India and Pakistan, though we did have one or two West Indians and the odd 'other' such as the Polish boy brought by his father. We discovered that he had had pins pushed into him one day in the yard in an attempt to find out if his blood was the same colour as everyone else's!

We were well-staffed in terms of numbers, though how well-qualified we were for this special task is questionable. Most of us had had experience of teaching overseas in one or other part of the erstwhile empire. Some had been missionaries and one a high-ranking officer in the Indian army. There were also two or three Pakistani men teachers. I think I was the only one who had had experience and some training in the teaching of English as a foreign language, though even I was to find these circumstances very different. The Huddersfield project helped. Our Indian army colleague was a great asset. He understood and could speak Urdu and Punjabi, the languages of most of our pupils. We were highly amused when, in his clipped army officer voice, he expressed his shock to hear the sweet little girls as well as the boys using words he had only ever heard on the lips of his roughest troops! But the 'brigadier' helped us enormously when the going was tough, in matters of communication, though we tried as far as possible to use English direct and not to resort to translation.

NATURE OF THE WORK

The centre had been going for only a short time when I joined the staff so it was still a new venture for all of us and we were able to try out many new ideas and methods, led by Shirley Sutcliffe who was an excellent Head. She had no separate office, only a desk in the place we used as a staffroom which became a workshop in various ways. One of my own particular ploys was to teach language through song. For each song I used pictures to which I attached magnets so that they could be put on a magnetic board (high technology in those days!). The authority was generous with its provision of equipment and I was fortunate that Shirley was very artistic. She made my pictures and figurines and was not at all dismayed to be asked, first thing in the morning, for such a thing as a lady sitting on the back of a crocodile going down the Nile, in time for my eleven o'clock class. Invariably she would postpone her desk-work and provide me with what I asked for.

I also found my theatre experience handy and used quite a bit of drama. I was happily amazed when my teenage boys accepted this (to them) very strange kind of lesson, an action song with repetitive structures which I later 'lifted' out of the song and used in other situations. It was interesting to hear my songs being sung in the yard at playtime and not in any mocking way. These youngsters seemed to understand that we were really trying to help them, and they took pride in using the language they had been given.

Another kind of breakthrough was the use of mathematics as a language-teaching exercise. I found this to be particularly useful when I worked with a Pakistani teacher. In front of the children we had a dialogue. We put mathematical operations on the chalkboard and then I would ask Mr Dhuper a question like, "What is the Urdu word for *minus?*" He would translate my question for the pupils and they would give me the answer. This was also a useful social exercise. It has to be remembered that most of these children, the boys at least, had been to school in their homeland, a very formal kind of school, with, at their level, all male teachers. We British ladies had to win our credibility, and to be seen as respected by a Pakistani gentleman teacher and working with him was very much in my favour.

But there were a few children who had not been to school at all. To be herding goats with eyes trained on the distant horizon one day, and sitting in a classroom in Britain the next, eyes down on this thing called a book, must have been a terrible upheaval and trauma. I began to read the signs, and to discern children who seemed to have particular needs. I recalled my work in Edinburgh as an 'adjustment teacher' and asked if could do something similar here. My part-time status allowed me greater freedom. In the end, another teacher was appointed to the establishment, and I was able to take groups from any of the classes.

It is difficult to express just how rewarding I found this work. I dealt with the pupils individually and tried my best to cater for their needs. The zenith of my satisfaction was reached one day when a lad who had been particularly frustrated and difficult began to sing a native song quietly under his breath. He caught me looking at him. With a big grin he said "Sorry Miss", and I hastened to try and convey that he was doing nothing wrong. I rejoiced that the boy was so obviously happy in what he was doing. He had really begun to achieve. I felt that I was learning so much about my fellow human beings and the ability to survive.

The work was not easy and called for great patience and understanding, not to say sense of humour. I remember a little girl who was taken off to hospital soon after joining the centre. She had been in one of my groups. Her stay in hospital was prolonged but she did return. When she went away she had no English at all. Now she greeted me with, "And how are we today?" I could just hear the hospital matron on her rounds. This child had caught not only the idiom but the Yorkshire accent, as most of the children did in the end. I realised that there was more than one context in which one could learn a language. Then there was the occasion when I had to present a school-leaver with a form from the labour exchange. He was fifteen, the then leaving age. Sadly he was also a very new immigrant and there was little chance of his acquiring enough English with us for coping with a secondary education. As the 'brigadier' was not available, I used a pupil interpreter. There was a question about health. "Ask him if he is poorly", I said, 'poorly' being one of the first words they all seemed to acquire! Back came the response, "No, Miss. He quite rich". I tried again. "Ask him if he is sick". And this time the reply came very quickly. "No, Miss, he Muslim". I should have known that 'sick' and 'Sikh' sounded exactly alike to these boys. I gave up and hoped that the lad got some employment. But I often wondered how far any of our pupils were able to cope, either with secondary education or work, other than the most menial practical tasks. Younger children had more chance of succeeding, and as more families arrived, Bradford opened language centres at junior level and eventually, to the horror of many educationists, infant centres were established. But more of this later.

Teaching at St Michael's

I look back on my St Michael's experience with fond reminiscence. We were a happy little community and there was a degree of social bonding which could have done only good for race relations. I had an interesting and heart-warming experience about thirty years later when I was visiting Bradford again. I was in a taxi. After some time, my Pakistani driver asked if I were a teacher. When I told him I had been and was now retired he went on to ask if I had taught at St Michael's. He had been one of my pupils there. He beamed his delight. The language centre no longer existed nor any other such place but it had fulfilled a need at the time and had meant a great deal to this taxi driver and myself. For me it was a part of my pearl of great price.

A Coming Together

For me also St Michael's became fertile ground for a link to be made between my teaching and my studies. The two strands of my working life came particularly together when, with the guidance of my tutor, Dennis Child, I carried out some research which seemed to suggest that these Asian children might be at risk when given intelligence tests, an important practice at that time. Their differing thought processes indicated that the tests were not really suitable and were not as objective as people liked to think. This was a special milestone for me. First I was encouraged by Dennis Child who wanted me to publish what he considered to be unique results although, sadly, I had no time to do this. And second, the Bradford Authority, concerned about the language problems of the younger children now, asked me to do a survey for them when my university work eased up. All this was a wonderful boost to my morale.

The Diploma Examinations

As the academic year of 1968 drew to its close and the Diploma examinations loomed, I stopped my school work altogether and concentrated on my studies. The authority was very flexible. I have strong memories of walking the streets of Saltaire on the long summer evenings, enjoying the fresh air after a day of incarceration with my books. I can still feel the terrible exhaustion of those last few months. Fortunately I no longer had housework to do. I had had to give up Liz's flat after a year and had found digs with an Irish lady called Chris O'Mahoney. Without the support of Chris and other special friends, I reckon I might not have passed, or at least not well enough, those vital examinations, which came on two Saturdays in July. Never will I forget the trauma of the 'battlefield' in the university examination hall, the clock ticking relentlessly on in the pregnant silence, as I raced for time. In one paper I was reduced to writing cryptic notes in order to cover what I wanted to say. It is difficult to express the tension and loneliness of this experience, which many readers will relate to.

Then came the weeks of waiting for the results. Had I qualified for the Diploma in the Behavioural Sciences? Had I qualified highly enough to be allowed to proceed to the M.Sc. degree by research? For most of my colleagues, given their full-time commitment to their schools, the Diploma would be sufficient reward for their efforts, though it would be a bonus to be allowed to go on. For me, having given up my Uganda University teaching in order to obtain the degree I never had, this was a critical and nail-biting time.

At last, one Saturday morning, the envelope came. Dear Chris was in the habit now of giving me breakfast in bed on a Saturday. She brought my post up with the tray. She guessed what was in this envelope but she left me to it and went downstairs, as she later told me, with her heart beating more quickly than normal. Even Sultan, Chris' lovely Siamese cat, in his usual place on the bed at my feet, seemed to be waiting with bated purr and suspended tail. There were twenty four names (the number who finally sat the examinations) on the typed sheet. Seventeen of these were asterisked and I saw that my name was one of them, the only lady. I took a deep breath and looked again. From out of the type swimming before my eyes, I gradually made out that we seventeen were the privileged group, allowed to go on to do the degree. I had made the first hurdle.

CHAPTER 7

And Apart from Work

The Framework

THE SUPPORT GROUP

Before continuing with my academic and professional journey, I must dwell a little more on what I am calling my support group, friends and neighbours, people in the church, colleagues in study and teaching, and also my ever-understanding family. There were in addition those in Sheffield and York and the more distant Uganda, who kept in touch regularly. To use Biblical language, I was very conscious all through my struggles of this seen and unseen cloud of witnesses. I felt shored up and strengthened. This chapter goes along with Chapter 6 in particular though its essence is also applicable to Chapter 8. It gives place and opportunity for me to express more fully my gratitude to all who saw me through one of the most difficult but enriching periods of my life, a period in which there were several important milestones.

And not only were the people of this support framework significant, so was the venue. Yorkshire, where I spent about a decade of my life, had its own kind of benign and stimulating influence. I thrived there. I have often wondered if some ancestral chord may have been touched. My grandmother on Mother's side was a Yorkshire woman, married in Manchester to a Cumbrian. The homely northern accent was part of the fabric of my childhood. Whatever the case, I felt at home. It seems to me, there could have been fewer places more suited for this 'focusing' part of my life, a time between 'fields'.

But having said this, it was in fact Chris O'Mahoney, an Irish lady, immigrant to Yorkshire, who became my closest friend. This is the landlady I refer to in Chapter 6. She was the same age as my mother and played a mother's role, spinster as she was. She and an 'uncle' had fled from Ireland in the 'troubles', been bombed out of Liverpool in World War II, and ended up in Bradford. The 'uncle' had recently died, Chris needed someone to care for and I needed care. So we came wonderfully together. Chris

and her cat, Sultan, became my family in Bradford and gave me a home from which I emerged to the fray and returned to recover. When I had had it confirmed that I would have to leave the Petersgarth flat at the end of summer 1967, I had to quickly find somewhere else to come back to for the start of the new academic year, and Chris' home became that place. My good friends at Petersgarth had known of Chris and had also known that I really needed the household tasks to be done for me while I was studying. So they brought us together.

MY NEW HOME

It was a beautiful June day when I went to see Chris. The roses, ablaze with colour, were fragrant in her little garden, and Sultan was stretched in the shade, eyeing me with feline suspicion. When I commented on him, Chris asked anxiously if I minded cats. When I told her I loved them and admired this particular one, I was in, and the amount I would have to pay weekly was not even mentioned! Much relieved, I was then able to take my holiday in Scotland, leaving my books and other belongings with my long-suffering friends until I came back to pick them up. Part of that holiday I spent with my parents in the Isle of Man. It was a pleasant oasis except that the hotel's resident band seemed to live underneath my bedroom. They had a limited repertoire and played the Beatles' *Yellow*

Submarine ad nauseam. But the summer now ended sadly with the deaths of Aunty Gladys and Uncle Billy who died within three weeks of each other. Cousin Norma came from Canada to attend the funerals, a terrible visit home for her.

I returned to Bradford in good time for the start of the school term, retrieved all my bits and pieces and settled in with Chris. I had a comfortable bedroom and a roomy wardrobe with many shelves. This housed both clothes and books. The view from the window over the valley was a never ending source of joy. Bankfield Avenue, my new address, was a small cul-de-sac, at the top of a very steep hill. We had some delightful neighbours, especially Frank and Mary who had an ever-open door. Frank helped me to become a driver again. I passed my British test and acquired a small German car called an NSU, the engine not much more powerful than that of a motor-bike, but it got me around and made my life so very much easier. The Bradford bus service was reasonable but we were a long way out from the centre and it was quite a walk from Bankfield Avenue to the main road. And later, as my life turned out, the car became an essential commodity for my work. The only problem was the snow and ice. We had several severe winters in my time there. Many a day I simply could not drive up that last bit of the road home, and had to leave the car on the road below where I rapidly came to know other helpful folks and eventually found a garage.

OUT AND ABOUT

Another memory of this little car is that it enabled me to become acquainted with the wider Yorkshire, and Chris loved to accompany me. We enjoyed in particular the haunting vastness of the moors, especially when heather-clad. As I write, I have a vision of lying amongst this heather in the Trough of Bowland, replete with one of Chris' lavish picnics, and feeding the friendly sheep by hand. But the moors at any time were awe-inspiring and it was easy to understand how Emily Brontë had her inspiration to write *Wuthering Heights*.

Chris and I loved the open air and the countryside, so easily accessible from our home. We loved to walk as well as drive, and often took ourselves across the fields, past a farm and on to Cottingley village; or we climbed up behind the house to enjoy an extended view of the Aire Valley, often lit up by the most amazing sunsets. People came from near and far to stand in wonder. Then there was the St Ives estate, recently open to the public. This afforded many beautiful walks. As we explored the countryside, my school botany came back and I enjoyed blinding Chris with science. I reeled off the Latin names of the wild flowers. In her turn, Chris shared with me her considerable knowledge of the birds and their habits. She had turned her garden into a bird sanctuary and introduced me to a highlight of the year, the gathering of the migrant swallows on the roof of Frank and Mary's house. As we watched with bated breath, the flock took off, moved by some hidden signal, destination Africa. And if we lingered to watch further, we saw the stragglers who had missed the flight. They would pause momentarily and then head off in the same direction. Why was it, I wonder, that Chris who claimed to be a lapsed Catholic and a heathen, helped me so often to see God at work?

On the occasional Saturday, when I had a little more time, we would visit other towns and villages in the West Riding and beyond. I soon became familiar with this delightful part of the world and enjoyed the narrow, winding roads which at that time were still uncluttered. A favourite place was Richmond. I was fascinated by the famous Georgian Theatre, which was, I was told, the oldest working theatre in the country. I became a member of its club, which brought concessions and a programme of events, most of them of very high quality, worth all the discomfort of sitting in an 18th century theatre with its wooden benches and double-thickness boards so that disgruntled audiences could kick and bang to their hearts' content.

CENTRE OF CULTURE

And, speaking of theatre, one of the great loves of my life, I soon came to realise that Yorkshire was a crucible of cultural events, particularly of the performing arts. From the brass bands spawned by the mills, to the Huddersfield Symphony Orchestra, the Gilbert and Sullivan productions in Bradford's Alhambra Theatre, and much more besides, one was spoiled for choice. How I longed for more leisure-time to indulge in all this, but with the way my life was now developing, performing and even spectating were forced into the sidelines, though I did manage a little concert work, especially at church socials. However it has to be said that my qualification in and experience of drama and song were standing me in good stead in my professional career, as I have described. Meantime I appreciated what I could and reckoned it an important part of the support base in my present life.

I kept in touch with my friends at Petersgarth by attending occasional services, particularly Evensong in St Peter's Church opposite the flats. But I had become a member of the Presbyterian church, St Andrew's in town. Here the congregation was liberally made up of Scots and some Northern Irish, expatriates who had gravitated to a worshipping community linked to the home country. It was natural that I should find my way here as I had to the Presbyterian church in York. Mr Barry, the Northern Irish minister was a grand preacher and a lovable pastor. He and his wife, Gertrude, whom I met also in the course of my work as she was a primary teacher, led a warm and friendly congregation which for most of us was our extended family. As in my York church, I was soon singing in the choir and reciting at socials. I also helped at sales and offered lifts in my car. I well remember one young lady I brought to church who was of Scottish background and had an uncle who was a famous mountaineer. She was known locally for her pet duck, which she took for walks round Shipley on a lead! My growing group of church friends were a colourful lot. I wish there were more time and space to describe them. I was realising once again how important it is to belong to *some* place of worship. It would never have occurred to me not to be. The bowling club or the pub can give you fellowship and lots of friends but they often lack that something extra which is the spiritual dimension, that something which empowers.

Because of the many Scots at St Andrew's the season of Burns was a great occasion. I polished up my poems and songs and leapt with enthusiasm into the ceilidh. I was able to enjoy my Scottish dancing once more and to revel generally in my Scottishness. I even danced a Highland Fling for my Pakistani pupils at St Michael's, much to their delight. At the same time the ecumenical and intercultural interests which had begun in Uganda were never far from my thoughts. In a letter home at the time I waxed lyrical on my views, remembering the frustration I had felt in Kirk Week. It seemed to me that it didn't matter if some liked bishops and some did not or some went for adult baptism and others preferred infant christenings. There seemed to be so much churchianity rather than Christianity especially when it came to matters like the form of prayer. Against the background of world turmoil and need surely all thinking and praying people should unite to sort out the problems, and that would include those of other faiths as well. Was I trying in a somewhat simplistic way to express what today might be called unity in diversity? Was I ahead of my time? I feel I could have written something like this today, forty years on.

Mr Barry was conservative and greatly worried about the pending union in England between the Congregationalists and the English Presbyterians. I could understand his concern as he was the minister of a small minority church. He did not want to see it disappear, but for me, much as I identified with this church community, the wider picture seemed more important. We had many an argument and disagreed in love, while the new United Reformed Church was in its birth pangs. And as a small gesture towards unity, I persuaded Chris that we might invite Mr Barry to tea along with Father Maguire, my Catholic priest friend from Uganda's university. He too was back in England. So it came about. The Northern Irish Protestant minister and the Roman Catholic Glaswegian priest came together, and we did not need to erect a barricade, a word much used at that time in the context of the troubles in Ulster. I *had* wondered how Chris might feel and react in the presence of so much 'cloth', but she went happily about her hostess task, leaving the conversation to the rest of us, and the whole event went off splendidly.

FURTHER SUPPORT

Although I had moved up the hill and away from my Petersgarth friends, as I have said, I did keep in touch. Indeed it would have been hard for them to forget me as my footsteps were 'set in stone' on the path just outside the front entrance to the flats. They are possibly still there now in 2006! I had dashed out one day in my usual precipitous manner, without reading a workman's warning of wet cement. There is more than one way of leaving one's mark on the community! In spite of this misdemeanour we remained friends and through these good people I met Patsy Wontner-Smith, who was to give me much support in all kinds of ways. Happily, at the time of writing, Patsy is still with us when so many others have passed on. She has a very warm place in my heart. Widowed early in her marriage, Patsy brought up her three sons and a daughter and still had time and love for others. She saw very quickly that it would be necessary for me to have time away from my books. She readily offered the hospitality of her home. I went to visit for a while every Saturday evening when we would play scrabble and chat about the week's events. We came to know each other well. Like Chris,

Patsy shared my highs and lows and I like to think I also shared hers. As the children grew, I experienced their schooldays and examination traumas, illnesses, accidents, and teenage relationships. I became a part of the family, so much so that Patsy played a large part in helping me through a serious operation in 1970. Chris needed her assistance and she gave it willingly. The neighbours and church folks were also supportive at the time of my illness as were my academic and professional friends.

Of the latter I must just mention Gerald Bevan. Gerald was a master at Bradford Grammar School where I gave a talk to the sixth form, having been introduced to the school by my old friend Harry Rée, who was once its Head. The topic of my lecture was 'Role-conflict', something I was deeply into on my university course. Gerald was particularly interested and invited me to his home where we discussed it further. The Bevan household was another where I continued to be made very welcome. Gerald became something of a sounding-board for me, a patient and helpful listener and a reader of my academic efforts. He shared my nail-biting moments as the university assessed and marked. Many a midnight's oil we burned amidst the deep concepts of psychology and sociology and how they related to education. I missed Gerald sorely when he moved away to work elsewhere. I found other support amongst my fellow students, all of whom lived either in Bradford or its environs. It was so useful to be able to mull over the subjects of our studies in the quiet peace of someone's home. There was one group of gentlemen with whom I thrashed out the mysteries and horrors of statistics and found to my joy that I could just about hold my own.

BACKGROUND 'NOISES'

I was so fortunate that behind all these wonderful Bradford people were my York and Sheffield contacts. I made regular visits to them and they came to me. I was also kept in touch with Uganda which at that time expected me back. I had renewed my Uganda driving licence. Also I was still writing supplementary readers for a language course being used there, and the tapes of my radio teacher-training work continued to be broadcast. So I was very much there in spirit at least. But the situation politically in Uganda was becoming increasingly dangerous. It was during my later Bradford years that Idi Amin in his megalomaniac excesses of ethnic cleansing cleared the country of its Asian community, much to the detriment of Uganda. I found myself being approached for job references, as my former students desperately tried to settle in Britain which at that time was itself going through a period of much industrial unrest. In some quarters, immigrants seeking asylum and work were looked upon askance. This was not helped by Enoch Powell's famous 'rivers of blood' speech which stirred the media into frightening prognostications about the outcome of accepting so many newcomers.

Events in the Middle East were also worrying. When have they not been? The Six-Day War between the Israelis and the Palestinians had taken place in 1967 and since then the area seemed to be in continuous tumult. Around me there was an atmosphere of panic, people in buses with their transistor radios glued to their ears. In the context of the Cold War, trouble in the Middle East where the big powers contended for allies could so easily have led into a third world war. But it did not and some of us are still alive to worry about the Middle East today. Is God trying to tell us something, I wonder?

A large part of my support group was my family. They were always there for me, and through regular correspondence and telephone calls I was kept up-to-date with all their happenings. I visited Scotland as often as I could and sometimes family members came to Bradford. A highlight was Mother and Dad's visit while I was still in the flat and could put them up. Alex continued in his advisory capacity. He and his new wife spent a year in America and their first child, Margaret, was born there. David came along two and a half years later. We were all very thrilled during the American year, that Alex's first book had been accepted for publication by the Cambridge University Press. In Edinburgh, Joan and Gavin had Alan and later, Linda. So the family grew. Dorothy never married. Perhaps this is why, over the years, she and I have developed a special bond. The fifteen and a half years between us never seemed to matter.

With such support and such a lovely and stimulating place to work in, how could I fail? After the hurdle of the Diploma examinations in 1968 there was still a long way to go. Had I known just what lay ahead, health as well as workwise, I am not sure that I could have faced it so easily. But, step by step, the way unfurled until that unbelievable day when I received my M.Sc. scroll from our Vice Chancellor, Harold Wilson, the Prime Minister who had just been ousted by Edward Heath. And so to the third and last part of my student days.

CHAPTER 8

University Student Part 3

Goal In Sight

YEAR OF RESEARCH

The last act of my academic venture began in the autumn of 1968 as the university started on another session. I had enjoyed what I reckoned to be a well-earned holiday on the Continent with my parents and sister Dorothy. I had returned to Bradford raring to go towards the final goal. With the Diploma examinations behind me I was now set for the two years leading to the M.Sc. degree. There would be no more lectures. I was on my own, with tutorial guidance, and I would proceed with my chosen research and then the writing of it in a dissertation. Although technically I could not call myself a graduate until I acquired the M.Sc., I was considered for working purposes to be engaged in post-graduate studies. I enjoyed certain concessions of the university such as more library tickets than formerly and access to more library areas with workspace if I wanted it. At first I missed the regular meetings with my fellow students, though we endeavoured to get together occasionally by arrangement. But soon we were all totally absorbed in our individual projects, with very little time for social contacts.

My own study, after much thought and planning and in consultation with my tutor, lay in the area of psycholinguistics. This was very much a virgin field at that time. It concerns the relationship between thought and language. My year of Linguistics at York and my experience of teaching English as a Second Language had made this an area of special interest for me, especially since I had done that study at St Michael's concerning thought processes. It would be good to go a little deeper into the processes connected with language. My first step was to read everything I could lay my hands on about language learning, a mammoth but fascinating task. There seemed, broadly speaking, to be two schools of thought. There were those who saw learning in general, and language learning in particular, as a matter of imitation and the forming of habits, while others saw it as the business of finding rules and applying them. My instinct was to go for the second of these.

I discovered also in my reading that there was a current interest in child language, in the context of these two theories. How did the baby acquire its mother tongue? Did the child simply imitate, or recognise rules which were duly put into operation? Again I supported the rule-finders. I then began to wonder about my Pakistani pupils learning a second language when they had at least one other. Did *they* use rules and how different was the process from that of the young child acquiring the mother tongue? Further reading showed me that in this latter comparison, the consensus of opinion seemed to be that the two things were very different; learning a second language was a related but quite separate topic. I had my doubts. Surely there must be some if not many similarities. My mind was humming and I longed to find out more.

Then I discovered Noam Chomsky, a psycholinguist who was interested in what he called language universals. He believed that the child had an innate capacity for language learning, a kind of set of basic rules or 'language acquisition device'. If this were true, I thought, surely this capacity could be used more than once, unless it disappeared as the child grew. There might well be a case for suggesting that the learning of another language was more similar to the acquiring of the first than had been supposed. One might even go further than this and say that the learner could be more efficient the second time round as he would be already a practised language learner. And, I wondered, how far is thought geared to the language and culture of the speaker and how far to a universal language and culture of humankind? Chomsky's universals of language chimed so nicely with my own ideas on the universals and particulars of culture, that I warmed to him and decided that here I had found my area of study. I would try a comparison of the language-learning processes of Pakistani teenagers in Bradford with those of young children from English-speaking homes, acquiring their first language, and, flying in the face of all the literature, I would hypothesise that the similarities would be greater than the differences.

I could investigate only a very small part of language and I chose the aspect of grammar known as morphology. This is about the rules for things like pluralising and indicating possession, notions which exist in most languages, though they may be dealt with in different ways. I was greatly helped by the work of an American scholar, Jean Berko, also a believer in rule-learning.

She had studied a group of young American children as they were acquiring their mother-tongue, English. Her object was to find out if they *did* use rules and if so how. Did they have an innate knowledge or 'language acquisition device' which allowed them to find these rules, and then to apply them to new experience? Her way of working was to use nonsense terms applied to funny pictures which would appeal to the children. For instance, she showed a strange creature which she called a wug. Then she showed another and asked what two would be called. If the child said "wugs" then she knew that a rule was being used, as the child could not have heard the nonsense word before and was not copying. She had a whole set of such tests covering the rules of English morphology and she was able to establish that her sample at least were discovering these rules and could apply them.

I decided to replicate Berko's study with my second language learners and to compare my results with hers. I devised my own set of nonsense words which went with a set of pictures drawn by an artistic and imaginative Bradford colleague. They became known as the 'ligs and gutches', after two of my nonsense terms. They became quite famous amongst my own circle of friends, especially later when I used a large presentation set in my teacher-training work. I was teased that I might not get my 'ligs and gutches' through customs! I do not intend here to go into the detail of my research, which like Berko's was complex and time-consuming. Readers interested will find the work in the copy of my M.Sc. Dissertation which is in the library of Bradford University. Suffice it to say that in that university year of 1968-69 I worked in seven educational establishments, the four secondary language centres and three mainstream schools. My subjects were all Pakistani immigrant boys, except for a group of English students at the university who acted as a practice sample. They were very happy to oblige. In fact, I am extremely grateful to all concerned. I and my tape-recorder were accepted with remarkable tolerance.

It is questionable which was more tiring, the physical plodding as I went about collecting my data, or the mental gymnastics as I applied the research methods and statistics learnt in the Diploma years. It was a year that stretched my every faculty and I knew great weariness. I also knew joy and excitement in a way I had never dreamed of, as my results began to show my hypothesis to be proved. The similarities to Berko's results *were* greater than the differences. I used a test called the Kolmogorev-Smirnov, after two Russian scholars. This allowed me to do the comparison. There was no significant difference overall though there were a few particular differences of a very interesting kind, but that is another story. Statistically speaking the lack of significant difference meant that, at least in this small bit of language learning, Berko's young children acquiring their first language and my older subjects learning another, were going through a very similar procedure. My initial, instinctive thinking had been proved right. Could this perhaps open the way to further and wider comparative research? Or was I being arrogant? I was to find a growth of interest in the years to come. I like to think that I might have had some small part in this minor revolution. Meantime I must return to my own immediate story.

EXPERIMENT AND TEACHER TRAINING

There were several important happenings for me while I was engaged in this research. During 1969 I continued on the establishment of the St Michael's Language Centre but found myself more and more in the role of training. One young male teacher was specifically appointed to act as my assistant, Mr John the pupils called him, and he must be my son! We worked very closely together, experimenting with all kinds of techniques for making the English language meaningful. My earlier attempts to use story, song and drama were developed further, with the additional technique of two teachers working as partners, much in the way that stage comedians work in pantomime. For instance I might say to John, "put the cup on the table", and he would put the saucer on the chair. I would look suitably exasperated, hoping the children knew why, and ask them to correct the situation. The pupils loved these deliberate mistakes. We developed the idea in all kinds of ways. Again, Shirley Sutcliffe came to our aid and designed a set of 'funny visuals' for example. The errors had to be found and corrected.

The number of visitors to the centre increased, not only from Bradford itself but also from other parts of the country. As I groped for further insight into the best ways of teaching English as a Second Language in this immigrant situation, I was greatly helped by all these others who observed and commented. I felt as though I were back in Uganda, training as well as teaching, and indeed it *was* the beginning of my official return to teacher education. It was also the start of work which took me out and about nationally as my visitors invited me to work in *their* schools and authorities, though until I had completed my university research, I had to limit my wanderings.

THE BRADFORD INFANT SCHOOL SURVEY

I have mentioned that the Bradford authority had become concerned about the language development of the younger children. They had now opened centres for children from eight to twelve years. But they were also troubled about the lack of prowess in the children at infant school level, as were other authorities with large immigrant populations. It seemed that the children from non-English-speaking homes were not achieving generally as well as their English classmates, and by the time they had reached the end of the infant school years at age seven, the gap was quite marked. These were children mainly born in this country and starting their schooling together with the English speakers. Surely without the ability, it was reasoned, to use fluently the tool of learning, they would be at a disadvantage during the rest of their education. Perhaps special measures of some kind were needed. A particular difficulty in meeting this need was that the current educational thinking on the education of the very young was not amenable to 'special measures' i.e. teaching! Just give the children a rich educational environment and verbal bath and it would all happen by osmosis! Following this practice, the infant non-English speaker would acquire the necessary language by sitting and playing next to Nellie. It can be imagined then how the advocates of this way of learning viewed the prospect of special language centres for the youngest children, a policy which 'Bradford' was contemplating.

Before rushing to implement their plan however, it was decided that a survey should be done, and some concrete results produced to justify such a programme. They asked if I would conduct this survey which meant reducing once again the hours I worked at St Michael's. It would also mean my carrying out two different lots of research at the same time, which in the event was helpful, providing many new insights. The pressure of the work was helpful to me in another way also. I lost my childhood friend, Mairi in that year. She died of cancer. The absorption with what I was doing took from the severity of my grief and heartache. I cannot dwell here on the significance of my loss. Suffice it to say that my faith was stretched to the limits. Why should a gifted woman of forty have to die? She had so much to give and so much to live for. I have often thought since about how my life might have been influenced had Mairi lived longer. So I concentrated on my research, both lots, the work for my degree and that for Bradford. In this last I was greatly helped by the team of Educational

Psychologists in the city, as well as by the teachers and Heads in the infant schools themselves, who were deeply concerned about their 'immigrant' pupils. I had become part of the mainstream educational scene, while still focusing on the particular needs of second language learners. This was another milestone for me, with a bearing on the future.

SCHOOLS COUNCIL PROJECT

The new work in Bradford was attracting notice nationally and I was somewhat apprehensive to discover that other places besides Bradford were anxiously awaiting the outcome of my survey. Would it demonstrate the need for special measures to be taken to help second language development at infant level? Educationists were preparing for battle. The 'sitting next to Nellie' controversy was very much to the fore. Meantime there was some interest being shown by the Schools Council, a body that had been set up by the government to establish action/research projects addressing current educational needs. These projects were usually based in universities. Leeds University had such a project in its Institute of Education. It was examining the needs of immigrant children acquiring English and providing guidelines and materials for the teachers. So far, work was well advanced for children of junior age, the guidebook *Scope* and materials for the pupils being well-used in the schools. Work was now progressing for secondary schools. The Director of the project, June Derrick, was considering adding a section to her team which would deal with the needs of the infant child, in spite of or perhaps because of the controversy. She cast an interested eye on Bradford and on my survey in particular. June invited me to see the work of her project and she also came to Bradford to discuss my work.

The upshot of this was that she confirmed her plan to add an infant section to the work in Leeds and she asked me to join it as the linguist. I would have two experienced infant teachers to work with me, and I would have lecturer status in the university though most of my teaching would be outside the campus, in various local education authorities. The infant section would start in the autumn of 1969, just as I had to start on the writing of my M.Sc. Dissertation! Had I realised the amount of work the latter would be, I might have thought twice about accepting June's offer. As it was, and with many regrets at the thought of leaving Bradford, I agreed to join the Leeds project, starting in September of that year and I

73

went off to the Isle of Wight for a family holiday, enjoying a glorious fort-night of summer weather and feeling surprisingly relaxed. I had reached an endpoint of a kind. The research for the degree was done and all that remained, I fondly believed, was the simple business of writing it up! I had also completed the infant schools survey, leaving the data with the educational psychologists for processing. I admit to some apprehension in that direction. Would the psychologists find from my work that some-thing special was needed to help the infant school child and teacher? If so then the setting up of the new section at Leeds would be justified. I was comforted by the thought that one of the local areas we intended to work in was Bradford so I would not be leaving that authority altogether. Jim Rouse had discussed the matter with June Derrick and seemed happy with the arrangements. Also I would not be leaving Chris. The journey to Leeds is not far and I intended to keep my Bradford home.

How thankful I was that I had had a good break over the summer! The next ten months or so were extremely strenuous but challenging and exciting. It was no easy task setting up a new unit of work from scratch, including making the necessary national contacts, but at least we were joining an established team in which there were artists and technicians as well as teachers and we would be able to make use of their skills. We would also be able to learn from the ways of working in the other sections though the particulars would be different. So I began my new venture, conscious of a race against time. These Schools Council projects had a time-limit of two to three years and limited financial support.

Then I had virtually about six months to complete the Dissertation for my degree so I was working on this alongside everything else. The writing was a lot more complex than I had envisaged. I think I wrote the first chapter nine times in my efforts to make sure that it cohered with the last. Also, some of my linguistic statements, as opposed to the psychological and statis-tical ones, had to be vetted by linguists in another university (Edinburgh), as the Bradford department did not have that kind of expertise. I remember the relief when my work was approved.

In addition to all this, there was a question-mark over my health. I had begun to feel unwell. I wondered if I might have bilharzia, an unpleasant tropical disease, legacy of my Uganda years. Tests showed that the problem was gynaecological and I would require a hysterectomy. Should I struggle on and complete my degree and the work on the project and then have the operation or stop now and postpone all the work? I decided to go on but I became very tired at times and lost a considerable amount of weight.

It was enlightening working with teachers in many parts of the country, including two areas of London. This way we met those on both sides of the educational controversy and learned a great deal from one another. It had never occurred to many that language was so important in the general curriculum. We spent a lot of time helping teachers to be aware of things they had taken so much for granted. Just what words and phrases did the young child need to know in order to count and learn to read? Were the songs, rhymes and games already used in schools really helpful to the non-English-speaking child or could they be adapted in some way? Could new ones be devised? The words 'adopt', 'adapt' and 'devise' became watchwords in our training sessions. How we struggled to find ways of 'teaching' without obviously doing so! But often I at least felt very frustrated and wanted to teach much more deliberately without feeling guilty about it! We left ideas and work with the teachers and spent hours back at base, and sometimes while travelling, analysing each workshop and endeavouring to build on what we felt had been achieved. Sometimes it was very difficult to assess.

There were many problems of a kind particular to the infant department, but one we shared with our colleagues working with teachers of older children was the tendency in schools to see the non-English-speaker as 'remedial', a child who today would be described euphemistically as having 'special needs'. In those days, most schools had a remedial teacher or even department and the slow learners were withdrawn for part or sometimes all of their school day. It is difficult now to understand how people could be so blind, that they could not see the difference between a genuinely slow-learning English child and a bright Pakistani who happened not to understand the language of the school. As it was, a great many children were classed as 'thickies' when they were anything but. The remedial groups became more and more full of children from the ethnic minorities who then suffered a particularly nasty form of racism. All the more reason that we should find ways of improving their English language abilities.

BOURNEMOUTH CONFERENCE

In February of 1970, my two teacher colleagues and I were invited to attend an important conference in Bournemouth. This was a national gathering for people at the top, the inspectorate and Heads of colleges which trained teachers of the very young children, including those involved in nursery work. The theme of the conference was 'language development', which is some indication of the depth of concern being currently felt. We three were somewhat overawed to be amongst this illustrious group, I especially, as I had been asked to give one of the lectures. The title of this lecture, whether or not of my choosing, was 'What is language?' It was a daunting prospect, particularly before such an audience. I had come so recently from my work with teenage children for whom the *teaching* of English as a Second Language was acceptable and encouraged. The people here, except perhaps for some of the male inspectors, would be very wary. Was I, with the authority of a Schools Council project behind me, about to preach a message unsuited to the preciously held notions of infant and nursery education? In my new capacity as linguist to the infants section of the Leeds project, I was expected to provide some answers to the question of 'language caught or taught?'

This was another time in my life when I really knew the power of prayer. During a very sleepless night in that Bournemouth hotel I felt strongly that I was not alone, and the next day I faced this large influential audience calmly, abandoned my notes, and allowed myself to become a 'channel' of my conviction. I realised just how strongly I felt about the language question and the feeling spurred me on. It was the start of a lecturing style which was to stand me in good stead in the years to come. What *was* my conviction in this case? All of a sudden it seemed very simple, as that teacher put it when I came to write about it, "just common sense written down". The learning of language needed both meaningful experience *and* teaching. It was not an either/or, and this for any age-group (shades of my time in France!). The skill of the teacher lay in a proper balance of the two. But the teacher needed three sets of knowledge in particular, first an awareness of the nature of language and its power as a human tool, including that of learning, second an understanding of the language demands of the curriculum for her particular pupils, and third a knowledge of the needs and interests of those same pupils.

This was the message I endeavoured to give in my lecture, spending most time perhaps on the nature of language as my title bid me do. In my summing-up I offered the terms 'Field and Focus', which seemed a succinct way of expressing my educational philosophy. There had to be an appropriate field of experience and there had to be help in 'pushing home' what had been picked up. Then as the learning was consolidated, the field could be widened and enriched. Little did I realise how important this concept was to be to me in the future.

To my great relief my lecture seemed to be well-received, and this was confirmed for me when, in the immediate aftermath of the conference, I received many invitations to speak in the teacher-training world. The work was useful for our project which now began to gather momentum and to widen its scope from the needs of infant teachers to those working at nursery level. It was a whole new world for me. We all three began to realise that, unlike our colleagues in the project working with teachers of older children, we would not be providing materials for the children so much as concentrating on guidance for the teachers in the use of their curriculum field. We began to focus now for ourselves on the means of this guidance and we continued to run our workshops greatly helped by the stimulus of 'Bournemouth' and what we had learnt from so many able people. Meantime, the results of my language survey which had been analysed by the Bradford educational psychologists, showed quite plainly that these children did have problems with language and were vulnerable to the difficulties of general learning. I felt more and more justified in taking my 'field and focus' approach.

GOAL ACHIEVED

At the same time as we were working with the teachers nationally, and I was lecturing in places where teachers and nursery nurses of young children were being trained, I was of course endeavouring to complete my dissertation for the M.Sc. I had persuaded the secretary of our Leeds Project to take on the onerous task of typing it, something she was used to doing for other staff in the university. In those days there were no word processors and it was a big job which she did very competently. I had to arrange for the binding. I found a firm in Bradford which would do this. And I had to provide a copy for the university library. These last days of my academic work were hectic and again nail-biting. I was on a strict deadline. I just could not believe it when the work was handed in. Adapting to the lack of strain was almost as hard as bearing it! It was a familiar pattern in my life. But this time, there was the additional element of my health problem. The postponed operation was scheduled for the autumn of that year, after my graduation which would take place in July.

What can I say about this latter event? My supportive family came from Scotland. Somehow Chris put everybody up. In my new academic regalia I took my place in the Great Hall of Bradford University and climbed the steps to the platform where Harold Wilson presented me with my scroll and shook my hand. Even as this was happening, the thought passed through my mind that Chris, somewhere in the hall, would be smiling at me and glowering at Harold. She had had no time for him and his Labour government and was immensely relieved that only months before, he had been defeated and we now had a Conservative government under Edward Heath. But I teased Chris later as we all enjoyed a celebratory meal in the Bankfield Hotel, saying that I would never wash my hand again since it had been shaken by the great and the good!

My goal had been achieved, and an even better one than I had envisaged in my Uganda days, vindicating my brother Alex's continual faith in me. The degree had come by research, giving me endless interest and excitement. I had had no idea in my early years how much I would enjoy

scholarly pursuits even if they also brought me much exhaustion. Now I possessed the key which could open so many doors to me, but first I had to deal with my health. As a way of unwinding and preparing for my time in hospital I went on a holiday to Austria with my parents during that summer of 1970. Amid the beauty of the mountains and the calm 'sanity' of the company, I gradually relaxed and faced with equanimity what was then a major operation.

Graduate of Bradford University

Family Note

In Book 1 there are family 'trees' (see page 12). I had intended to update these in this volume, but in attempting to do so, I found myself becoming bogged down in a spreading network, no doubt interesting to family members, but probably tedious to the general reader. My niece, Alex's daughter Margaret, is working on the family annals, and has already produced (2006) an excellent record of the Garvie side. She aims soon to work on the Tysons. Members of the Garvie and Tyson 'clans' therefore should be in touch with Margaret. Suffice it for me in this book to say by the time of writing, both Alex and Joan in my immediate family had become grandparents, and cousins Anne, Graham, Doris and Norma likewise. I have a growing gallery of children's photographs and I am enjoying being a great-aunt-cum-first-cousin twice removed.

Edie Garvie
January 2007

Edie's immediate family in 1975 – The Golden Wedding
Dorothy is behind Edie and Joan is behind Alex

Book 3

Milestones of the Widening 'Field'

1970 and beyond

*"All things are simply God to you,
you who see God in all things"*
Meister Eckhart

"Be the change you want to see in the World"

Mahatma Gandhi

Part 1

The Bridge

1970 – 1981

Bradford/Leeds

TURBULENT THOUGHTS

Back to Bradford in the short time before my operation, I went through another period of uncertainty about the future. It was in fact the start of eleven years which formed the bridge between my 'focusing' years of study and the 'shore' which I finally reached, the wider 'field' which I believe was right for me. I endeavour in this section to telescope these bridge years. At the risk of mixing my metaphors, finding the right door for my new key proved to be more difficult than I had imagined. The bridge was not an easy road, especially in the beginning. In fact it was a veritable bridge of sighs!

There was the problem of Uganda, still strongly pulling me back. There were many calls for my return which had been taken for granted. My teacher-training tapes were still being used in the country. I had even kept my Uganda driving licence which people coming and going had continually renewed for me. Sadly the situation for expatriates was becoming more and more untenable because of the political upheavals, and the stories I heard from those coming out persuaded me towards caution. Perhaps Uganda would have to wait. At the same time, I was beginning to realise it would not now be easy to extricate myself from the British educational scene. Rightly or wrongly, and more since joining the Leeds national project, I had become embroiled. The lecture I had given in Bournemouth had resulted in many requests for my services across the country. And if truth be known, I had enjoyed this challenge. So, there was a strong pull in this direction.

But of course I was committed to the Leeds project for now. It had about a year to run and there were problems in this sphere also. The 'language caught or taught' controversy, which I spoke of in Book 2, had penetrated the project itself, especially our infants section. We were supposed to be producing some kind of guidelines and materials for teachers, but the nature of these and procedure for writing were eluding us. Then, just as I needed to be there to give linguistic leadership, I had to go into hospital for my operation. I did so, my thoughts very much in tumult, and it was to be some time before I could contribute to any project.

ILLNESS

For about five months I was virtually out of commission. The hysterectomy itself, an operation which was a much bigger event then than now, was successful, and I seemed to make a quick recovery. My parents were even allowed to see me on the day of the operation. But, on leaving the hospital two weeks later, I haemorrhaged and had to go back. This happened twice, the first time at Chris's and the second at Patsy's home. Patsy had realised that the bleeding could happen again and she offered to take me to save Chris another trauma. She was right. The same ambulance men came and cared for me with typical Yorkshire cheerfulness and kindness, which I was to meet from friends and nursing staff alike, a tremendous boost to my flagging spirits. It was depressing and debilitating to be afraid to leave the hospital, and I shall be for ever grateful to my many visitors. Chris came in every day and neighbours and friends very frequently, including people from university, language centre and church, and of course colleagues from Leeds. On one occasion, I had three vicars in one day, Brandon Jackson from St Peter's (later to become the controversial Dean of Lincoln Cathedral), Andrew from Sheffield and Mr Barry from St Andrew's. The hospital staff were much impressed, declaring at least one of them to be 'dishy'!

At last, just as I was preparing to spend Christmas in hospital, and the Salvation Army was already playing carols outside my room (I had been given a side-room to myself), my surgeon pronounced, "You will be all right this time" and chased me home. Chris alerted our good neighbours and they took me in their car. I remember sitting in the home of Frank and Mary, my eye fixed on the gleaming horse brasses which hung either side of the mantelpiece, in an effort not to worry and panic. When several days had passed with no more bleeding, I began to relax and even thought of going to my family in Edinburgh for Christmas. This was arranged. Brother Alex, with Dad as companion in the car, came for me. It was decided to go north by the A1 and not by the more scenic and bumpy way over the hills. It was brave of the men to risk the hazards of carrying a passenger who could haemorrhage again at any moment. Thank God for Alex's sense of humour. He produced a small piece of elastoplast and declared he was ready for all emergencies! We reached Scotch Corner and all was still well; then we were home and Mother took over.

The next four months are difficult to describe. To say that I was grateful to my family is an understatement. They were so caring. Even the little ones, now on the scene, were encouraged to play quietly. Physically I healed more quickly than mentally. I was depressed and tearful and must have been very difficult to live with. In my weakness I worried about my colleagues at the Project, and all the work I could not face. A group came to see me from Leeds, but had no joy from me. I told them I was not going back! And things were far from right there, they told me, not only in the infants section. June Derrick, the Director, was very troubled apparently. Much of that time for me is now a blissful blank. All I can remember is that suddenly it was spring. The sunshine and the renewal of everything about me made me feel better. I returned to Bradford and Chris, and with a new-found motivation, tried to sort out my life.

INFANT CENTRES

In this I was greatly helped by my old friend, Jim Rouse, in the Bradford Education Authority. As planned, and in accordance with 'the children need to be taught' side of the language controversy, Bradford was to open eight special centres for the youngest children. When the shouts of consternation reached them from some quarters, they said that if they *had* left the children in the ordinary schools, these schools would have been full of 'immigrant' children in any case, because of the catchment areas. By having them in special centres for a time they could aim in particular at *their* needs, could work out methods of enhancing the language programme and of training staff to cope with this. They could also work on ways of assessment and when the children were deemed ready, they would join the normal infant schools.

Fine in theory, but who was to coordinate and train? The reader is probably way ahead of me. God moves in mysterious ways. I am convinced that my illness and its aftermath gave Him the opportunity for one of his quirkier interventions. I eventually found myself recruited for this role. The work of the Leeds project was finally fulfilled through the Bradford infant centres and all parties except the extreme 'language caught' adherents were satisfied. But, how did this miracle come about?

Unknown to me in my absence, there had been some frenetic activity of various kinds. June Derrick had discussed the work of the Project, and particularly the infants section, with Margaret Thatcher, then Secretary of State for Education. June and the Director of Leeds University Institute of

Education had talked with Jim Rouse and also with Bradford University, which had considered taking over the Leeds infants section of their project in a new networking of town and gown. The infant centres in Bradford would be an experimental field of operation.

I arrived back in Bradford at a crucial point of these negotiations and the upshot was that I was offered the job of coordinating the centres and training the staff. Bradford University, in the event, did not take over the Project, but were helpful to me personally, especially my old tutor, Dennis Child. The infants section of the Leeds Project would no longer exist, one of the teachers on it being offered the headship of a Bradford centre, so we would still be working together. The others were to go back to their schools or to move on to others. But as a team we were still committed to producing a publication of some kind and this was finally achieved, helped by the work in Bradford. I returned to Leeds only to clear my office, and now was known officially as a teacher/research-worker in Bradford.

But I was still not a hundred per cent fit, and it was a while before I could work a full day, let alone take up an experimental new post. This was recognised by 'Bradford' and I was eased into the work with a writing commission. It could almost be called a recuperative exercise. The authority required a written raison d'être for its infant centre policy along with a clarification of aims. My previous time in Bradford when I conducted the language survey and worked closely with the educational psychologists, enabled me to tackle this assignment. I did several reports on various aspects, and included suggestions for the way forward. These were accepted as a kind of blueprint which was strongly supported by the Director of Education who promised staff and equipment accordingly.

THE TEACHERS' CENTRE

To begin with, and until the new Teachers' Centre was established, I wrote in corners of schools which Jim Rouse found for me. It was strange to be in an active community without taking part. But I was made very welcome and both staff and pupils accepted me as a familiar part of the scenery! This was particularly so in Wapping Junior School where I spent most of my time. Mrs Barry, the minister's wife, taught here, so I already had a friend at court. And the Head, Mr McDowell, became a very good sounding-board for my writings. He was a warm, down-to-earth

Yorkshireman. We got on very well together and I was touched when some years later I was invited to his retiring party.

But the time came when I had to move to this mysterious new 'animal' called a teachers' centre. The concept had been taken up all over the country and there was now such a place in most authorities, sometimes purpose-built, sometimes, as was the Bradford centre, a large house converted. Ours was called Rosemount, once I believe the elegant home of a mill owner. At the time of its building it would have been on the edge of the city. Now it was very much in the centre and a convenient place of access for most teachers. I was excited to be based there. I was given my own room and became part of a team of advisory teachers. There were about twelve of us at that time, each with our own responsibility for a curriculum area or age-group of pupil or both. My own interests lay within the area which dealt with particular needs. There were several of us in a sub-team, one of them being Marcel Leclerc, who had also been part of the Leeds Project at one time. We had our own technician and artist and lots of opportunity for doing innovative things. Part of our work called for research. The staff of the Teachers' Centre offered advice to schools in general. We ran in-service courses, offered a library service and gave provision for the designing and making of teaching materials. The place became a hive of professional activity. It was also a social centre with its own cafeteria and bar.

As I drove down the drive on my first visit, a drive which swept round a circular lawn surrounded by old-established trees and flower beds, I had the feeling of a new beginning and that this attractive ambience would encourage us and enhance our work, which certainly proved to be the case. None of the eight infant centres I was coordinating was more than three miles from my base. I was out and about amongst them every day and we all became part of an experimental new venture which gathered momentum. Soon, in today's jargon, it began to deliver. There was still much interest all over the country, including an on-going opposition, but this quietened down when useful materials began to emerge, the outcome of some fine team-teaching, not only within each centre but across centres and eventually drawing in teachers from the infant schools to which our centre children would go. I hardly had time to notice my improving health, so happily occupied was I, and all my old enthusiasm seemed to have come back, so much so that when I had to return to hospital yet again, this time to have a small growth taken off my nose, I took the 'ligs and gutches' with me (See Book 2 page 70) so that I could go on working, much to the amusement of the nurses. Luckily the growth was benign and I returned to the fray with still more vigour.

The three years or so that I spent based at the Teachers' Centre gave me many happy memories, not only of professional satisfaction, but also of social pleasures. There was, for instance, the Burns Supper we organised, ably assisted by members of St Andrew's Church. There was the group of Japanese young people who came for a course in conversational English which I was asked to run. This was an event which mixed work with social activities and for me personally had a further happy outcome. One of the girls, Junko Egashira, kept up with me later and I became godmother to her first son. I also visited the family in various parts of the world. Junko's husband was a Scot who worked for the Reuters News agency. I was accumulating 'children' and godchildren all over the world. I have always felt that this was some compensation for my not marrying and having children of my own.

As the centre became more active, there were many interesting visitors both from other parts of the country and from overseas, some of them to be considered as V.I.Ps. An amusing memory for me was the time that Mrs Thatcher came. For some reason I had missed the rules of protocol, and after meeting the lady in my room, I hastened to my car and to my next appointment. I had not realised that we were all supposed to stay put until our important visitor had left. Hers was to be the first car to depart, instead of which it was mine that had that honour! I did wonder why the drive was so quiet and why there were police at the gates and some cheering from bystanders as I came past. They had taken me for Mrs Thatcher! Another memory of that time, as I record the period, was the changing of our money. Britain went decimal.

LANGUAGE ACROSS THE CURRICULUM

The great clarion call in education which emerged from the famous Bullock Report of that era was 'Language Across the Curriculum'. This was to affect all teachers working in every part of the system, no matter what subject or age of pupil they were teaching. It chimed very nicely with our infant centre policy of helping these little non-English speakers to acquire the language of learning. We set up working-groups to study the curriculum of the infant school, in other words the 'field' of learning. We looked at the special measures needed for 'focusing' on this learning and I developed the notion of a 'language-teaching kitbag' which contained toys and various articles of interest to the children, carefully chosen to highlight such things as colour and plural. The bag became famous when I went round the centres, especially as it contained a strange animal called a glook which sat on my shoulder and told me what the children were doing! I worked closely with staff, experimenting with techniques, discussing and pinpointing what made for success, then going back to base and writing about it. Duplicated papers were sent round all the centres so that everyone could share what was going on. The words 'adopt', 'adapt' and 'devise' became key and all the resources in every centre were stretched to the limit. For instance, the Head of one centre was particularly musical. She worked out a special course for her colleagues in the use of the guitar, simple chords for beginners. The casual papers produced soon became work units and these were accompanied by other papers on, for example, social and community matters. Bradford had appointed teacher-social workers. Our working-parties included these people. They also included a group of bilingual teachers and parents who were able to guide us on cultural and language problems. For instance, we discovered a word in Punjabi which means 'in' and is pronounced like the English word 'under'. The prepositions are difficult when languages are in contact. We had been trying to demonstrate an 'in/under' contrast in English and we wondered why there was so much confusion!

THE SUCCESS OF 'FIELD AND FOCUS'

The work grew over my three years. It was exciting and exhilarating. I looked forward to joining a centre and taking part in their day. I took particular pleasure in being there towards the end of the afternoon and participating in a 'community happening', a friendship circle where the parents waiting for their children would join in. I like to think that *their* English was also helped by the songs, stories and games. To my great satisfaction I found that my concept of 'field and focus' was serving well. It seemed to be a useful construct for learners, teachers and teacher-trainers alike. I found myself building programmes and planning courses with this concept in mind. The various working-parties seemed to find it helpful and we were all singing from the same hymn-sheet. So much was being carried forward on a broad front, the idea of which I illustrated by the use of a tartan stole. This made an even better aid when I put the stole across my chest. The teachers would not forget the broad front!

Eureka

Then came the day when we all came together in a conference held in one of the bigger centres. We mounted an exhibition of ideas and materials, the outcome of many months of work. Each working party had its stance and spokesperson. I sat in the centre like a spider in my web and acted as coordinator. From this conference there came a booklet which I was honoured to edit. It was called *Language for the foundations of Reading and Mathematics* and it exemplified the Bullock Report's maxim of 'language across the curriculum'. In a sense, the whole of the infant child's curriculum, including the stories, songs etc. is a foundation for these two important areas of learning. The booklet reflected the hard work and tremendous enthusiasm of so many. We had reached, I felt, an important staging-post and justification for the infant centres. Sitting in my car one day in a lay-by on the A1 during the time of the booklet's construction, I had a sudden sense of the rightness of all this, a kind of professional eureka or epiphany. I had a vision of how 'Bradford', at the infant level at least, might proceed. I also felt that the concept of 'field and focus' and the notion of 'language across the curriculum' were important for me personally. It was a significant moment. It seemed that Destiny – God – was very much at my elbow.

Forced Decision

Bradford had its own press and our booklet was produced in great quantity. The requests for me to give talks nationally were coming in again and I took copies of the booklet with me. I can't remember it being sold but it certainly was dispersed and became well-known. Now that I was fit and well again, and now that the work of the Leeds Project had been chan-nelled, as it were, through that of the Bradford infant centres, it was time for me to consider again my own future, to start seeking once more that elusive door for the key I spoke of earlier. One of my options it seemed just then, was to stay on in Bradford, at least for a while, and to see my vision fulfilled. The ideas had been well received by my colleagues and the people at the top in the authority. But this was not to be.

The state of the country in the early seventies was rocky. There were strikes and redundancies and three-day weeks. In candle-lit gloom the leadership seemed helpless to do anything about it. There was little money about and new ventures were out. The Bradford authority, which very much wanted to take up my ideas, virtually disappeared into a regional 'rationalisation'. They even lost their Director who had been so supportive. He was devastated, as were Jim Rouse and myself and many others. Jim and I realised that this was, almost certainly, my point of departure. If I stayed on in Bradford, it would be a matter of going round in circles with more of the same. I needed to be where I could use the things I had reached. This was perhaps the first glimpse I had of the door I was meant to enter. It had been apparent on several occasions. I just hadn't seen it. I needed to freelance. I was a pioneer with a mixture of madness and courage! But, there was also a feeling of 'not yet'. I needed to be prepared and equipped for this ultimate adventure. Hence, I believe, these frequent stops and starts, this wide and varied experience of many things.

So, if not Bradford, what? It so happened that a publisher's representative had visited me at the Teachers' Centre. He had browsed amongst my papers and asked if I had considered publishing. While I was so involved in the work of the infant centres, I could not face such a task, but now, if I resigned, might be the right time for writing a book, to put into more permanent form a record of the Bradford/Leeds Project and at the same time to record the 'things' I had reached. I began to warm to the notion. So it came about. I was commissioned by Blackwell to produce a book which was eventually entitled *Breakthrough to Fluency*. It would be a very practical manual, the story of the infant centres and all that they stood for.

It seems now, in hindsight, that the current difficulties in the country and in the Bradford authority actually contributed to the finding of my way. I was propelled out of the local scene in which I had become embedded and at least pointed in a direction which gradually took me to where I was meant to be. But the accent was on 'gradually'. This was only the first step. I was on a long bridge. To cut a long story short, I resigned from Bradford and went to Edinburgh, where for eleven months in my parents' home I concentrated on my writing, apart from one exciting excursion (see below) and frequent short visits back to Chris.

Edinburgh Sojourn

My First Book

Angus Doulton, my editor, was very helpful and trusting. First he introduced me to two others of his authors who were writing in the same genre as myself. I am not sure now if this was in-house policy of the publisher or just a thing that Angus did, but it was a very useful ploy. And second, he left me to it. I should simply get on with the writing and he would come back to me when the book was finished. There was no request to see any of my work as I went along. So I had initial chats with my fellow-authors and then settled to my writing. I had a small portable typewriter, suitable for a nomad like myself! It had been a gift from Mother after the writing of the university examinations had left me with very bad writer's cramp from which I never quite recovered. Writing by hand had become increasingly difficult and when the time came for me to write the dissertation for my M.Sc. I needed to teach myself to type. Of course there were no word processors in those days. But I found my little typewriter a godsend and so it now became again.

My time in Edinburgh was a strange period. Once more my understanding family gave me their support, allowing me time and space to write. I worked for most of the day in my bedsitter on the top floor, a small radiator just winning the fight with the intense cold. There was no central heating. Mother would call upstairs when meals were ready, and at some stage in the afternoon I would desert my desk and go down to the lounge to play scrabble with Dad while Mother rested. The scrabble session was a sacred hour which we would not miss. I was greatly blessed in so many ways.

I had always enjoyed writing and had already produced articles for newspapers and several professional journals. This had started when I was in Uganda and increased in Britain, especially after I became a member of the International Association of Teachers of English as a Foreign Language (IATEFL), and that of the British Association for Applied Linguistics (BAAL). Both these bodies held numerous seminars and conferences and I had sometimes been a speaker, with written follow-up. One memorable occasion, and quite a milestone for me, was the lecture I gave at the University of Copenhagen in 1972. This was at an international congress to which BAAL contributed. It gave me a chance to offer my research to scholars from all over the world, and I recall the thrill of having it well received. This had put me in touch with several universities. I remembered it now, when in spite of the concentration on my book, I was pondering the future. Should I perhaps go for the academic road? I had so much enjoyed my research work. On the other hand I knew I would miss the 'hands on' in the school classroom. I did in fact apply for one or two university posts, mostly overseas. My yen to work again in distant lands was still strong. Again, in hindsight, I realise that it was not meant. A post anywhere in the world would still be 'local' and I would have to become what my sociology professor at Bradford called an 'organisation man' as opposed to a 'cosmopolitan'. I was very much the latter.

So I plodded on with my writing. The book was the end product of several steps. From my language survey in Bradford and the reaction to it, the setting up of the infant centres and the methods used, I had gone from casual papers to organised curriculum units, to booklets and now a complete book. I illustrated my philosophy (see illustration after Preface). I had used this diagram in teachers' courses. Some called it a turnip, others a thistle, when they matched it to my accent! The book and its philosophy was another important staging post in my life.

UNESCO AND THE BRITISH COUNCIL

It was while I was in Edinburgh that I made contact with these bodies. The United Nations Educational, Scientific and Cultural Organisation, with its headquarters in Paris, recruited me as a so-called expert (a term I cringed at!) and put me in their data bank for calling upon. I was short-listed for a very exciting post in Nepal and was just pipped at the post. Again, when the disappointment had died down, I accepted the hand of fate. These things, I believe, were straws in the wind. The British Council too put me on their 'books', not in a full-time capacity but as a candidate for short, sharp assignments here, there, and everywhere. The first of these occurred while I was in Edinburgh in 1974. I was invited to direct a course for serving secondary teachers in Sri Lanka. The course would be for three weeks in December of that year. Of course I agreed to go. It was a taster of things to come.

Renewed Friendship

It was while I was in Edinburgh too that there began a renewed friendship with Jean, an ex-member of St Katherine's Club and Community Centre in Aberdeen (see Book 1). We had kept in touch over the years but at this time we started to go on holiday together. As I now had a car, we were able to explore our beloved Scotland, and we did just that, much of our travel in the north and west. Bed and Breakfast was then incredibly reasonable and we enjoyed wonderful hospitality.

These holidays, which began in a small way, became a regular part of the summer. I think we both found them restful. It was good to be with someone who came from another world, as it were, someone who could listen objectively. Jean was head of tailoring in a prestigious Aberdeen outfitters, and regaled me with tales of the great and the good who came to be fitted for 'the kilt' etc. And I shared with her the excitements of the educational scene. I had the additional perk of being able to benefit from Jean's tailoring skills!

In later years we explored further afield, with or without the car. We went to Dublin, to Jersey and Rome, and many parts of England. And now, in old age, we still come together annually at my place or hers. It is a friendship difficult to describe. We are such different people but we have shared so much, and we know each other at a very deep level. Jean understands what I mean.

Assignment in Sri Lanka

In the glorious sunshine of that beautiful island I recaptured my Uganda excitement and I met delightful people of a culture new to me. My immediate contact in the country was Lenny Gunewardene, Director of Education, English Units. He had recruited eight highly competent tutors to work with me. I divided the two hundred course members into working-parties each led by one of these people. I had frequent meetings with my team of tutors, and during the working day I went round all the groups and sat in with them. The lovely Peradenya College campus, where the course was held, was on the side of a hill, lush with tropical growth and ablaze with colour. It was an enchanting work environment but quite physically tiring for me going from group to group, especially as it was very hot and I had come from the opposite extreme of weather in Scotland's winter. But I knew a wonderful peace and a sense that it was right for me to be there. My 'field and focus' worked once again and my emphasis on 'language across the curriculum' in so far as English was used as a medium of learning. What I had to do very quickly was to learn about the curriculum of this particular group of teachers. It was a steep learning curve and a procedure which was to become important for me. I learned here, for instance, that there was quite a difference in classroom approach between English as a Second Language (ESL) and English as a Foreign Language (EFL) and I glimpsed something of the problems, both educational and political, when changes were made from one approach to the other. English Language teaching (ELT) was not always as straightforward as it seemed.

Every so often the working-groups came together in the college hall and we did plenary things like talks and discussions while the fans whirred in the ceiling and the odd wild dog looked on curiously. On one or two occasions I was able to work with children, though the schools were on holiday. I demonstrated teaching methods, including the use of song for teaching language. The teachers sat round the 'class' of children and joined in the singing, something which was an innovation for them. A poignant memory is the lunchtime walk I had with one of the tutors. I was suddenly conscious that there were others in the vicinity. Gradually, one after the other, some young children, probably of the college staff, made

With course members at Peradenya, Sri Lanka

their appearance from the ditches beside the path. They had been curious about what they called 'the fair lady', and had plucked up the courage to come nearer. They followed us on our walk and I felt like the pied piper. It was a wonderful opportunity for teaching English. By the time we had completed our walk and were back at the main college buildings where the course participants were waiting to go into the hall, these little followers had acquired quite a Scottish accent as they repeated my phrases, and I finished up having the children in a friendship circle doing all kinds of activities. It was an impromptu demonstration lesson which might have done at least as much good as my organised programme.

Would that I could give time and space to some of the accompanying adventures of this assignment, particularly the time when I went to watch the elephants bathing and later sat on the back of one of them. This was a working elephant and it was not a set-up for tourists. There was no special seat and nothing to hang on to. The mahout gave a warning shout as I reached for the animal's ear at one stage, informing me that if I held it the elephant would take off! The British Council might just have been one operative short! Another wonderful experience was a visit to Sigariya, a very special holy mountain. It was quite a climb in the heat. At one level I stood on a precipitous ledge and saw some ancient rock paintings, the colours still clear after two thousand years. There were hornets not far away, ready to pounce on the unwary. It certainly was an exciting expedition. I was also able to spend a little time in Colombo when the course was over. I much enjoyed the hospitality of Lenny Gunewardene and his family. His wife Indra and daughter Indi made me feel very much at home. They took me for a sightseeing tour of the city.

An exciting day out

97

My Sri Lanka assignment was followed by a lovely holiday in India, with my missionary friend Irene Glass. I spent Christmas with her in Ajmer. It was amongst her Indian friends that I first heard the tape of *Jesus Christ Superstar*! I also had excellent treatment from the lady doctor there when a mosquito bite went septic. The problem with my leg meant that I could not do all the sightseeing that Irene had planned for me, not a bad thing perhaps, as I was in need of a rest and it was pleasant to relax with Irene and her friends. My travel to the UK had to be postponed but all too soon I was back in the winter cold of Edinburgh, back to the typewriter and to continuing thought of what next. Although The British Council had paid me a fee for my work in Sri Lanka, I was not on a salary and I could not go on living as an 'indigent gentlewoman' for much longer. I had to get a job of some kind. Birmingham Education Authority were advertising for a Deputy Director of their Language Centre. I applied and was successful. So began the next span of my bridge and an extremely useful one it was, even though in a sense, it was a kind of holding operation.

Birmingham

A Wider and Different Spectrum

In Birmingham, the 'probation' for my final work was to be further enriched and nicely followed my Sri Lanka experience. I met one or two more immigrant cultures. In particular I came to know better the people of Afro-Caribbean background. Now I had the whole range of age to deal with in the schools where most of my teacher-training work was done. These courses in situ gave me more experience of assessing the needs of a curriculum so that I could gear my advice to it. Sometimes they were held at lunchtime and sometimes, referred to as twilight courses, they were held at the end of a shortened day and they spilled over into late afternoon. The Birmingham Language Centre was the base for peripatetic teachers of English as a Second Language who went out into the schools to work. There were one or two centres for children at secondary level but this authority preferred the teachers to go to the schools. There were also courses for teachers at the Language Centre, complementing those held in the schools. It was good for schools to come together at times and to discuss common interests.

Once again I found myself in an excellent team of dedicated teachers. After an initial period of wariness, we went forward together in some exciting ways. Our Language Centre Director, Bob Chapman, knew Jim Rouse well. They were two of that vintage which had been appointed by metropolitan burghs when the numbers of immigrants in the schools had jumped above the skyline. But Bob and Jim differed in that Jim was office based and Bob was out in the field, running a centre. Happily for me, Bob dealt with most of the administration, leaving me to do the things I enjoyed doing. He also gave talks nationally and understood the calls for me to do so. These were steadily increasing again.

Because of my recent concentration on work with infant age children and the booklet published by 'Bradford', I made a quick contact with the local Adviser for Infant and Nursery Education and found myself concerned with language development per se, not just second language learning. This was all further grist to my mill. There were many new challenges in this different and very large authority, and I shall always be grateful for the time I was there, time made easier because I was so happily housed. I spent the first month or so with Beryl Chandler, Head of a nursery school in Smethwick whom I met at a conference. Beryl then found, through her teaching contacts, the Worrall family who also lived in Smethwick. Hilda was Head of a primary school. In her home, a large, rambling Victorian house, I was able to have what was virtually a flat of my own. But I was far from isolated. I very soon became a welcome part of this big, hospitable family. It is difficult to believe now that I was there for only about eighteen months. Both Beryl and the Worralls have remained valued friends into old age.

PUBLICATION OF MY BOOK AND OTHER WRITINGS

It was during my time in Birmingham that the publication of my book took place. The Blackwell editor came to collect the manuscript. It was like parting with a child! Because of all my new work, I was thankful that the book was finished. The publisher expected me to go on writing but it was a while before I tackled another book, though my writings for journals increased and continued to be a large part of my life for many years. I also published in the edited books of others. Much of my writing now reflected my widening interests. While language would always be important for me, I had come to understand more, its place within culture, and the larger context of multicultural education took on a whole new meaning for me in Birmingham. I came to understand there that whole-school change might be necessary in pluralistic Britain, and I began to see Education in the same way as Edward Burke had seen the country two hundred years ago when he said, "A *state without the means of change is without the means of preservation*".

ANOTHER ENDING

In my usual inimitable way, I went off in all directions, relishing the opportunities for initiating such change. It was in Birmingham, for instance, that I developed the notion started in Bradford, where teachers role-played in front of second-language learners. I was inspired by the comedians in the pantomime and the ways in which they encouraged talk-back from the children in the audience. There was lots of scope for experiment and innovation, and most of the schools and parents seemed to be with me, as were my colleagues at the Language Centre. They too had moved from a purely language orientation to one of multicultural education. We had some exciting times.

But there came a stage when I realised that if I were to continue working in this country, I needed a patch of my own. This was Bob's territory. We were like two cooks in a kitchen, each of us with some expertise, but tending to get in each other's way. I applied for a post in Peterborough, a city in Cambridgeshire which was advertising for an Adviser in Multiracial Education. Though I preferred the name 'multicultural' to 'multiracial' because of the (to me) negative vibes that seemed to go with the word 'race', I was attracted by the fact that this post was for an Adviser/Inspector, which meant in all probability a particular patch of one's own. I applied, was appointed, and would start in the autumn of that year, 1976. But, before I left Birmingham, The British Council asked me to do an assignment in South Africa. And of course I accepted.

ASSIGNMENT IN SOUTH AFRICA

The Birmingham Director of Education was much less amenable to my gallivanting than the one in Bradford had been and it was only when he had received my letter of resignation that he consented to let me go to South Africa. This again was a short, sharp assignment, helping on courses for black, serving teachers. It seemed that two 'experts' were required in this case and that the direction would be the responsibility of John Foley, the cultural attaché at the British Embassy, who was also the English language officer. This time I was ready for my introduction as an 'expert'. I would give the course members my definition of one: "An expert is a person who comes to a country to find out things and leaves before she's found out!" If the audience laughed knowledgeably then I knew I had a fairly sophisticated level of English to cope with.

My experience in South Africa in 1965 meant that I approached the work with some reservations. I was surprised that Britain had a foot in the country at all and had not realised that we had an embassy in Pretoria. Many of my colleagues, knowing my views on race, were amazed that I had accepted the assignment but I reckoned that I must give it a chance. My British colleague was Hywel Jones, a college lecturer from Wolverhampton. He had worked in South Africa before, with John Foley. My first task was to win my credibility with these two 'buddies', first as a woman and second as a professional. That I must have done so is perhaps evidenced by the fact that when I left my slippers in a rondavel as we were travelling, John took the trouble to retrieve them and send them to me in the diplomatic bag! I kept those slippers for many years.

Seriously, I had now one of the most wonderful experiences of camaraderie that I have ever enjoyed. We shared our disgust of apartheid but loved our black clients in the midst of it. For two days we travelled from Pretoria, John at the wheel of the Landrover. This constituted something of a holiday before the work began. We went through a game-park, lived rough in the wilds and skidded on terrible roads or got bogged down in the mud. But through it all, and perhaps John had designed it so, we became very close and enjoyed one another's company enormously. It was also an opportunity for John to brief us in leisurely fashion. We were to give three courses, the first of which was in a remote part of the Transkei, one of the so-called homelands. The place put me in mind of the kind of frontier post I had seen in American films. I almost expected the U.S. Cavalry to come charging out. Amongst my many poignant memories, and I can still taste it, is the brown chocolate porridge we had for breakfast. Another is the sound of the chapel bell which woke me before the sun was up and I could just see from my bed, the nuns going in to mass while the priest's dog howled outside. We were in a Catholic mission.

There were frequent blackouts as the electricity failed and it was fun

In the Transkei, South Africa

in my room when I played Scottish records to some of the teachers in candlelight. Oh, the joy of working with Africans again! These people were mainly Xhosas and Zulus, delightfully pawky in humour and hugely talented as teachers. I was back in Uganda and loving every moment of it. I came away with an additional name. They had made me a matriarch of the tribe! For some years after, the postmen in Peterborough puzzled over this long, complicated jumble of letters which appeared regularly on mail from South Africa. I came away also with a beautiful beaded pipe, the work of the local people, and a gift of the Mother Superior, after I had admired it one evening in the nuns' parlour.

The second course was more of the same, enjoyable work again with people from different tribes but this time in an urban area. Then came a problem. Because of political unrest, the third of our courses had to be cancelled. We found ourselves, instead, tutoring a course for white Afrikaaner teachers in Johannesburg. This was something else! I had to keep reminding myself that the teachers were not responsible for the regime. In fact we got on well together and I was presented with a tiger's eye brooch at the end the course. I had 'collected' yet another culture, a different set of particulars, and, despite apartheid, was perhaps a little nearer the universals than before. I returned to my friends in Birmingham with lots of stories for them and just in time for my farewell party at the centre and another at the Worralls, who had encouraged me to invite as many people as I wanted! I had a wonderful send off. But, as with Bradford, it was not goodbye. I kept returning, sometimes to lecture, sometimes for social occasions; Birmingham is only two hours drive from Peterborough.

Leisure-time fun

Adviser in Cambridgeshire

THE INITIAL SCENE

But it is, or was then, many miles away in its ambience. This was a shire county as opposed to a metropolitan burgh. What had not been at all clear when I applied, was that Peterborough was part of the wider Cambridgeshire authority at that time, a kind of sub-authority living somewhat uneasily with Cambridge, Huntington and Fenland. Each had its own area office and staff. This was to affect my work quite considerably, especially as it was only 'Peterborough' that saw the need for it. Ken Stimpson, the Area Education Officer there, backed by those like Richard Paten, working for good race relations, had made great efforts to obtain this appointment and all praise to them for it. Sadly Ken died in office during my time with Cambridgeshire and was much missed as he was a hard worker for Education generally. He had a new school called after him. But these early efforts rendered this shire county the first of its kind to appoint an Adviser for dealing with inter-ethnic matters, whatever the person was to be called, even if many saw the job as a matter of only help with language, restricted to a few schools in the centre of Peterborough. But more of this below.

The reader will be pleased to know that I have now reached the last span of my bridge! This one was the longest part of it. It lasted from 1976 until 1981, and contained many more important milestones and experiences which I needed to have if I was seriously to consider the freelancing destination of my growing conviction. The years in Yorkshire had taught me much about dealing with particular needs, especially those of the second-language learners, and my Birmingham experience had widened my horizons so that I now saw language much more clearly in its cultural context. I had also learnt there the importance of whole-school change to meet the needs of pluralism. In a situation of increasing immigration, with the richness this brought to the country, it was not so much a case of changing children to fit a system but of modifying a system to accommodate diversity. It was at this level of awareness that I entered my very new situation.

In a sense, Cambridgeshire, or more correctly Peterborough, was at the stage that Bradford and the other metropolitan burghs had been at a while back and which had led to special measures of one kind or another for the teaching of English. When I arrived in Peterborough, there was in fact a language unit attached to one of the schools so attempts had been made to cater for this need. I was asked if I intended to keep the unit or did I have other ideas. But there was one particular school where the Head had moved further than most. With her extremely high proportion of immigrant pupils, Joan Beale had truly appreciated the wider context and was doing some fine multicultural work. This, and the work being done by Community Education, were areas of growth. It was an interesting and hopeful scenario.

THE 'MULTIRACIAL CENTRE'
But there was something looming in the midst of it which made me very uneasy. It had not been made clear in the beginning that a special centre was envisaged in Peterborough for multiracial education. As I was leaving the interview, having been appointed, I was handed the plans for this building which I should mull over and modify if necessary. Should there be a snooker table for instance and if so how would this affect the flooring and furnishings of the room? What exactly was to be the purpose of the building and how should the rooms be arranged? I would be required to supervise the place and perhaps even to have my office there. I was not at all happy about this situation.

While applauding Peterborough's attempt to move a step away from seeing immigrant education in terms only of language teaching, I worried about the kind of signal this centre would give to the schools. Whether for language work only or something wider, its exclusive purpose seemed to be saying, 'This will serve the needs of the immigrant people, take the problems away from the schools, and we, the host population, will be able to go on as normal'. Also, it seemed to me that the authority was mixing education needs with those of a social nature, or could the two be dealt with in the same building? And there was another misunderstanding. It was unfortunate that in the minds of many, 'immigrant' meant 'black'. It seemed not to be recognised that there were those who were not. In fact the largest minority group in Peterborough at that time was Italian. There were also Poles, Ukrainians and many others. Was the multiracial centre to be for them too?

Now that it can be told, I have to say that I would have preferred not to have the centre at all, and at that early stage I felt sure that I could have done my job much better without it, so much of my energies going into its justification. But in the end and many months and heartaches later, the place became a useful base and focus under its new title of 'Resource Centre for Multicultural Education'. A warden, hard-working Roja Ali, and first class staff were appointed, my own desk being in the Education Office along with all the other authority Advisers. I disbanded the language unit but the staff of the Centre took language work on board, going into the schools to do it. They also ran courses, offered advice, and built up a library of books and other resources concerned with multicultural matters. The role of the Centre became a reflection of how I saw my own, looking after the particular needs where this was appropriate, and a wider aware-ness-making for all. And once the Marcus Garvey Community Centre was established in the same compound and other such places for various immigrant groups made their appearance in the city, the building's role-conflict was sorted out.

With Roja Ali and Ken Stimpson at a conference

ROLE-CONFLICT

Not my own however! I was at the receiving end of a number of different expectations. First, within Peterborough I was seen as a trouble shooter, taking away a growing problem in the schools, and that was where I should be spending most of my time. Also within Peterborough, the Council for Community Relations (PCCR) and, to quite an extent, the immigrants themselves, saw me as a 'big stick' with which to hit the authority if it did not seem to be championing their needs. A new Race Relations Act had just come into force. Nationally the somewhat bland Community Relations Commission had become the Commission for Racial Equality and authorities could be penalised for not falling over backwards to work for 'blacks'. Statistics should be collected on, for example, examination results, and comparisons made. Racial differences were emphasised, in some ways all very right and proper, but liable to generate, in my opinion, much bitterness and unpleasantness. I did not like the 'big stick' approach, and certainly did not see myself in that role.

Then, along with my fellow Advisers, I had to face the role-conflict of being based in Peterborough while in fact having a county brief. There was a loyalty problem. As far as I can remember, the degree of autonomy in the four areas varied and was somewhat vague. For instance, sometimes appointments were made by the county and sometimes, as in my case, at area level. I discovered that there had been much argument over mine, within the county and even in the Association of County Councils. As I have said, Ken Stimpson in Peterborough was alone in considering such a post necessary. Others had seen it as something esoteric, not very affordable and hardly relevant for the shire county of Cambridgeshire which had no real 'problems'! They saw the UK in general as a host country with immigrant minorities which would have at worst to be contained, at best helped, but without disturbing the even tenor of the status quo. I was a change agent, liable to stir things up, and changes cost money. The county officers needed to see value for this. There was no room or time for famtoosh (very Scottish) theories! As a trouble-shooter in the few schools in the centre of Peterborough they could just about accept me, and the degree to which these schools were satisfied was the gauge of my success. Anything beyond that they didn't want to know. It can now be seen, perhaps, the kind of vortex I had entered.

And there was an ironic twist to the situation. If they were honest,

'Peterborough' saw me in that narrow role too, virtually as an advisory teacher for about half a dozen schools, but at least they had made the appointment and were fiercely cross if I ventured south of the river or into the Fens. They did not see me as a wider Adviser. And yet the very first memo to cross my desk was one from the Cambridge Area Officer, who had just appointed a teacher for English as a Second Language and wanted me to advise her. I had the impression that the city of Cambridge didn't want to admit to having working-class immigrants, though the percentage in the school population was not unlike that of Peterborough, and when you added the children of university personnel, also immigrant with a first language other than English, the numbers of those requiring language help shot above those in Peterborough. I recognised the Cambridge Officer's request to me as possibly the reluctant acceptance that there was a need and that help should be given. All this I discovered as I struggled to find my way through a great number of demands I had not expected.

Then there was the rest of the county, most of which either did not 'see' me at all or saw no role for me whatsoever. An experience early in my time in Cambridgeshire springs to mind. I was in a classroom in a Wisbech primary school. "Will you tell the children who you are" said the teacher. I duly told them that I was the Adviser for Multiracial Education. The teacher went on, "Oh, I wonder what that is". The 'multi' bit was got around by reference to multi-storey flats which the children knew about, and once 'race' was seen as not the thing you ran at the sports, the way was made a little clearer for me to say what I was doing. The teacher finished up by saying, very dramatically, "And do you know, children, Miss Garvie goes into classrooms with black children"! There were suitable gasps of amazement and the class looked at me again, as though I had sprung from some other planet. And that was 1976.

Very occasionally I would receive a frantic phone call from a school in the hinterland, asking for a rescue operation, always in terms of language. I found one Pakistani child here, two Chinese brothers there. What to do? As these calls grew in number, I welcomed the opportunities they offered for fulfilling the two prongs of my role as I myself saw it, the particular needs on the one hand and the awareness-making in general on the other. But all this added up to enough work for two or even three people. I found myself working flat out and continually on the edge of exhaustion. I did seem to have a penchant for generating work. Perhaps I should have accepted the role that Peterborough area saw for me and stuck to trying to solve the language problems in the half dozen schools with a high proportion of immigrants in the centre of the city.

Traveller Education

But, my wider role was now being more accepted by my colleagues at least, and this led me into two other areas of work which brought me great interest and richness. One concerned the children of the Traveller or Gypsy people. Cambridgeshire was a big centre for Travellers then. Up to the time of my appointment the Advisers generally, but especially the one responsible for Primary education, were supposed to supervise the children's schooling. But this was not something they relished and it seemed to me that they were only too glad when an Adviser who saw herself as having a special brief for the handling of minority groups could take this on board. So I learned about yet another culture as I visited the two official sites in Peterborough, the one in Wisbech and the scattered and unofficial ones elsewhere. I got to know Robbie Britton, the teacher in her little school on one of the Peterborough 'encampments' and greatly admired the understanding she had of her work and the way she had endeared herself to the Travellers and earned their trust. Another experience comes to mind.

It was my custom to visit this teacher at the end of the school day. She would see the children out, lock the door and put the kettle on. Then we would chat about the work generally and the problems in particular. On one occasion, just as I was coming in and the children were leaving, Robbie called after one boy, "And remember to tell your mother about going to hospital or she might die"! (The Traveller people were very loath to go near doctors). "Yes Miss", the boy replied and ran off. But while Robbie and I were enjoying our tea and chat, the same boy came back. Knowing the door to be locked, he shouted from outside, "Miss Britton". "Yes", Robbie responded. "My mother says, has she to take a sample?" "Yes", replied this intrepid teacher. Very few in the authority had any real idea of the humanitarian role Robbie played. She later became a close friend.

Adult Education

The other area of work which I just touched and would have liked more time to spend on was that of Adult Education. I did visit the further education colleges and tried to advise and help where I could, but it was a limited contribution and the work really required another person. Fortunately the department of Community Education shared our open-plan office and I began to work fairly closely with John Webb and his staff, particularly his Adviser, Jill Navid, another who became a personal friend. We shared a number of projects and acted as sounding-boards for one another. I have many happy memories of multicultural events where the various immigrant groups, including those from the European continent, came together to share their richness and I remember the pleasure I had in joining the English classes especially those for the Asian women, which Jill and her colleagues set up.

And I must record an event which we still remember with amusement. Community Education was entertaining an adult group from France. They asked me to help as they knew that I spoke French. We ended up having a party in John's garden at his home in Peterborough with me teaching our French friends Scottish dancing. I had never done that in French before and found it quite a challenge! I think John must have warned his neighbours about the party as I cannot remember any irate voices from over the fence.

SOME SOLUTIONS

As time went on, I battled in this conflict of roles, and found a way of working which I could just about cope with. In Cambridge I managed to persuade the powers that be to appoint its own team of teachers similar to those in the Peterborough Resource Centre for Multicultural Education. Accommodation was found for them and they gradually built up their own centre of advice and resources, relevant to the university city. On the Traveller issue, I discovered from Robbie that there was another teacher, working peripatetically amongst the gypsies in the Fens. She also visited the site in Wisbech. I began to work with her too. I found ways of delegating on all fronts and became peripatetic myself, constantly visiting the outposts. A great deal could be left to the able and hard-working teachers who gradually became one large county team. And this included a teacher of Urdu, Mahmud Hashmi, an appointment the Pakistani community had persuaded me to make, and one, already in post when I arrived, Louisa, who was of Italian background. Wife to Sam Shippey, one of the ablest and most forward looking Peterborough Heads, she was bilingual in Italian and English and was a tremendous asset in a city with a large proportion of immigrants from Italy. I was able to have her 'used' more widely and the poor lady became quite over-worked. Both Mahmud and Louisa were excellent teachers.

I think the breakthrough came when I started to work more closely with my fellow Advisers, sitting in on their courses while they joined me on mine. It was good for me, for instance, to observe Brian Walsh's work in English per se as I continued to be concerned with English as a Second Language. 'Language across the curriculum' was still very much to the fore and something else now called 'Language for Special Purposes'. I needed to know about this. The Religious Education Adviser, busy with rewriting the syllabus to take in other religions besides Christianity, found some of my courses helpful and the Music, Art and Home Economics Advisers began to enrich their work with input from other cultures. This was a big step forward. Multiculturalism was beginning to be seen as a dimension of everything else. But it was when I began to work particularly closely with the Adviser for Modern Languages that there was movement on a large scale. We launched a venture that we called 'International Focus'. It involved all age-groups and schools in both town and country and touched every part of the curriculum. It brought about a whole new degree of cultural awareness. For the first time it was recognised, for instance, that the Traveller people had their own Romany culture and language and that there were Irish gypsies as well as Romany. The events were multicultural and international and if we couldn't find a community within our boundaries, we found resources for what we wanted to do. The world was our oyster.

Becoming a Housewife

So, some of the conflict was resolved and the burden shared but before I leave the topic of role, there was an additional challenge for me personally. I had to learn that of housewife! It was in Peterborough that I acquired the first real home of my own. The Development Corporation rented me a maisonette or townhouse in the new township of Orton Malborne. I became part of a new community in more ways than one, many of my neighbours also professional people who, like myself, had been recently appointed in this expanding market town. Meanwhile I had to learn how to set up and run a home. I even got a little cat, a real symbol of domesticity. Though I was to travel far and wide in the coming years, I kept my Peterborough base. It was convenient for all kinds of reasons. I live there still although in a different part, and have no regrets. I have become very fond of my adopted city.

This was my life in Cambridgeshire in the late seventies, new home and new work, the latter radiating from my Peterborough base like the spokes of a wheel from its hub. And some of that work, increasingly since the publication of my book, in other parts of the country. The book was selling well. It is interesting to note that I had now become officially Edie Garvie rather than Edith M. Garvie. My name on the Bradford booklet was the latter but somewhere along the line it changed and my book showed me as Edie, which was the name I was known by amongst family and friends. I have no idea why or how this happened. Was it a professional *promotion* or *demotion*?! As Edie I progressed on my journey over the bridge, the work within Cambridgeshire augmented by that outside it, including other writings. The demands were heavy and I was becoming very tired again. How long could I go on at this pace, doing national work from a local base?

TIMELY ACCIDENT

There came the night in Peterborough in the autumn of 1977, when the PCCR called a meeting which was held in our Resource Centre. I forget now whom the meeting was meant to be for but there seemed to be a great variety of people there, teachers, head teachers, area officers and advisers, perhaps also, community workers and parents. The chairman of the PCCR at that time was a particularly abrasive and difficult gentleman. He was white, English, and an ordained clergyman! This meeting brought to the surface his growing frustration that the 'big stick' had not been applied to the authority as he and his colleagues had expected. Why was the School Meals Service not serving Halal meat? What was being done about this, that and the other to fight the corner for the black pupils? What had my appointment been about if not to concentrate on these things? The atmosphere in the room became very unpleasant as I endeavoured to explain what we *were* trying to do, with the audience apparently taking sides. My role conflict enveloped me once again and I went home that night very depressed. I did not sleep well.

The next day I had occasion to meet with Advisory colleagues in the south of the country and had to drive on the A1. It was the worst day of fog I ever remember in England. Six people were killed in accidents on the

Al alone. I too had an accident. A lorry had overturned on the Brampton roundabout. The vehicle ahead of me, another lorry, had stopped just before this roundabout and its lights were either not on or were very dim. I went straight into it. The car was a write-off but I had only minor injuries. It was an amazing escape. Whether or not my normal driving care was impaired by the fog or by my state of mind and general tiredness, I shall never know. It was probably a mixture of things. The upshot was a spell off work. There were cuts and bruises to heal. My right knee and ankle were particularly tender and I had to walk with a stick for some weeks. Also, in gripping the steering-wheel fiercely, I had put pressure on my dodgy right wrist and I was unable to use that hand at all now for writing.

As can be imagined, there was some stirring in the dovecote! The accident had been on the local radio and television news and my colleagues and friends were very upset. I think they blamed the previous night's meeting more than the fog and my 'attacker' got short shrift. *His* letter of sympathy was amongst the flood of others which arrived on my doorstep. With the blessing of the authority, I spent some time once again with my long-suffering family in Edinburgh where the quiet peace of the place was a blessed relief. I had time and space for some much-needed reflection, one of the reasons why I have called the accident 'timely'. I realised that I could not go on for ever in this multiple role. The freelancing goal seemed ever more attractive as the only solution, but was I yet really ready for it?

The accident was timely in another sense. My father, now nearly eighty five, had been ill for some time and was in hospital. My stay in Edinburgh allowed me to see more of him and I shall always be grateful for this, and also for those scrabble sessions in 1974, when we became particularly close. Dad died in the early hours of New Year's morning, 1978. Mother, Dorothy and I were with him. We all missed him sorely. That spell in Edinburgh at the end of 1977 for me seemed meant.

Article for The Times Education Supplement

In a somewhat drastic way, the accident had been a means of making me pause in my professional tracks. In the time of reflection I came nearer to my final goal. I also learned to write with my left hand. I must have had some degree of ambidexterity, because after practice the writing came easily and was in fact much better than that of my right hand. I felt stimulated to write an article for the Times Educational Supplement and they must have been able to read it as it was published and given a centre spread. I called it, *What's in a Name?* It traced the journey, as I saw it, of the way Britain had handled the immigrant children 'crisis' over the recent past.

First, there were no special measures, the children simply 'disappearing' into the ordinary classrooms, then came the start of something being done as the numbers grew. This was 'immigrant education', a time of help with the English language. Thirdly came multiracial education when language was seen in its community context and the wider needs were recognised and catered for, but still in an exclusive way. I suggested that this concentration on race differences was divisive and could only cause conflict. I preferred the notion of 'multicultural' education because for me it catered for all groups and individuals and that was where we should be now. This is why I had changed my title from 'Multiracial' to 'Multicultural Adviser'. Education needed to think again about its handling of minority groups whatever the nature of the group. I was thinking of a certain school in Peterborough, for instance, where the minority was English and white. I was thinking of the children with particular needs, of the Travellers and of the Barge-People etc.

The reaction to this article took me back to my time in the Leeds Project when the Times Educational Supplement published my piece, *Language Does not Rub Off.* It stirred controversy and was seen as a kind of landmark. The present article led me to two further significant milestones. One was the writing of another article, commissioned by BAAL on behalf of the University of Graz in Austria. This institution seemed to have a particular interest at that time in matters of immigration. So I wrote for them along the same lines as my TES piece. They published it as *Education for Immigrants: A Changing View in Britain.* This brought more contacts and increasing offers of work. One of these, the other milestone, was an invitation to be the keynote speaker at a conference being organised by the American Embassy in Britain. The theme was 'Minority Groups in Education'. The audience were a mixture of American nationals and British teachers, and people from the Commission for Racial Equality. The Americans were kind enough to applaud my contribution and I was happy with the discussion which followed. It did us all good to share thoughts with those who had similar concerns on both sides of the Atlantic.

I received invitations to lecture in the States, including one to the

Pacific Rim. Oh to be freelancing and able to accept immediately! The need to be that was highlighted yet again. Whilst I declined these particular calls, there were some that I did take up in spite of the pressures within Cambridgeshire and my duties there as Adviser/Inspector in the authority. The following potpourri of adventures describes a few of them. I found my bosses and colleagues amazingly tolerant. We were way ahead of the rest of the shire counties. It was almost as though they were saying, "See how clever we were to make such an appointment" (I refer to the post and not me personally, I hasten to add!). "Feel free to borrow our incumbent!" And so they did!

A Potpourri of Adventures

SRI LANKA AGAIN

I was pleased that they wanted me back. I must have done something right. While the course in 1974 had been for secondary teachers, this one four years later was for those who taught in primary schools. It was held on the same lovely college campus and I worked once again with Lenny Gunewardene and his colleagues of the English Units. New materials for use in the schools were being produced and sample copies were sent to me in advance. I found copies of my own book in Sri Lanka, which was flattering, but I did wonder how exactly the work of the Bradford infant centres could apply here. However, my 'field and focus' continued to go down well and the notion of 'language across the curriculum', whether or not we were talking about English, Singhalese or Tamil. The Sri Lankans seemed to be on the move politically from English as a second Language to English as a Foreign Language, two very different educational situa-

tions as I have said. I had to listen and learn quickly and advise accordingly, the constant requirements of the so-called expert abroad. It was on this assignment that I discovered the importance of having certain key concepts which could be exemplified in a number of ways. This became a lifeline, as I found myself in so many and varied venues. Both Sri Lanka courses were a significant part of my 'probation'.

A local tutor holding a copy of Edie's book

On this occasion I spent more time in the capital, Colombo. I lectured to teachers on a university course, in the garden of one of the big hotels, as the university was on strike. It was an uncomfortable experience as there seemed to be little shelter from the searing heat. I visited the broadcasting (radio) studios to advise on possible teacher-training on the air for those teachers in the more remote areas, work I had organised in Uganda. I had forgotten just how vulnerable the broadcasting media can be in countries liable to have coups d'états and I found it amusing, if somewhat embarrassing, to be taken there in the British High Commission car with flag flying bravely on the bonnet. The place was like a fortress, swathed in barbed wire, and the armed sentry jumped to attention as my car swept up the drive. I only hope that the help I gave merited all this pomp and ceremony. I enjoyed once again the hospitality of the Gunewardene family and also that of the British Council representative and his wife. The latter saw me off at the end of the assignment to Singapore where I spent Christmas in the famous Raffles Hotel, a whole new other adventure. I was able to visit the Regional English Language Centre (RELC) which was doing some interesting and excellent work, and to have my first glimpse of Malaysia across the Causeway, a pointer to the future. I decided that I liked the Far East.

JERSEY

It was a surprise to receive a telephone call from St Helier. This was early in 1979. The voice informed me that he was speaking as a representative of the States of Jersey. Could I come and advise them? The children of their Portuguese hotel workers were causing some problems in the schools. How could the teachers be helped? I don't think this was a British Council assignment. The call came direct. I was excited at the thought of dealing with yet another culture though how much I could really do, in the few days they were suggesting I stayed, was doubtful. But of course I agreed to go, leaving my car at Heathrow and flying from there.

One of the strongest memories of this event was the snow. Few in Jersey had ever seen it before. The strange thing was that there was none in London just then, though it came later. 1979 was a bad winter. In Jersey, the schools were closed and the shops shut early because of this snow which rapidly changed to torrential rain. Cooped up in my hotel room, members of the Education Department, head teachers and myself,

117

thrashed out ways and means, once the problems had been made clear. So far as I can remember, these were mainly to do with discipline stemming from lack of communication. It was difficult to know where to start. I couldn't even visit any schools as they were closed. I did my best and, in a funny sort of way, enjoyed my first visit to the Channel Islands.

STRASBOURG

In the spring of 1979 I was invited to a colloquium in Strasbourg, on the languages of Europe and issues of their contact. This was my first experience of an event where there was simultaneous translation. The interpreters, English, French, German and Italian, sat in their own special gallery. They inspired me, at least, with awe. On the two occasions when I ventured to speak, my tummy turned over at the thought of the vast company of participants pushing their language buttons and the interpreters springing into action so that my words of wisdom could reach all who wanted to hear them. Our tiered seats were numbered and if you wanted to speak, you pushed another button which alerted the Chair, a remote figure in the distant depths of the hall. On your number being called (in French), the floor was yours. It was quite a nail-biting experience.

I remember feeling very European. I also felt ashamed that I could speak only English and French. Our continental friends were so adept. This was particularly marked in the group meetings. Somehow I tried to manage with my two European languages as well as a smattering of German. I felt very alone and hugely responsible in one meeting where the person chairing asked me, "And what does our British friend think about this?" I was the only person from the UK there. As time went on and my international memberships took me to various global gatherings, I began to feel more at home on this stage and my Britishness was put in perspective. Usually the language medium was not a problem for me as English was widely used in most congresses. On this occasion in Strasbourg, however, French was the main language of communication, with English taking its place with the also-rans. It was very good for me.

Strasbourg is an attractive place and to be there in spring is a joy. I loved to walk on the avenues with the cherry trees heavy with blossom. I also loved the quaint corners and old-fashioned inns. I had one or two happy evenings when I sampled the tavern scene with fellow conference-goers. In this European camaraderie it was still possible to cherish my Britishness and specially my Scottishness, and yet to feel that I was a citizen of Europe and indeed of the world. We all need, in my view, to have this kind of experience.

ZURICH

The year 1979 was the UNESCO Year of the Child and the organisation had commissioned FIPLV, the Féderation Internationale des Professeurs de Langues Vivantes (the International Federation of Teachers of Living Languages), to produce a book about teaching foreign languages to the 4-8 year olds. They maintained that learning a foreign language led to better cultural understanding. For some reason, Margaret Thatcher, who became our Prime Minister in 1979, took Britain out of UNESCO, though we were able to return some time later. In spite of this, I was asked to be one of a group representing seven countries, who would meet and produce this book together. It would be called *Teaching Foreign Languages to the Very Young*. The venture was known as a UNESCO B project.

We met in Zurich in May at the elegant premises of what used to be the Italian Embassy. We were a 'round table' each with her/his country's name on a card in front. There were four or five days of intensive work. We had each been allotted a chapter which had to be completed before this meeting and sent to our Chairman, Reinhold Freudenstein, who was also the Editor of the book. These writings were duplicated and shared and we came to Zurich ready with comments and suggestions. The chapters were analysed and criticised with great candour. It was the first time that I had written along with others in this way. Though I have articles in other edited books, the task was not so onerous as this where we were all in at the beginning, endeavouring to understand where others were coming from in more ways than one, and moderating our own work accordingly. Again I grappled with the distinction between ESL and EFL. Fortunately the discussions were in English. We even had an American 'ombudswoman'.

Professor Freudenstein was an exacting chairman. "Ladies and gentlemen, you have precisely seventeen and a half minutes for coffee", and we had just that. Our meeting was in May and the book was published in August, in English and later German. It was a marathon effort. Besides our various chapters, the work contained a record of our discussions and a useful compendium of resources. The Editor's wife, whom I later met

at a conference, confided to me jokingly that she nearly sued for divorce
during the months of the book's going to print!

THE VIETNAMESE BOAT-PEOPLE

Back in England and an assignment of a very different nature
found me in Lincolnshire. I spoke above of my being 'borrowed' by other
shire counties. This was one of these borrowings. I had been working in
Hertfordshire, Buckinghamshire, Norfolk, Suffolk and other places, all
very interesting and tremendous experience, but none quite so demanding
as the assignment in Lincolnshire. I was asked there to advise on the education of the Vietnamese boat-people. The political situation in Vietnam
had forced many of its people to flee the land. They went all over the
world, seeking refuge. A number came to Britain. Cambridgeshire did not
have many at that time but Lincolnshire did. A fairly large contingent of
families were housed at Swinderby, a former RAF camp which had sub-
sequently become a borstal! The prison atmosphere was still there and
also some of the staff. My work, in the beginning, was as much a matter
of social welfare as education. I found myself drawn in to a huge project
involving people from the cradle to the grave, people in a state of terrible
trauma and shock. I joined the Lincolnshire folks in their planning as to
how best to bring help and comfort to these very disorientated refugees.

A means of communication was one of the first essentials and 'classes'
were set up in the different age-groups. At first I did a lot of teaching
myself and others watched. Lincolnshire at that time had a pool of redun-
dant head teachers, on supply. I can't remember why. But it was these
mature and experienced people who were assigned to this project. They
were able professionals, glad to accept a new and challenging job. We
became a team, and for some weeks I travelled north on the A1 every day.
The journey to Swinderby took about an hour. Then I spent most of the
day with them. There was a time when my mother joined me. She had
come to stay for a while. I think she found the whole experience uplifting,
and both staff and refugees seemed to enjoy having Mother there.

A SECOND EUREKA

Indirectly, my work with the boat-people and that in the country
at large, especially in the shire counties, was the final spur towards my
decision to freelance. I had a sense of a growing number of places with

new needs, calling out for help. In a sense also, I saw this wider picture as that of Cambridgeshire writ large. In my home county I had been able to use the opportunities offered by the special needs and cries for help, to fulfil the other prong in my role, that of making people more aware of the richness of diversity. I had a vision now of this being applied to the whole country whether or not I should be its instrument. However if I *could* have been given this brief, which seemed to be mine already, and paid at national level, I would have been happy to accept. Cambridgeshire would then have become one county amongst many for me and no longer my long-suffering economic base.

I had some very interesting and hopeful discussions with people in high places, in the Home Office and the Department of Education and Science, and I had the backing of UNESCO. I tried to make out a case for suggesting that the presence of the Vietnamese, for instance, in so many places which never before had to consider multicultural education, was a learning opportunity not to be lost. But in the end, after a massive amount of buck-passing, the idea of a national project along these lines was dropped. I continued in the status quo for some time, feeling a kind of Bradford déjà vu. Once again, was this the time to move? Should I now take the plunge and risk going off on my own? I was a pioneer, an innovator, and no good at plodding or building in one place. Thank God more were not like me or nothing would have developed! The summer of 1980 saw me in Jamaica on holiday. I was able to mull over all this once I got through the distraction of Hurricane Allen!

JAMAICA

I had two lots of friends there with whom I stayed. Claire and Kenneth were black people who had been immigrants in Bradford, but who had returned to Jamaica for health reasons. Mollie and Leonard, of mixed race, had also been in the UK. Mollie had been secretary to my father. I had been promising to visit for some time. But August, the time I had chosen, is hurricane month and Hurricane Allen was just approaching as I landed. Politically, things were in turmoil too and my friends had very nearly warned me not to go. But I did and I survived both the hurricane and the politics. I was there for three weeks, the first of which was full of tension and worry as the hurricane came ever closer. The television was never off. It was hoped that the storm would veer and blow out to sea, but this did not happen. We watched it on our screens coming nearer and nearer to Kingston, where we were, a horrid gremlin out for its prey, and the announcers were as obviously scared as the rest of us.

There were no storm shelters. People near the coast were moved inland. I helped Mollie and her niece (Leonard was in the States) with whom I was staying that first week, prepare as best we could, stuffing window cracks and blinds with paper, filling baths with water as the pipes could be affected, buying food and candles to tide us over. The shops were soon completely empty, the malls deserted and ghostlike. We had been given 7.00am on the Thursday as the time when the storm or 'breeze' as it was euphemistically called, would strike Kingston. The night before, Mollie and niece Kathleen and I climbed, fully-clothed, into the large bed in the master-bedroom. We clutched our important papers. The bath in the en suite bathroom was filled and the large guard dog was in the room with us. Mollie and Kathleen had been through all this before, and I had listened to some fearsome tales. At worst all the roads could become rivers and we might be swept away in the floods; at best the roof could come off and we might survive within the crumbling walls. As the wind became stronger and the tall trees in the garden swayed and creaked ominously against a sky which was darkly purple edged with fiery red, we clung together and waited. I remember holding my passport and thinking about a British warship which was supposed to be somewhere out there. I had a vision of swimming down a road turned river and shouting to the ship, "Take me home"!

What a strange night that was! Against the roar of the storm which rapidly increased towards midnight, we exchanged stories and I recited some of my poems. We became amazingly calm as we prayed and somehow we slept. I was the first to waken. I looked at my watch and it was after the time the hurricane was meant to hit. The roof was still on and we were alive. The storm noises were receding but it was very dark as the foliage of fallen trees covered the windows. I woke the others and we switched on the radio. The storm *had* struck Kingston but because of the Blue Mountain behind, it had split and been deflected round the island. There had been severe coastal damage and one hotel had been swept into the sea but there was much less loss of life than expected.

With deep sighs of relief we rose and looked around. The garden seemed as though a bulldozer had given it the once-over. People were emerging from holes and crannies everywhere and there were shouts of

Relief after the hurricane

neighbourly concern. "Is your water on?" "Does the telephone work?" and so on. There is nothing like a crisis of this kind for bringing people together and helping them to forget politics. The island seemed to settle down very soon as people worked together to clear the debris and put things to rights. I endeavoured unsuccessfully to telephone Scotland. I knew that news of the hurricane would have reached my family. Fortunately, by means of a satellite in the French island of Martinique, I was able eventually to give a brief message of reassurance. And I continued with my holiday.

But before I leave the storm there is one story I must tell. The gardener at Mollie's found that a very tall tree had been cut near the base and lay on the ground. He felt sure that if we could raise the tree he would be able to seal the cut and the tree would stand upright again. We all helped. A rope was fitted and we pulled it up. The tree stood. But what was particularly remarkable was that the little yellow birds, which had lived in that tree before the hurricane, came back as though nothing had ever happened. Where had they been during the storm, I wonder?

I stayed for the first and last weeks of my holiday with Mollie and family and the middle week with Claire and Kenneth. They all gave me a wonderful time and a whole raft of experiences to add to my collection. Mollie's university friends introduced me to the educational world and I was privileged to be able to see something of the adult education work and to visit an impressive institution which designed and produced books and materials. From the creation of ideas to the final printing and making, all was housed under one roof. When I was later interviewed on the local radio, I was happy to be able to express my admiration for this venture. I took a set of materials back with me and there was much interest amongst the West Indian community in Britain.

Claire and Kenneth introduced me to their friends in the black community. They lived in a 'cosy' street where people sat on their verandahs and played dominoes. There were few tourists in this area and not many white people. One evening as I walked down the street with Claire and Kenneth, I was conscious of heads looking up from the dominoes, and there was much cheerful banter in the patois, which I found hard to follow. "What are they saying?" I asked. My friends laughed. "They are asking us to look after you. As though we wouldn't!" Once again, I was back with Charles Kabuga in Kigezi (see Book 1). Uganda was never far from my thoughts, though it was now fifteen years since I had left.

AUSTRALIA

So, back to the UK for the start of the new session, with more of the same, a full-time job in Cambridgeshire plus commitments nationally, including much writing, and the pressures building up again. To freelance or not to freelance, that was the question. Though my concern was not quite so drastic, I felt haunted by Hamlet's ghost! I had not yet decided, but I was nearly there. I could now see that shore at the end of the bridge.

One day, not long after I had returned from Jamaica, a lady came to see me in the office. She was from Sydney and to my astonishment she told me that New South Wales was using my book, *Breakthrough to Fluency*, in their teacher-training programme and could I please come and talk about it at a conference they were to hold in January. They were calling three key speakers from outside, to specialise in primary, secondary and adult work respectively, and all in the context of English as a Second Language, linked to multicultural education. It seemed that Australia, after a period of resisting immigration, had now opened its doors and was experiencing many of the things we in Britain, and those in the U.S., had already been

124

through. They were inviting me to be the primary education specialist and an American gentleman to be the secondary one. Evelyn Davies, with whom I had worked in London, was to cover the adult work. This was all immensely exciting. I looked with some apprehension towards the door of Alan Jones, my boss. The office for the Advisers was open-plan but the officers had their own abodes. Alan Jones, Ken Stimpson's successor, was smiling in his doorway. He had obviously been talking to the Australian lady and had already given his consent to my going to Sydney, probably with a great sigh of resignation! I would be away for five weeks, as other parts of Australia wanted to 'use' me after the Sydney course was over. Again I would be supported by The British Council.

Sydney Conference

So it came about that I found myself 'down under' in the hottest part of their summer, an experience, apart from the heat, that I wouldn't have missed for anything. The conference in the Sydney College, now part of the university, was a real eye-opener. I met people from all parts of the Commonwealth and began to have some idea of the vastness of Australia and the diversity of its needs. I learned at least as much as I gave. The social side of the week was also stimulating. I even encouraged the participants to have a Burns Supper and in some mysterious way a haggis was found! My mother was startled to receive a phone call. "It's Edie in Sydney. Just checking. How do you cook a haggis?" And The British Council gave us tickets for the opera. I just could not believe that I was actually sitting in the famous Sydney Opera House. I am ashamed to say that I fell asleep at one stage, nothing to do with the performance, which was excellent, but through sheer exhaustion. The heat and the intensive work were taking their toll.

Wollongong

After the Sydney course I went to Wollongong, another place in New South Wales. My two colleagues were sent elsewhere. I travelled there in a very rickety train, reminding me of a journey I had made in India. The gauge seemed narrow so the speed was kept down, but the lurching and bumping were considerable. However, there was a big welcome and lavish hospitality at the end of the ride. I lectured to the local inspectorate who gave me a very good hearing followed by many interested questions. I was also favoured by nature in this area. On a road journey through a forest, a lyre bird crossed in front of the car. This was apparently a rare sight. I was amazed by the magnificent tail.

Melbourne, known as the Garden City, was my next destination. It is an impressive place with many tree-lined boulevards and lots of lovely parks. My 'minder' (I had one in each port of call) met me at the airport and took me to my hotel. Throughout the tour my needs were well catered for and I was grateful for all the hard work and care which had gone into the planning. Here, in Melbourne, I worked with serving teachers for two very long days in a teachers' centre which was not air conditioned. It was very trying for all of us as the heat was intense. But a happy memory of this time was of meeting with my good Birmingham friends, the Worralls, who were visiting family. They introduced me to a nun of their acquaintance who took us all to her hospitable convent for lunch and later took me for a wonderful day out to the Dandenong Hills. I was so thrilled to see a koala in the wild and to hear the kookaburra of my Girl Guide song, laughing in the old gum tree.

At Captain Cook's house in Melbourne

Canberra

Canberra next, the federal capital. I spent several days here, lecturing to large groups of serving teachers. I was surprised that there were so many working in this strange, contrived city. It had been built in the middle of the outback as a capital for the Australian Commonwealth. At the time of my visit there were sixty embassies and a university. I was told that bridges had been built and the water put there later! But that was probably an apocryphal story. My talks also 'sucked in' some from the scattered outposts in the hinterland, a few teaching the Aboriginal children. I was happy to see that Australia was now concerned for *their* welfare. These children were of course not immigrants but they were of a distinct other culture, and much was now being learnt about the different tribes and languages. I was invited to visit the department which was studying all this, and advising and designing materials for teachers. Although each state in Australia had its own education department and ways of working, it also gleaned help from the federal capital. I was able to see some of this in general and to hold interesting discussions on the big questions of the handling of minority groups. Familiar issues came to the fore. How special should we make our provision? How far should we concentrate on the needs of the minority while keeping a sense of whole community? How far can all benefit from the special things of some?

Perth

I finished my tour in Perth, capital of Western Australia. Straddling the Swan river, where the elegant black swans give the place its emblem, it is often considered to be the most beautiful Australian capital. Here I was looked after by Alaister, of Scottish origin. I had helped him to organise an intensive course, again for serving teachers, when he visited me in England. I was now joined by my British colleague Evelyn, and we worked together again. Our American friend had returned to the States.

In a college which boasted a television studio, I agreed to give a demonstration lesson on video. My 'class' were Vietnamese boat-children. I couldn't help contrasting the conditions with those I had experienced in Lincolnshire. Here, all was bright sunshine and colour, probably more like home for them. The ex-borstal in grey England must have been a shock. I had hard work in my Perth lesson to keep the children's attention. They were so fascinated by the gadgetry of the television process, which is not surprising.

Here in Perth I celebrated my 53rd birthday which had somehow become known to the course participants and I was duly feted. The huge chocolate birthday cake which appeared at the end of one of my lectures, just on tea time in the morning (the Australians were then greater tea than coffee drinkers), had to be demolished quickly or it would have run in the heat! Those nearest to me in the refectory stood to benefit. It was also here in Perth that I met a kangaroo close-up. It was in the arms of a ranger, its mother having been killed on the road. The little mite, with its surprisingly soft fur, looked so vulnerable. I remember too, in some rare time off, being taken to caves and admiring the stalactites and stalagmites in a blissfully cool atmosphere. Somehow I had not expected this. Australia was full of surprises.

But for me personally, Perth was the place where I finally made up my mind. The time was right now for me to freelance. I had been 'trained' in many fields and now I was on my own. I would have to do without the local work which had been my main source of income, but whose commitments had been at times a large source of strain. Evelyn, who knew me well, agreed, and I was grateful that she was there. I appreciated her wise advice. She was even able to give me the name of an accountant firm in London which could look after my financial affairs. I would require this. I returned to Britain very tired. It had been an exacting assignment but a most satisfying one. At the same time, I felt much at peace in the knowledge that the die was now cast and that I had at last arrived at where I was meant to be. The probationary period was over. Of course there were moments of trepidation when I thought about no regular cheque at the end of the month, and then I looked again at something which had been sent to me by my Birmingham friend, Beryl. It reads, "*Do not follow where the path may lead. Go instead where there is no path and leave a trail*". If this was what God was asking me to do, then the means would be found. I accepted that freelancing would carry hazards as well as joys but I felt confident that the latter would win the day. The next section of my story I think bears this out.

Part 2

The Freelancing Years

1981 – 1993

An 'Expert' at Large

FINISHING OFF IN CAMBRIDGESHIRE

Until the summer of 1981 I had to carry on in my local base of Cambridgeshire, while at the same time looking ahead and planning for the freelancing years. Much of this time was taken up with fighting for my successor to have the same salary as the rest of the Advisers. I had not realised till I was well into the job that I was on what was known as a Group 7 rate while my fellows were on Group 8. I cannot remember what this meant in terms of finance, but the message was clear. The Adviser for Multicultural Education had a less prestigious position. It was not a 'normal' post and was much less onerous. In fact, I believed, it was a bigger job than that of any of the other Advisers, as it had to cover all areas of the curriculum and all age groups. My colleagues eventually agreed with me and so did many of the county officers. My successor duly gained his Group 8, but the salary was not backdated for me. Ah, well! Many reap where others have sown.

ENTREPRENEUR

I devised a leaflet saying what I offered as a Consultant, and distributed it nationally and internationally. See the front and back covers of this opposite. Inside I put the case, as I saw it, *for* a roving Consultant, and a brief description of my qualifications and experience which had led me to offer this service. I realised that I was virtually starting my own business, that it was necessary to 'sell' myself as efficiently as possible, and to try not to be embarrassed about it. In fact, the leaflet did very well and the business began to grow. In many ways it was more of the same, running courses and speaking at conferences, reviewing for publishers and writing, and giving advice to both individuals and authorities. In the UK I found myself more and more in shire counties with no Adviser of their own in the multicultural field, just as I had envisaged the national need, and I felt somewhat justified in what I was trying to do. It would have been good if I had been paid nationally as I had also envisaged. As it was I had to charge consultancy fees and this, at times, became a real hassle. I was glad of my accountant who worked, at a fee, on my behalf. The financial side

E D I E   G A R V I E

author of Breakthrough to Fluency

**LECTURER/WRITER/CONSULTANT
IN MULTI-CULTURAL EDUCATION**

Special interest in: Curriculum Change and
Development

and,

The Place of Language
in Education

— To help you start

— To support what is on-going

—— General awareness in all schools

—— Ethnic Minority group needs in some

Curriculum Change   Attitudes – Policies –
                                    Strategies

                        Resources

Language   Vital component of the 'new'
           curriculum
           Language 'awareness' for all
           Catering appropriately for the
           bilingual child
           School language policy

Teacher Training   Initial and In-service

           Help offered at:
                    conferences
                    courses
                    informal meetings

              – institution or centre based

of freelancing was the least enjoyable part of it, including the problems of pension and insurance, and there is no doubt that I would be in a better position financially today if I had remained with Cambridgeshire. It was unfortunate too, that in the early eighties the country was faced with a number of strikes, as the government battled with the unions. These included industrial action by teachers and postal workers. As the former were my clients and the latter brought my cheques, I frequently found myself in lean times. This is something of the down side of my new work.

On the other side was the glorious freedom of managing my own time and of being able to pick and choose the tasks. It was wonderful to be able to extend the jobs I liked doing most, without feeling guilty about commitments in the home base. This applies to work in both the UK and overseas, the latter especially. I had always revelled in my work abroad, which lent itself to the short, sharp assignment whose challenge I seemed to thrive on. The British Council could now give me much more of this and some countries invited me direct. I began to rove more and more widely. Also I could take an increasing part globally in the conference circuit. Not only did I continue to attend meetings of bodies like IATEFL and BAAL which kept me up to date with the current thinking on matters of language, but I became involved in work new to me such as World Development Education and Peace Studies. My alma mater, Bradford University, had established a Chair in the latter. And how badly this was needed at that particular time when the Cold War so very nearly became hot and the News was at its gloomiest. In my own area, a man was offering places at £2000 each in the nuclear bunker he was building! It was not easy to carry on with normal life and work in this kind of political climate. I was only too happy to keep busy, and felt that perhaps I was contributing in my own small way to bettering that climate. I became involved, for instance, within the UK in a strong move to increase equality of opportunity. The National Association of Multiracial Education (NAME), linked to the Commission for Racial Equality, became an increasingly vociferous voice in the land. I spoke and wrote for both bodies. I also helped to promote Harmony, an interesting private venture started by Carol Palmer, a mother of mixed race children. Her work eventually attracted government help.

New Interest in Mother Tongue

As a part of the move towards greater equality, there was a new interest at this time in mother-tongue, and a special linguistic project was set up to survey the picture in Britain and to consider possible educational implications. People were looking hard at the child's total lingualism and how best this should be catered for in school. How was the teaching of English as a Second Language affected? The issue was of course equally important in other countries and often became a political matter. As far as English was concerned, EFL could jostle with ESL and what of the mother-tongue in that situation? It was a complicated scene but an extremely interesting one. There seemed to be more and more components for me to juggle with and an increasing need for me to understand the different contexts.

Problems of Identity

I left the Cambridgeshire county employ in August 1981, and almost immediately went to Nigeria. It was a useful distancing operation, and as a result I was better able to cope with these contexts and with the changes in my life. Not the least of these was my status as a freelance Consultant. Many people looked askance at someone who was not part of a reputable 'firm', and were not quite sure what to make of me. Could my advice be trusted?! Although in a very different context, I must just relate the story of a little boy in a Glasgow infant school, one of the many children there of immigrant background. The pupils had been told that Edie was coming as that seemed easier to say than Miss Garvie. This child stared hard at me and then asked if I were E.T., the creature from outer space in a current film. What a terrible let-down for him when I was not at all what he was expecting.

THE BACKING GROUP

However I met expectations and whatever my status, I very much preferred what I was now doing and my ex-colleagues were amazed that it seemed to work so well. As I remained living in Peterborough, I kept in contact and several of them became lasting friends, backing me all the way. And as always my family continued to give me *their* support. Mother and sister, Dorothy, had really been with me on this venture from the beginning as they had come to my home to give me a welcome when I returned from Australia, and so were the first to hear my decision to go it alone. They would never know just how much I appreciated their unexpected gesture.

This was all the more important to me as only three years later we lost Mother. In fact the eighties for me was a time of several family bereavements. By the end of the decade I had lost all the aunts, uncles and cousins of my parents' generation. At this time too I lost Chris, my wonderful Bradford landlady who had been a second mother to me, and also Oliv, a friend I had met when we were four years old (see Book 1). I speak of these events in a group like this because I am beginning now to treat my story more thematically. In the next section, for instance, the African tales range from 1981 to 1988. But naturally other things in my life went on apace.

The Immediate Circle

Special mention must be made of my friends and neighbours in Orton Malborne, without whose help and backing my roving life would have been much more difficult. There were Jean and Tony who adored my cat, Rusty, and cared for her as their own. She was an attractive tortoiseshell with a friendly purr and an amazing tolerance of my comings and goings. They were always there with a cuppa or a full meal as sustenance for the weary traveller. Jean helped with my washing and Tony kept an eye on my car, making sure that it would start when I was away for a while in winter. My fridge was always filled up and the plants cared for. The acts of kindness and understanding were innumerable and my debt to them enormous. Then there was Dora, an elderly lady with a cat of her own, who also had a key. She would let Rusty in or out. She loved to hear my travel tales and I brought her thimbles which she collected. Mary, a deaf Orcadian lady, lived a few doors away. She too loved Rusty, which seemed in her quaint, feline way to be the focus of so much fellowship and fun. So many people all around me formed an enclave that was warm and reassuring to go from and to return to when I was facing the unknown. Finally there was Liz. In 1988 she bought the house which was attached to mine. Liz virtually took the place of Tony and Jean when they moved away and she became the daughter I never had. I say more of her in Part 3 in my church story there but at this point let me relate two instances in particular when Liz gave me *her* backing.

First the burglary. I was in Scotland when it happened. Liz dealt with the police and got in touch with me. There was no need for me to return at once, so long as everything was left for the police to cover when I did so. Liz had coped admirably with the immediate hassle and saw to it that my door was boarded up. And when I did return, she looked after me though she was suffering with flu. The other event was Rusty's disappearance after a cat-fight. This is a long, strange story, the details of which I cannot go into here. Suffice it to say that my pet was gone for three weeks during which I frenziedly sought her, advertising her loss in all directions. Liz was a great smoother of anxiety. Then, when by a miracle, one of the answers to my questing brought Rusty back, from a place on the other side of the city, Liz came with me to fetch her. I had her for five weeks and she needed tender love and care in which Liz supported me still, and then was a great comfort when I had to put my beloved wee pal to sleep.

Church in particular – Mick-the-Vic

Not long after I was established in Orton Malborne in 1976, Michael Scott, and a bit later his wife Gretta, arrived. They had come from an orthodox Anglican church in Reading, where Michael had been a conventional Anglican priest. But there he had met the hippies in their camp, he had gone to help 'convert' them and, as he would tell you, had ended up being 'converted' himself! Whatever happened, it was a new Michael who came to Peterborough, appointed to start a community church in the new township of Orton Malborne. Although a full priest in his own right he accepted the curacy of this post and was virtually assistant to the rector at Holy Trinity, the church in Orton Longueville village. This lovely place, along with Orton Waterville village, was part of the old rural environs of Peterborough. Surrounded now by the buildings of the new Orton township, the two old villages had been absorbed into Peterborough, although electorally speaking, they are south of the River Nene and geographically therefore in the wider Cambridgeshire.

So, the new church, to be known as Christian Presence, was in the diocese of Ely, on the very edge of the see. Perhaps that made it easier for our Michael, quite a character as we were discovering, to develop this 'alternative church' as he saw fit. He visualised the church as being the people in the community, and would not have a special building. We met in the Leighton Community Centre (the townships had these centres all over the place), at the heart of where the people were.

Michael worked night and day for his flock, welcoming each new family as it arrived, anticipating their needs and helping them to find the necessary furnishings. He became a familiar figure, dragging a hand-cart with the help of Jonny, a community worker, as they went round delivering fridges and cookers etc. Michael and Gretta were always there to welcome newcomers, people very often uprooted and endeavouring to settle. Many years later the place is still doing this for immigrants and asylum seekers. They would be happy to think that something of their early influence is still helping those in need.

There had been a Presbyterian church in Peterborough, now like most, absorbed along with the Congregationalists, into the United Reformed Church. I nearly joined it, the familiar métier of my upbringing. But I decided to go along with Michael in his new venture, this being on my doorstep. I liked the notion of the 'parish' church. I was also attracted to the pioneering nature of this particular one. So I became a member of Christian Presence, if 'member' is the right word. We were a very open worshipping group, members by virtue of living in the neighbourhood. Inevitably, this made us ecumenical and although Michael, becoming known now as Mick-the-Vic, remained an Anglican to the end of his days and flavoured the liturgy accordingly, he introduced many things which would not be accepted as Orthodox. For instance, the local Methodist minister, who had become his friend, was asked to take services on a regular basis, including the communion. A special service order was produced which in many ways merged the patterns of the two denominations. This was put on a card, issued to the people as they came in. Michael also had church members taking part in the running of the service, long before this became common practice, and on one occasion at least, he had a lay person presiding at communion when he was to be away. We had a special song book and our singing was accompanied by guitars, at that time not so usual as it is now. As I write, I have a vision of three people in the band, two of Methodist background and one a Catholic. And sometimes Michael himself would join them.

Michael was also in the Peace Movement and supported the Campaign for Nuclear Disarmament (CND). He did what was seen by many as outrageous things, and had himself arrested on several occasions. The people of the Christian Presence were instructed not to pay his fines, and so he went to prison, welcoming the opportunity this gave for reading and reflection.

The church members accepted his behaviour with degrees of tolerance ranging from mild amusement to avid discipleship, but there were a few also who disapproved, even if they agreed with the sentiments. On the whole, Gretta was one of these. She had married a conventional priest, and seemed quite bewildered by this strange Michael. She was certainly not best pleased when he brought peace-campers home to spend the night on the floor in their sleeping bags, or when Michael came home very late, having walked and hitch-hiked somewhere to a rally. For a man in middle years all this took a physical toll and must have been very worrying for Gretta who had to care for him when he was ill. He had a mild form of epilepsy and so was unable to drive. I remember being amused on one occasion, when I overheard Michael asking Gretta to drive him down the A1 to the point of meeting with other peace-campaigners, and she vociferously refused!

Michael rode a bicycle in the township itself, a much more appropriate means of transport in the area. We were constantly replacing this as the machine was frequently stolen. Again, in my mind's eye I can see our bearded cleric, complete with cassock, long black cloak and hob-nailed boots, large wooden cross and numerous keys on bands round his neck, cycling around the township, about the business of his people. The bicycle, with no padlock, would be propped against a wall while Michael strode, like a prophet of old, to serve the needs of his parishioners. He became a well-known and well-loved figure and not only to the members of his church. On his hospital visits he had a word for those of every denomination and faith and those of none. He always reckoned that his mission was also to the unchurched. Mick-the-Vic may have been an eccentric, going to extremes at times and raising not a few eyebrows, but I came to the conclusion that in all fields of human endeavour, extremists may be necessary to arrive at a proper blend of eclecticism.

Church Becomes A Large Part of My Life

The Christian Presence, along with Holy Trinity, the more conventional place of worship from which it derived, became a large part of my life at this time. I would attend the former in the morning and the latter in the evening, where I began to sing in the choir and read a lesson on a regular basis, vested in my choir robes. I had always liked Evensong which I had gone to in Uganda. Indeed my acquaintanceship with things Anglican had begun earlier than that when I was chaplain to those schoolgirl camps (see Book 1) and my team of officers was mainly English. They had introduced me to the various services, one called Compline, which to their dismay I confused with 'complan' a special kind of food! But they forgave my irreverence when I agreed to learn about it and to celebrate it one evening. Now, in my Orton home, I became a member of two very different churches and throughout my time with the Cambridgeshire authority and into the freelancing years, I followed these two strands in my spiritual life.

But in fact I was able to attend less and less as my travels increased. Church friends teased me that I was like one of the Canada geese which live on the lakes in Ferry Meadows, our lovely country park nearby. I was always flying overhead but hardly had time to land! I was conscious, nevertheless, of this church bulwark at my back. I joined in with what I could and this included a little time for social events. I organised a St Andrew's Night (very Scottish!) for the Holy Trinity people on one occasion and spent time in homes. That of Michael and Gretta in Malborne was a favourite base. I would play scrabble with them and have long discussions. Then the Root Group started. These were young people sent by the United Society for the Propagation of the Gospel (USPG), to live and work in the community for a while. I got to know a few of them well. We had many a happy peaceful evening in the house which had been set aside for them, sometimes in Bible Study and prayer, sometimes in story and song. Our growing church and Sunday school benefited much from the work of the Root Group who were with us for several years with changes of personnel. I think they also benefited from working with us. Some went on to full-time work in the Church.

LINK PIECE

Although church affairs had become such a large part of my life, the Christian Presence at least was very much alive in the community as a whole and I had a glorious sense of belonging. At this time too I did manage to join a few things in the wider Peterborough, organisations such as the Film Club and the local branch of the United Nations Association. I was also invited to become a Soroptimist. I attended these things when I could and remained with them into retirement.

In what follows I have selected some of my freelancing ploys, mainly from my work overseas, where I was so blissfully happy, though the developing of my work in the UK carried its own excitements and stimulus and was a large part of my freelancing. The stories form another potpourri of adventures which gives a flavour of my life at this time. I hope that the narration helps to show that my various life journeys were still proceeding. I was still learning, as I am yet. I start with Africa, the 'Uganda factor' remaining in my conscious and sub-conscious mind, and I make the Nigerian and Togo experience my first tale, as it came so quickly after my decision to freelance.

Tales of a 'Spectourer'
and
Other Stories

In Africa Once Again

NIGERIA 1981

Conference in Ibadan

Picture if you can, a small crowded minibus wending its bumpy way across a stretch of very dark and somewhat ominous country, the passengers tired and jet-lagged, with one in particular endeavouring to cheer on his fellows by a continual passing round of a vodka bottle! This was my arrival in Nigeria in August 1981. I was one of these passengers. There were twenty-eight of us from various parts of Europe. We had travelled from our different countries. Some of us had met in Zurich first; all of us had finally met in Frankfurt where we took off for Lagos. We were heading for a conference at the University of Ibadan. The conference had been organised by both African and European language teaching organisations, and the participants would reflect this, an interesting coming together of people whose common interest was language and its place in education.

We had arrived in Lagos and experienced the somewhat chaotic immigration procedures. I remember I was first off the plane and last to go through the barriers, not realising the necessity of bribing the officials! After an interminable delay for one reason or another, we twenty-eight found ourselves in this minibus with our luggage in another. So began this weird journey, with our Polish friend passing the bottle (he was trying to drown his own sorrows I discovered as Poland was in a mess politically at that time) and Nigerian police stopping us every now and then to ask what we were doing there. Our baggage transport was also stopped and there were threats of opening and searching though I don't recall that ever happening.

More chaotic procedures at the University of Ibadan when we arrived very late in the night. The Guest House Reception seemed overwhelmed and it was some time before keys and rooms were sorted out. So far as I can remember, there was no welcoming meal or even a cup of tea! Our Polish friend had his vodka; the rest of us whatever we had managed to carry from the journey and we prepared to settle for our first Nigerian night.

I can only speak for myself, though I know that my fellows shared my experience. Nigeria in the early eighties was not comfortable for Europeans and in many ways, because of its own political situation, preoccupied and even bitter. We were there for such a short time and it is all so long ago. But my overriding memory is one of physical discomfort, much disorientation of one kind or another, and shock at the way in which things just did not function. It was hard to concentrate on the business of the Congress. It was hard to prepare my own paper when much of the time I felt hungry or queasy. Most of us had tummy trouble. Why was I there at all? This was not a British Council commission. It had all come about because of my contacts with BAAL and other language organizations, and I was fascinated by the idea of a joint meeting with Africans. Also, my book *Breakthrough to Fluency* had been ordered by a bookseller in Lagos and my publisher was keen to follow its progress. Would I check up on it? So I applied for the Congress and offered a paper dealing with the language development of the young child; a first step in my freelancing years towards the specialism I was to become known for, that and story. For this reason, Nigeria/81 was particularly significant for me.

Conference at the University of Ibadan in Nigeria

143

The university was on vacation, otherwise we could not be there, but a number of the staff were in and about and it was good to meet and talk. It had been a pretty campus. I was shown round the fairly extensive grounds especially when I said I wanted to make a phone call to Scotland! My colleagues were very sceptical that this could be done from the university but I was assured by one of the staff that it was possible. He took me in his car to a remote corner of the campus. In a rickety out-building some ladies in the attractive Nigerian dress were sitting in front of a console of plugs. "What number you want?" I told them. They then suggested that I go and sit on the verandah and wait for the connection. I noticed on a shelf behind me that there were one or two black telephones, covered in dust. The air was heavy with insect drone and the musky scent of flowers. I dozed and became part of the somnolent scene. After about half an hour, I was brought quickly awake by the sound of a phone ringing behind me. I picked it up and heard the voice of my sister, Dorothy. I just could not believe it, nor could my friends when I told them. They had been less successful.

The hub of this community was the swimming pool. There was no water in it but it still represented the centre of activity of a social nature. There was a bar, one of whose operators was a red-haired Scotsman who was married to a Nigerian. I met his handsome daughter, all Nigerian with her hair magnificently plaited. Chief John, as her father was known, had been in Nigeria a long time. He was training engineers. We struck up an immediate friendship, and when I rendered some of my Scots recitations, he rewarded me with the present of a beautiful caftan which has become a most useful garment over the years. He got his wife to bargain for it in the market. With all his Nigerianisation, he could never do that as well as those born there.

I have memories of invitations to the homes of one or two of the university staff and other local notables. Parties went on well into the night and hospitality was overflowing. Many of the Congress participants came from French-speaking countries. The catchment area was wide. It was fascinating to mix with such a varied and interesting group, both at work and play. I made several useful contacts. I also reached the important bookshop in Lagos, experiencing some horrendous roads in order to do so, and was able to discuss the buying of my books, though the man I should have seen was not there. Now, having some idea of the financial situation in the country, I was not at all sure that the money would be found for the books. As it turned out eventually, I was right to doubt. They were sent back to the UK and my royalty statement showed a minus!

For much of my time there, like my companions, I was hungry and also unwell. The commissariat left much to be desired and the organisation of meals was a nightmare. But somehow we survived even if we felt uncomfortable most of the time. For many in our party this was a first visit to Africa. I was sorry that it was so difficult for them. For me at least, it was a shock of another kind. Sixteen years ago I had known a very different African scene. The old questions returned. Why were things like this? Why had the situation degenerated? What had 'we' done to Africa?

Togo

With my mind buzzing and the work of the Congress wound up, I joined a few others, about fifteen all together, to go on a holiday to Togo, a French-speaking country further up the coast and next to Ghana. We were due to fly out from Lagos. More adventures getting to the latter, but we made it, only to find that our plane to Lomé (a place of an important political summit) had been cancelled! The next, on a different airline, was not until the morning. With aching tummies, we stood disconsolately (there was nowhere to sit) and pondered the next step. There were two options. We could stay in the airport all night, or we could find a bus/cars and travel by road. The latter would mean going through Benin, a country which at that time was having considerable political trouble and bandits were rife. I for one did not fancy another night journey through an ominous unknown. But neither did I fancy the airport all night. To our relief, a little minibus appeared out of nowhere with a hotel name on its side. We asked the driver if there might be accommodation. He assured us there was. He piled us all in and found another vehicle for the luggage.

This night was quite an experience in itself. The place had just opened and was looking for custom. It was clean and the proprietors were helpful and friendly but there was little furniture and the amenities were lacking. The water stopped running and the men had to shave in rum! I shared a double bed with a Swedish lady and slept remarkably well as I remember. Breakfast was in a basement room. Most had tea. I asked for coffee and that had to be searched for on the market, also other things. We were Europeans in a very African world, a world still recovering from the end of colonialism and not yet attuned to world tourism. We decided to move on as soon as possible. At least Togo was supposed to be catering for tourists. A Swiss travel firm had become ensconced there and it was under their auspices that we were going. There was an amusing incident while we were at breakfast, which contributed to our moving out quickly. A telephone was ringing persistently in the room and no one came to pick it up. Our Polish friend eventually did so and to our horror he said, "KGB here". For readers who remember, the KGB was the secret police organisation of the Soviet Union, and in the West had a very unsavoury reputation. We were not at all sure who might be listening or where we stood. So we left as soon as possible.

Back at the airport, we found places on the plane going to Lomé. A somewhat surly stewardess attended to us reluctantly. I called her over and told her how smart she looked in her uniform. And she did. She was a good-looking woman with a fine figure and the colour and cut of the dress really suited her. A big beam appeared on her face when I said so and she then couldn't do enough for us! I remember being annoyed when one of the men in our party expressed reservations about the skill of the pilot. He did not fancy being flown by an African! Both take-off and landing were smooth and the flight very pleasant.

The hotel in Lomé was that place we all dream about, a tropical paradise on the beach, individual rondavels with thatched roofs, linked by winding paths edged with flowers of all kinds and the whole lapped by gentle waves. Palm trees clustered about us, silhouetted against a radiant sky when the sun went down. What a shame that our party felt so ill most of the time and could not fully enjoy the perks of this lovely place. Whatever we had caught in Ibadan was still much with us. We supported each other and were particularly grateful to one of our number who seemed to have escaped. He really looked after the rest of us. And, in spite of all this, we did manage to enjoy one or two excursions. A touring bus took some of us to Benin, for instance. The Swiss guide pointed out some crocodiles as we crossed a bridge, but warned us not to take photographs as they were communist crocodiles! It was interesting to read the graffiti in several languages, telling the imperialists to go home! On another day we were taken, suitably clad in large sun hats, to a remote creek where we climbed into canoes which meandered amongst the reeds. We were able to glimpse all kinds of exciting wildlife. At one stage in my canoe, a lady

146

from Papua New Guinea, wife of one of the conference participants, took over the punting. She was quite at home in this kind of milieu.

It seemed no time till we were leaving for Europe once again. For me it had been simply another experience to 'clock up', another face of Africa which I tried very hard to understand, my 'Uganda factor' still working in me. Back on home ground I soon recovered from the ills of the Ibadan 'bug', reckoning that the useful contacts and knowledge gained more than compensated.

ZAMBIA 1985

This was a British Council assignment. The previous year I had been a speaker at a IATEFL conference in Groningen in the Netherlands. Here I met Peta Constable, the British Council ELT advisor who worked in Zambia. I had been recommended to her. She was looking for someone to advise the Zambian government on the educational implications of a change in the policy of teaching reading. A feasibility study had indicated that it was better for children to have their initial reading experience in their own language, a policy which scholars of the time were advocating and which was becoming popular internationally. In Zambia this would mean a change from teaching the first steps of reading in English to doing it in one of the many Zambian languages, and bringing English in later. It was a big change and rendered a great many implications, not least a political one. I sensed this and realised, though not fully at that stage, that it would be a far from easy assignment for the 'adviser'. But I agreed to go and The British Council supported me.

Unlike most of my overseas work where I was in close contact with teachers and those who trained them, and working mostly in places of higher education, on this occasion I was based in the government Education Department of the Curriculum Development Centre and working with the Zambian Languages section. Next-door was the English Department where there were one or two European staff. There was a complicated set of relationships and it was difficult to pinpoint my exact role in it all. First I had to win my credibility. What did this white woman from Britain know about Zambian languages? How thankful I was to have learnt some Swahili which was related to them! My black colleagues were able linguists and highly qualified, with degrees from Yale and other institutions of prestige. I had to prove my academic competence if my advice was to be listened to.

Lusaka Orientation

The first week was a battle of minds. I stayed during that time with Peta Constable and this was very pleasant and helpful. I gained many insights into the work and relationships, not always easy, between the two departments. I also met several of Peta's friends and acquired access and acceptance socially into the European community. And I learned of the tensions politically and of some not so pleasant happenings like letter bombs. Every house had its guards, one for day and one for night. There seemed to be a thriving industry in means of protection. As in Jamaica, the baying of the guard dogs was a nightly feature and barbed wire surrounded all properties in Lusaka. In spite of this my memories of the capital are happy ones. Much of it was very attractive and leafy suburban. I felt at ease as I walked around. One particular place of great interest to me was the Namibian Institute. Here in Lusaka was a government in exile and an amazing place where Namibians of all ages and both sexes were learning how to do a variety of jobs which would contribute to the infrastructure of the country when it gained its independence. Lusaka then seemed to be a hotbed of underground activities of one kind or another.

At the same time that I was becoming acquainted with my colleagues in the office, I was taken to several schools to meet teachers and pupils and to watch the then processes of the teaching of reading. It was a whistle stop tour and should really have been much longer (a problem of most British Council assignments) but it gave me some kind of picture and suggestions for what might need changing. I took copious notes and discussed my findings with my office colleagues and Peta in the evenings, though this later stopped as I was moved into the Ridgeway Hotel, which was more central. I enjoyed my stay here too, in a quite different way. I had a large room right over the entrance which was strangely quiet in spite of this. I could spread my working materials and I could relax in the evening in one or other of the lounges. Several of the staff became particular friends, especially the waiter who 'reassured' me about the crocodiles. There was a central pool round which were tables. The pool contained a number of baby crocodiles. As I was having breakfast one morning, I asked this

148

waiter how long they kept the crocodiles. With straight face he replied that when the tourists started to disappear, it was time to clear the crocs! We laughed together and became great pals. There were also two 'Cool Knights' with whom I became close. The Cool Knights was the name of the hotel's resident band and I often sat in the lounge where they were playing. Two of their number would join me later and we enjoyed each other's company.

Gwembe Valley and Beyond

But perhaps the most memorable part of my Zambian adventure was the trip to the Gwembe Valley in the south. This was to give me some experience of rural Zambia and its schools and training colleges in the interior. It also served the purpose of giving remote places a visit from the outside world. One school I went to had had no visitors of any kind for seven years! I well remember my progress round this school, a pupil walking behind me with 'the chair'. As I entered a room he placed it carefully for me to sit on. There were so little resources in these classrooms, five children to a double desk, one pencil between them and the only book in the hands of the teacher. What price all our theoretical discussions in Lusaka! These visits really brought me down to earth.

School in the remote Gwembe valley

And speaking of earth, a lasting memory of the Gwembe valley is the miles and miles of earthy wildness we traversed, much of it in the dark. And how very dark it was! There were five of us in the Landrover, Peta who drove with wonderful competence, me in the passenger seat, my special duty to pull on a large lever if we got into a skid, and behind, three of our Zambian colleagues in smart office suits appropriate to their important government roles but who were nevertheless quite willing to mess up these suits if they had to help shovel us out of the mud. We carried a whole kit of safari equipment. Once again I was back in my beloved Uganda, this time sharing the wildness with others. And the hazards! Crossing a very dicey creek one day on a rickety bridge, I closed my eyes and prayed. When I told Peta I had done so, she replied that she (the driver) had done the same! Our African friends almost went white at times!

How Peta found our various stopping-places I will never know. There was one rest-house in the middle of nowhere reputed to have been visited by our Prince of Wales. I was able to believe this story as I surveyed the marble and chrome bathroom fittings and many other luxuries of the en suite bedroom which Peta and I shared. The contrast with the other places we stayed in was very marked. Here too there was quite a community of travellers, one of whom knew and had worked with my Charles Kabuga. Is Africa such a huge continent? Another lasting memory is our arrival out of the inky darkness of a long journey at a point of light and an Irish voice greeting us, "Welcome! Come in and have some tea and I'm sure you would like a bath!" We had reached a convent whose hospitality was extremely warm.

Victoria Falls

And this excursion was not all work. For the second time in my life, I visited the Victoria Falls and just could not believe this was happening to me. The last time had been on a holiday from Uganda and I had approached from the Southern Rhodesian (Zimbabwean) side. Now in what was then Northern Rhodesia, I was at this Zambesi River once more, and again the falls were full and roaring as ever – *the smoke that thunders* – spray rearing above and visible for many miles. Can mere words ever describe this phenomenon? We lingered and explored and scrambled down through a rocky cleft just below the Falls. I was still aglow with the excitement of the game we had seen on our way, particularly the white rhino, rare even then.

It was hard at times to keep my eye on the ball and to remember that I was here on a job. In the town of Livingstone I met several professional, middle class people who were very much against our project. We had great difficulty putting the educational case when everything was so politically hot. Their professional, class snobbery, it seemed to me, was too strong. English was paramount and to start the children's education in Bemba or one of the other Zambian languages was a retrograde step to them. And before we in the UK condemn or criticise, it is as well to remember, for instance, how Welsh or Scottish Gaelic-speaking children were at one time punished for using their language in school. It was discouraging but we plodded on. I was more and more convinced that the project was right.

Final Seminar

This became even more evident to me at least and I think to my government linguist colleagues, as we proceeded with a seminar, back in Lusaka. The meeting was to bring together our thoughts in some kind of curriculum plan or syllabus. In the event, it was quite impossible for me, in the short time I had left, to help produce a syllabus. But what could be done was to give pointers and leave concepts of the reading process which could then be turned into classroom objectives after I had gone. So it turned out. For two weeks we examined the question, "What is reading?" Had I put this to my friends when I first arrived they would have thought me mad. Everyone knows what reading is. Once again my experience in Uganda came to my aid, as one or two still murmured. I tell this story in Book 1 but perhaps it is worth repeating here. I had set up a little school in the hospital for long-stay polio patients. Most of them were Luganda speakers and I could not speak to them. The work had to be practical, art and craft etc. But I longed to tell them a story. I brought a primer used in the schools and 'read' it to an adult Luganda speaker who assured me that I made sense. In other words I *barked at print*. The children did understand me and for a short time we seemed to be in communication. But when I stopped 'reading' the communication stopped. *Was* I reading? I asked my Zambian colleagues. They agreed that I was not and the reasons for this occupied us for two weeks as we explored both the mechanical and the message sides of the process and what this means for education and the work of the teacher. It was incredible just how much we all learned and how our enthusiasm grew.

Final Conference

The last week of my stay in Zambia, I conducted a conference for the tutors in training colleges where I was able to share the findings of the previous weeks. I also gave a lecture at the university and some of the lecturers there attended the conference. It was a wonderful coming together of so many strands. During this period too I enjoyed a little time off. In particular I remember going with Peta on one of her bird-watching expeditions. This was a special hobby of hers and she was part of a group of Europeans who met regularly. We were taken on a hay wagon into the country. One of the gentlemen in the party was particularly knowledgeable. Not only did he recognise the sounds of the birds, but he was able to imitate them very accurately and call them to us. I found myself caught up in the whole fascinating business. I also felt a frisson of trepidation as we left the wagon at one point and walked through the long grass of lion country. One had been seen there recently.

So my five weeks in Zambia came to an end. At one stage I had been scheduled to go on to Botswana but for some reason, probably financial, the plans were aborted. I was sorry in some ways, especially as David Kiyaga Mulindwa, my ex-Uganda student, was working there and it would have been nice to see him. But in other ways I was happy to go home and unwind. The Zambian assignment had been exacting even if all the original aims had not been fulfilled. At least I may have helped to bring a little cheer into the lives of those lonely souls in the Gwembe valley. I needed time to digest the experience and write up my report for the Council. The nature of these short, sharp assignments made the reports necessary and important if there was to be continuity in the work. As in a relay race, 'spectourers' (the British Council nickname for we wanderers), passed on the baton to the next one. But it was mostly done through the office in London. We seldom met our fellow operators, and even the office staff were remote, disembodied voices who spoke on the telephone, "British Council here." "Far East desk." "Angela speaking." "Will you go to Malaysia for us?" for instance. It was all very exciting and I loved it.

SOUTH AFRICA 1986

Problems of Apartheid

One of the joys of the work was its variety. A call came for me to go to South Africa in 1986. I had started work on my new book and my emphasis on young learners and story as a vehicle for language teaching was beginning to be known. The work on this occasion was a consultancy on the evaluation of English materials and methodology in use in the black primary schools. The EFL/ESL distinction would come in again amid tremendous political overtones! A second part of the assignment was to act as tutor on courses for the African Teachers Association or ATASA, one in Durban and one in Johannesburg. I swallowed twice before accepting this work. South Africa was still deeply immersed in its apartheid policies and the rest of the world had ostracised it. Sanctions of all kinds were in place. My friends and colleagues in Britain and elsewhere looked askance at my even contemplating going. They could not understand how I could, knowing my views. So, why did I go, and why return in 1987 and again in 1988?

I wanted to see for myself. It was as simple as that. I could not believe that all the people in South Africa were monsters, white or black. Could it be that there were people of all races within the country who wanted change and could do with some help? I did find this to be so. There were a number of quite significant differences from the time I had been in South Africa before in 1976. I could write a whole chapter about it, but perhaps one incident will suffice by way of illustration. This was in 1987. Working in the Cape Town area, I was lodged in a luxurious guesthouse in a leafy suburb, feeling very white and very guilty while enjoying wonderful amenities and at the same time working in Crossroads, a black township of unbelievable squalor and sadness. On my first evening when I had just come from this place at the end of the day, the lady of the house came to my bed-sitting-room to inform me that there would be sherry before dinner in the drawing room. Swallowing four times, I went along and mingled with my fellow-whites before a roaring log fire and other luxuries. All through dinner I wondered and chuntered.

At the end of the meal, as I left the dining room, I saw a group of black people entering the house at the end of the passage, being conducted in by the lady of the house. They were ushered into a room. I discovered later that this white lady belonged to the African National Congress (ANC), and she was using her guesthouse as a front. In this fortress of South Africa with its siege mentality, there were innumerable stories like this as I was to discover over the three years of my visits. Change was happening from within and history records for us all that the expected blood-bath did not come. It was a very sick society at that time, turned in on itself with no news of the outside world and no part in it. I wept for the many thousands of ordinary, decent folks who suffered, most succumbing but many resisting and doing incredibly brave things. I reckoned that I wanted to help and that educational sanctions were a nonsense. How could things change without the educating of the population?

Pretoria

In 1986 then I went, first to Pretoria to join a meeting of a body called the Human Sciences Research Council, where academic and professional people (white) examined the books and other materials being used in the African primary schools. There was one black participant! She was an extremely able and knowledgeable teacher who knew the primary school scene and whose expertise was much used by this august body. She and I became good friends. And when I had time to think outside the politics and the hectic business of these high-powered gatherings, I revelled in the beauty of the place. Pretoria and its environs exemplified so much of this attractive country, geographically speaking.

My British Council 'minder' on this tour was a pleasant young man called Rainey Colgan. Besides being responsible for the English work of the Council here, he had a diplomatic role, as John Foley had in 1976. I discovered that my own movements were much monitored by our Embassy in Pretoria. I remember being quite surprised that we still had one there. It was an extremely uneasy presence. Rainey, who had his home, Spanish wife and baby in Pretoria, was completely snubbed by his white neighbours and his life in the republic was difficult to say the least. I experienced some of this when I stayed with him for a few days between jobs. Rainey looked after me and tried to give me a good time when I was off duty but I could sense his difficulties.

Durban and Johannesburg

In Durban and Johannesburg it was easier. I was surprised to find now a mixing of races without embarrassment at many levels. One place was the Market Theatre in Johannesburg where avant garde shows were staged and plays risky to the republic's official line were flaunted in the face of hovering police. Players and audience could be swooped upon and arrested at any moment.

A risky bit of behaviour of my own was to ask for black children to work with in Durban where there was on-going tension and rioting. The course I was helping was held in an Indian community centre for some reason. I think the African premises which had been booked were in the middle of the trouble area. The irony was that the friction was between the Indian and the African communities, and here we were, guests of the Indian people, a white woman and about twelve African teachers. Unheard of! Then when the class of African children arrived with their teacher, brought there I have no doubt by devious routes and with much difficulty, the furore was heightened. Somehow we got everyone safely inside and the children into the lift. This was a completely new experience for them. I can still hear their cries of wonder mixed with apprehension as this strange vehicle rose above the city and they saw the streets from on high.

Somehow the course progressed and there was much fun and laughter when I launched my usual stories, games and songs and showed the teachers how to make the materials. I remember a lady arriving late one

Self-help group of teachers in Durban

morning. She had been collecting shoe-boxes from all over the place. These gave cardboard for making the reticulated figures I had shown them and which were extremely popular. Unlike the group I was to work with in Johannesburg, this one was new to work of this kind. They had only just come to the self-help situation and they welcomed any idea I could give. And what a delight they were to work with, both the teachers and their inspectors! Once they saw that I had no political axe to grind and that I treated them as fellow-human beings, they became delightful friends.

Johannesburg was a different picture, not in friendliness, but in the environmental particulars. I worked in Soweto, the city's township which was larger than Johannesburg itself. Grey and forbidding streets of mean houses, the streets patrolled by hypos, large tank-like vehicles manned by police with guns, it was hardly an inviting place to visit. Very few whites did at that time. As the car taking me there reached the outskirts of the township, I had to click the door locked. We travelled as quickly as we could to our destination, usually the Funda Centre where my course was held. Alice, the leader of the group, was an enthusiastic teacher and whipper-up of others. She certainly kept me on my toes. The group had been self-

Excited by new teaching materials

helping for some time. They were interested and somewhat cynical to hear that I had been working with academics in Pretoria, whites who purported to know what was good for blacks! They had a point. But they soon forgave me this aberration and again we worked, played and laughed together. Alice longed to take me to her home but it would have been unsafe to do so. How sad it is when friendship has to be surreptitious!

SOUTH AFRICA 1987

Making Reading Functional

The Council asked me to return, this time to work with an organisation called READ (Read, Educate and Develop). The acronym also stood for its aim of making reading functional, not only as a tool for learning but also as a means of making the black people aware politically and able to help themselves. It was an interesting follow-up to my work of the previous year and a very big awareness-making exercise for me. The organisation bled me dry! But I gained so much in return. I was all over the republic, into every corner of their vast network. It was an operation sponsored entirely by private business and individuals and the staff were from all races. Through READ I was able to meet with other projects such as the Molteno work, another big venture with language development as its short aim and enlightened, non-racial South Africa as its longer. The hopes that I had cherished since my last visit returned now and I was happy to support these efforts and to identify myself with a new South Africa.

I worked some of the time in the headquarters in Johannesburg but mostly I was out and about, in Soweto again, in the High Veld, in the townships of Cape Town, Natal and the Eastern Cape and in the Ciskei homeland, taking with me an exhibition of books and educational resources, lecturing and conducting training seminars to groups large and small. In each region the READ coordinator had planned my itinerary and I had very little time to prepare or draw breath. There were occasions in fact when I really wondered how I could go on but I felt sustained by the tremendous sense of need and by the overwhelming enthusiasm of students, teachers, community workers, librarians and members of the general public with whom I came in contact. I was sustained also by the staff of READ itself whose untiring efforts impressed me greatly. Cynthia

Hugo, the Director, with whom I stayed when I was in Johannesburg, was a remarkable lady with a finger in so many pies, and it was an effort to keep up with her. On one occasion she whipped me off to a remote, beautiful place where we talked endlessly, walking on the mountain and sitting by a log fire. I shared her South African dreams and felt honoured to be considered worthy of doing so.

Story Telling Lady

While I was engaged in this work, my book was progressing. It had been commissioned by Multilingual Matters Ltd and would be called *Story as Vehicle*, to be published in 1989. It was to be the summation of my educational philosophy, 'field and focus' geared to the use of story for language teaching. This book became a kind of hallmark for all my freelancing work, particularly in its links with the education of the very young, in which I tended to specialise more and more. It was in South Africa, and to some extent in Malaysia, that the work really developed. In South Africa I was known as the 'story-telling lady', and the whole business became much more than a useful methodology for the teaching of language. It was seen as a means of possible change in society. It is interesting that even as I write, a similar process is going on in China now. English Language Teaching, for better or worse, has taken off there and the Macmillan Publishing House is overwhelmed with orders. It is song and game and particularly story in education that the Chinese are discovering!

SOUTH AFRICA 1988

Training Colleges

And I returned to South Africa the following year, this time to work exclusively with training colleges. The READ college project, under its able leader Pat Haak, was making great strides and it gave me much joy to be able to share in the work for a short time. In April 1988 there was a conference for colleges held in Johannesburg. I was invited to be the keynote speaker, after which I toured the country once again, presenting workshops at fourteen colleges. A great deal of enthusiasm had been generated countrywide. A story pack had been developed by READ and during my tour it was distributed widely. I felt myself being caught up in this great wave of excitement and once again felt privileged to be a part of it. The title of that film which I quoted in Book 1 kept coming back to me, *All this and Heaven too*, especially as I travelled much of the time with Pat Haak by car and was able to enjoy at close quarters some of the loveliest parts of the land. South Africa really is a very beautiful country.

Apartheid Cracking?

Once again I was able to meet a great many professionals as well as members of the general public and to sense a groundswell of yearning for change. A particularly interesting experience was my talk over dinner with a high court judge. This man was endeavouring to start youth activity in a multiracial way, feeling instinctively that if he and like-minded colleagues could reach the young people, and 'tell the story' of inter-race equality, through joint and enjoyable ploys, they would be contributing to a new South Africa. I wonder if he was able to meet Nelson Mandela and if he realised just how soon some of his dreams were to come about. Though no one could say today that perfection has arrived in the new 'Rainbow Land' of South Africa, the fact that the blood-bath so many expected did not happen, and that apartheid was ended officially, was a big step in the right direction. I have no regrets at having visited during those apartheid years. I had dipped into the country in the sixties, the seventies and now the eighties, and I had seen much to worry over and be sad and frightened about. I had discovered at one stage for instance that I was being followed in my tracks by the police! But I had also seen change and signs that the apartheid structure was cracking. And so it was.

At a college for 'coloured' students

Malaysian Saga
(1983 – 1987)

A Beginning in England 1983

Hilderstone – Broadstairs

It began in Broadstairs, in Kent. As part of my freelancing, I helped a young woman called Janet Higgins, with her training of teachers from Malaysia. Rick Collet, the Kent Adviser for Multicultural Education, had found me for her. Janet was on the staff of a language school called Hilderstone, a place which concentrated on the teaching of adults, and it must have seemed that the place was appropriate for the training of these mature people from Malaysia. The difficulty was that they were in fact trainers of primary teachers who had to teach English and were what their country called key personnel in this field. Hilderstone had no expertise in the teaching of primary children and Janet had been landed with a hard job. Hence my contribution. Shades of Makerere in Uganda (see Book 1).

I have vivid memories of driving to Broadstairs every Monday for about three months during 1983 and staying for most of the week. Janet had found me Bed and Breakfast accommodation with a delightful seaside landlady. It was yet another experience, a glimpse of a different life and a sharing for a brief period of other people's ventures. The boom of the waves below the promenade, the rumble of the refuse wagon which came early before anyone was up and resounded in the empty streets, my wanderings in the Dickensian byways of this place which has an annual festival in honour of the great man, are all components of my Broadstairs syndrome, an unlikely background for my introduction to Malaysia.

Hilderstone and several other institutions in the country had taken Malaysian 'students' for short periods. It was a lucrative venture, paid for by something known as the 'Pym' money, Pym being the Defence Secretary at the time. He had negotiated a special relationship with Malaysia. It was fashionable for higher educational establishments to acquire a group of fifteen Malaysians, seemingly the statutory number, and this was happening all over England.

For Janet and me, it was a time of close companionship and easy professional understanding. We learned a lot from each another. For me

With Janet and her 'students' at Hilderstone

especially, there were two interesting and important outcomes. One was that my story methodology was really put into practice here and much advanced. I have in my kitchen even today a large glass bottle holding spaghetti, the bottle being the gift of the Malaysian teachers at Hilderstone. I had told them the story of 'the woman who lived in a bottle' and developed with them a methodology and teaching kit to go with it, which would enhance the teaching of English for their young pupils. We had enjoyed this operation and we all learned much about language, its learning and teaching. This kind of close group-work was to stand me in good stead as a modus operandi in future assignments.

The other outcome was an invitation from The British Council to work in Malaysia itself. I accepted eagerly but asked if Janet Higgins might come too. We were by now such a team and I could visualise a fruitful extension of this in the country from which our present 'students' came. The British Council agreed and we set off in March of the following year.

Seminars in West Malaysia (1984)

We ran three seminars, one in Kuala Lumpur, one in Johor Bahru and the third in Kota Bahru, on the Thai border. In the light of my Sri Lankan experience, I had asked for the assistance of local tutors and this was granted, though there had been some reluctance at first. Staff were coming to the course to learn and not to teach. They underestimated their own capabilities. It was a different story when we arrived and they saw how we worked. Also, one or two had been in the Broadstairs group, and at least two of these went with us to all the seminars. Again, using my Sri Lankan memories, we formed a teaching team in each seminar, with Janet and I guiding so that each local tutor was then able to lead a group of the course participants, all serving primary teachers. The on-going group work was interspersed with talks and demonstration teaching, often with children. We were five days in each place and could have done with longer, but perhaps the sense of urgency to complete the project in time for the final exhibition of materials aroused greater motivation. The project was the making of a story 'kit', our prototype 'kits' acting as patterns for the teachers to use for stories from their own culture. On the whole, it worked very well. And how helpful all this was to the writing of my book, *Story as Vehicle*. When I wrote later I could hear the voices of the teachers as they questioned, and my own as I responded.

With Janet and teachers in West Malaysia

Edie behind the picture

The Working Environment

In all three places where we worked, we were taken out to homes and restaurants, and were able to sample the local cuisine. On occasion we went to the markets, even at night, and sometimes ate at the stalls where the food might be just the same as that at the hotel, at half the price. It was interesting to see how the stall-keepers worked together. If you asked for something that was not available it was sought from a colleague. And speaking of colleagues, I found it interesting to meet so many Westerners there working in one capacity or another, some of them ex-colleagues of my own. There seemed to be much interest and focusing on things Malaysian and many wanting to work there even though the place had become a difficult 'wicket' and was to become more so, for Westerners. There was a kind of battle going on politically. On the one hand the country wanted to have the latest expertise and state of the art, the latest thinking on language teaching for example, something known as the communicative approach; and on the other, they did not want to be obliged to a Western country, especially Britain which had once ruled. There was also a drive to push the interests of the Malays or Bumaputra, as against those of the large

163

Chinese minority or others. This included the emphasis on Islam. You were left in no doubt that this was a Muslim country. One of our assisting tutors was Christian and was finding it more and more difficult to be so. It was Easter while I was there and I almost forgot! I was to find when I returned in 1987 that the country was more of an Islamic state than ever, and now in 2006 I believe that to be a Christian, or an adherent of any other faith, is still very difficult.

Before the first seminar began, we were able to do a little sightseeing. The visit to the limestone Batu Caves was especially memorable for the squeaking of the bats and the pungent smells. There were also statues of gods and goddesses and some strange lurid paintings. The whole experience reminded me of Forster's book A Passage to India where Mrs Moore is overcome by an incomprehensible, almost atavistic feeling of gloom, on one of her sightseeing trips. It was good to return to the outside world and the sunshine even if the latter did become a bit much at times. We were in fact very fortunate. If we wanted we need not be out in the hot sun at all. We could move from the air-conditioned hotel in an air-conditioned vehicle to an air-conditioned place of work. It was easy to forget just how hot it was.

Three Different Places

It was interesting to work in three very different places and to see something of the country outside the capital as well. In the latter, Kuala Lumpur, we found ourselves in an enormous urban conurbation with a sea of traffic careering madly amidst modern high-rise buildings, and that was before the building of the Twin Towers. In Johor Bahru things were quieter and lower and we were within a stone's throw of Singapore. I could see the famous causeway from my bedroom window. During some time off we crossed it and explored a few of the sights there. In Kota Bahru, near Thailand, we could have crossed the border there too, had there been time. We should have liked to see more of the puppet and shadow-play which is a feature of the area. But we were much preoccupied profession-ally. In addition to the main work of our seminar, we were asked to advise on the very new resource centre of which the area was immensely proud. The request for help was reluctant as here again was an example of the 'conflict' I spoke of earlier. The staff knew that they needed advice but we had to be very careful how we offered it.

Concluding Thoughts

I came away feeling generally happy that things had gone smoothly and according to plan, and it did seem that our 'customers' were satisfied. We had been greatly supported throughout by Christine Nuttall, English officer of The British Council whose speciality was the teaching of reading, and she had shared this with us. We had offered the starting premise of 'Children need experience to develop language and they need language to cope with experience' and we then offered story as an experience which was structured, the staging-posts of the tale giving pause for language work, and somehow we had steered our way through the muddy political waters of EFL not being quite sure that it was not ESL or the other way round, while Bahasa Malaysia, the language of the Malays, was gaining more importance in schools. And all this in the context of my 'field and focus'. I rejoiced that this seemed to work in yet another culture.

So I returned to the UK, leaving Janet to stay a little longer and do some follow-up. I was expected at the IATEFL conference in Groningen where I met Peta Constable and arranged for my assignment in Zambia. I realised in retrospect just how much one thing was helping another, and how my book was being written as I went along. What I did not realise at this time (or I had forgotten the possibility), was that I was not yet finished with Malaysia.

IN ENGLAND ONCE AGAIN (1984 – 1985)

Twickenham and Brighton

The next step in the Malaysian saga was further teacher-training with the 'Pym' groups in England. During the seminar in Kuala Lumpur I had had visitors from colleges in Twickenham and Brighton, tutors who were to be responsible for acquiring and training Malaysian groups. The colleges were duly successful in attaining such groups and I was offered a visitorship in each college. In 1984 I worked in both, half the week in one and the other half in the second. In 1985 I was full-time at Brighton. It was very hard work and involved much travel. It was a kind of Broadstairs situation once again where I became a carbuncle on the main college body, and it was sometimes difficult to relate to other staff. At the same time, I was offered useful insights into the workings of colleges, some of which helped me on my return to Malaysia in 1987 when the assignment was to train the trainers in colleges there.

SEMINARS IN EAST MALAYSIA (1987)

The years 1983 to 1987 yielded a kind of Malaysian package. This assignment to East Malaysia squared the circle. I had begun by working with teacher-trainers in the Hilderstone language school in Broadstairs, had then gone to West Malaysia to conduct seminars for serving teachers in the country itself, and this was followed by further work with young teachers and administrators in England. Now, in Malaysia once more but this time in the East, I was to work with personnel in situ for the second time.

The assignment was to direct seminars for the English Departments of Teacher Training Colleges in Sabah and Sarawak, the two eastern states of Malaysia which lie in the north of the island of Borneo, the southern part being Indonesia. This was a very different adventure, fulfilling all the exotic expectations the name 'Borneo' had always conjured up for me. The steamy jungle, the mangrove swamp, and the wide yellow rivers which are features of most of the country, the breath-taking mountains, the compact kampongs or villages with their houses up on stilts, and the larger towns with their vibrant mix of races, were to be the context for my work and travel during four wonderful weeks. I loved the work and I loved the place. Once again I found myself reciting the quotation, "All this and heaven too".

It was a different adventure workwise also. In West Malaysia I had worked directly with classroom teachers. Here in the East, I would be training those who trained them. Although I had been involved with both on the courses in England, it was only now that I really began to comprehend some of the enormous problems in the colleges. The post of a training-college lecturer was a promotion from that in a secondary school and most of the trainers had never taught in primary schools. They were supposed to be training the whole range. To add to their difficulties, there were new syllabi in operation reflecting a whole new educational approach. Malaysia, like most countries where English was taught, had been touched by global change. In language work for instance, grammar was out and communication was in! Trainers had been sent on courses overseas to study applied linguistics and had returned to their country full of exciting concepts with exotic terminology which they would pass on,

166

Impressions of Borneo
Iban Chief, Mt. Kinabalu, Orang Utan

Photos by Albert Teo © 1994, Published by Sabah Handicraft Centre, Malaysia

undiluted, to their pupils. On the blackboard in one primary classroom for example, I found the words "Anaphoric reference" written!

I had to let my trainers know that I understood these things or I would have had a repeat of my Zambia experience and perhaps lost credibility, while at the same time I had to try and bring them down to earth and demonstrate ways of being communicative in a primary classroom, and perhaps show that grammar had not gone away! I was to concentrate on primary school work. It was a tall order, especially as I had only a few days in each place. The work had to be very carefully planned. I based it on the materials I had brought with me and as before helped them to make their own, using mine as prototype. Language in the classroom had to be meaningful, I told them, and a story which offered structured meaning was one good way of going about it. So to some extent the work I did in the East Malaysian training colleges was similar to that in the seminars in West Malaysia, except that in addition I had to help my students here to draw inferences for training their teachers. The idea that you must first know all about it yourself and be able to manage a primary classroom before you train others to do it was revolutionary!

In all I directed six seminars, three in Sabah and three in Sarawak, and whilst in essence the work was similar, each had its own particular

167

flavour and emphasis. I learned a great deal about group dynamics and the influence of circumstances. Each seminar had its own special 'chemistry' and the main line of attack had to be adapted accordingly. In other words, I had to put into practice in a wider context, the current notion of 'language across the curriculum'. Not only did I have to familiarise myself with the new school syllabi and course materials, something I had been gradually doing since 1983, but I had to try and ascertain very quickly how far these things were known by the college staff and how far they had been put into practice in the local schools. There was many a night that I burned the midnight oil and many a morning when the Malaysian dawn chorus acted as background music.

A Good Start

John Stoddart, Christine Nuttall's successor, was a great help, also a sprinkling of Key English Language Teachers (KELTs) and young folks who were offering Voluntary Service Overseas (VSOs). John accompanied me for the first part of the assignment so we shared quite a lot. The others, especially in Kota Kinabalu and Kuching, appeared in various nooks and crannies of the work and helped me enormously with their information and support, though with varying degrees of wariness. An 'expert' has to be approached cautiously! Also, *they* were the sitting tenants and I was an outsider. It would have been helpful if I had been told more about the various individuals and groups concerned with the English Language Teaching business, and then I could have prepared better for their input. This assignment, perhaps more than any others I did overseas, needed a careful 'mapping' on a large scale. There was little time for sightseeing and socialising was in short supply, but in each place the college community and/or the people in the hotels where I was accommodated, went out of their way to make my visit memorable.

Seminars in Sabah

The first seminar was in Kota Kinabalu, the state capital of Sabah. It was a good place to start. Staff of two colleges came together and I learned a great deal about the nature of the challenges facing me here in Borneo, as well as about the island and its peoples. But I was particularly fortunate that while I was in this place there was a public holiday and I was invited by the hotel staff to go on a picnic to one of the lovely off-shore islands.

168

On this trip I had the opportunity to learn much more. The ebullient cook had organised a day out for the entire staff, or so it seemed, though I suppose somebody had to remain to keep the home fires burning. Almost before I realised what was happening, I found myself in a small speedboat and part of a little flotilla, going over to a palm-fringed island. The large party of adults and children came from all parts of Malaysia and as such were a cross-section of its many races. At that time, and probably still, the Malays predominated, the Chinese coming a good second. But there were many other groupings. It was a useful introductory microcosm for me. And what a wonderful experience to be so readily accepted as a friend and to spend the best part of the tropical day relaxing with them and sharing their well-earned leisure and food. It was restful by its very remoteness. I shall never forget that day.

Keningau

The journey by road to my next venue was a special experience in itself. Keningau lay on the other side of the mountains. We climbed high before decending again, with Mount Kinabalu, the highest mountain in South East Asia, on our left. We were in the land cruiser belonging to the college where I was to work next, John and I in the back and the college principal beside the driver. The breathtaking scenery made up for the hazards of the road, putting me in mind a little of that journey I had in the Gwembe Valley in Zambia. Here in Borneo it was rare to go by road, the preferred and often the only viable way often to go by river or air. But each college had its own four-wheel drive and driver and on this occasion, there being no airport near or handy river, access had to be by road.

A particular memory of that journey was the discovery, once the college principal began to make conversation, that he had spent six months in Peterborough, 'attached' to our education department, as a placement from a course he was attending. He was so excited when he discovered that I lived there, he nearly fell off his seat. He spoke of schools and people I knew well. I was assured of red-carpet treatment in his college and this was certainly so.

As always my work was greatly inspired by the adventures en route. During my short visit to Keningau I managed one day out. John and I were taken to a tamu or market. This was a very special event which lasted for several days. In the West we would have called it an expo. There was an exhibition of homes and lifestyles both past and present, representing the different peoples of the area. There was also an intriguing mixture of sports, of which blowpipe shooting was a prominent and somewhat dicey feature! This merging of history with the present in Malaysia was to impress me time and time again.

We went from the market to see the hydro-electric scheme which lay in a most peaceful and secluded valley. Instead of a dam the water had been directed up the mountainside through a vast pipe and made to plunge down four miles further on through another pipe, to work the turbines. At the entrance to the pipes the swiftlets flew in and out and their squeaking echoed in the sunny stillness. Apart from the birds and one man who appeared to be guarding the gateway, our little party was alone in the world.

The next stop was an orchid farm, exhibiting the most amazing blooms of all colours, some of them entrenched in the hollows of trees to where the seeds had blown. We wandered on the lush wooded paths with large butterflies and brightly coloured moths accompanying us on our way. We chatted with the keepers and learned some very interesting facts about the plants and their propagation. There were many there, exotic to Malaysia and not all orchids. It was the first time I had seen vanilla growing and had not realised that it came in a pod!

From Sandakan, my third place of work, I had what was probably the most exciting of my experiences. I met the 'wild men of Borneo', not men at all though very nearly so. These are the orangutans, our closest neighbours in the animal world. As the only lady in our little party, I was a great source of interest to one of the females who tried to take my hand and even touched my skirt. How this incident might have finished I don't know, but a keeper smacked her bottom playfully and she scampered up the nearest tree. These friendly and trusting creatures gave us so much amusement and enjoyment. They lived in a bit of jungle which had been preserved and where a visitors' centre had been established. It seems that such a good relationship had been made between man and beast that the animals came to the rangers when they were in need. They suffer from colds and malaria in the same way as humans and respond to the same medicines. I often think of these delightful creatures and pray that they are still living in their Borneo paradise and being cared for.

On to Sarawak

My first seminar in Sarawak took place in Miri, very near the rich oil country of Brunei, a strange little state within a state. It was a very Chinese area and I have strong memories of a wedding party in the hotel where I was staying. The wedding seemed to take over the whole place. The Australian and other white oilmen moved out at this time and I was catered for at a special small table in the bar, from which I witnessed and heard the frenzied proceedings. I watched the bride, in red, going into the large banqueting hall, and the hundreds of guests. The hotel staff rushed back and forth carrying huge platters of rice. The speeches at the wedding feast went on interminably, usually ending in a high screech which sounded almost menacing, but I was assured it was a sign of joy and good wishes. Over the years and travels of my life, I have been privileged to witness and often to take part in the ways other people do things, things I/we also do, things universal. It is a small world and very wonderful.

Miri

It was in Miri that I met again one of the people I had helped to train in Broadstairs. This was a great joy for both of us and very helpful to the work. My friend could 'interpret' in several ways. She was instrumental in setting up a miniature classroom and finding children so that I could demonstrate teaching, which I continued to do in Sarawak.

A Very Special Experience

My second venue in Sarawak was the college of Rajang, deep in the interior. I think that of all my Malaysian experiences, this one stands out for me. I make no apologies for sharing more of this than any other. As though I left the world and disappeared into a kind of time capsule, I became for the few days part of the old Borneo scenario which I am sure has greatly changed in the past twenty years. I flew from Miri to Sibu, a memorable event in itself. There was one other non-native on board. I was to learn that the people treated their internal flights as they would a bus service. "Are you stepping down here, dear?" There was no luggage in the hold most of the time and I could spread mine. I was not charged excess though I should have been. We flew very low and I could enjoy the marvellous scenery below. We flew over a very blue sea for a while with boats like toys leaving silvery wakes. Then we were flying parallel to

171

the coast. It was fascinating to see the many rivers pouring their waters into the sea. The colours were so lovely, turquoise, blue, fawn with white breakers, and as we turned landward, the green and brown patchwork of the cultivated areas followed by the deeper and darker greens of the jungle.

I was met at Sibu airport by Ranjit, the Sikh Head of Department who was to be my 'minder' for this seminar, a charming and very able man. He was all smiles as he whisked me away by taxi to the Rajang river and the somewhat rickety jetty where we boarded a ferry, another bus-like vehicle. The journey took an hour and we even had videos being shown for entertainment. But for me, it was entertainment enough to be on this boat, sitting with the regular customers on one of the longest and widest rivers in Asia, its waters yellowish brown from the timber growing in the thick jungle on either side. The fans hummed as we closed the windows against the flying spray.

Ten miles from the college we disembarked and Ranjit led me to his car which he had parked ready. The road was a mixture of gravel and tar, the latter referred to here as 'sealed'. As we bumped along Ranjit told me something of the college. It was called Rajang, after the river. It had been built by the Canadians with the help of something called the Colombo Plan. The idea was to bring education to the Dyaks, the people of the area. I think this *was* happening but there were also students from all over Malaysia, people who wanted to experience a very different geographical scene. So once again, I was to meet a great variety of races. In the car also I was asked if I wanted to stay in a hotel or on campus. When I realised that the hotel was in a little town about eighteen miles from the college and that I would have to be fetched and taken home every day by the land cruiser, I opted for the campus, thinking it more practical. In fact, they were not expecting me to make this choice and it caused some hectic last-minute arrangements. There was an empty staff house but it had not been lived in for some time, that is by a human being!

To this house now in the middle of a thunderstorm Ranjit took me and with many apologies left me, as he had to take his wife, also in teaching, back the way we had just come to catch a plane to Singapore where she was going on a course. The next couple of hours or so was one of the strangest periods of my strange life. Here I was sitting on the verandah of a little wooden house, which rested on stilts. The early monsoon rains

172

poured down and the surrounding jungle seemed to crouch in the stormy darkness. I had to pinch myself to make sure this was true. But what a useful time of quiet it was, apart from the thunder. It gave me an opportunity for reflection and thanks. I thanked God for my safe travel just ahead of this storm. I gave thanks for my warm welcome and for the anticipation of exciting things ahead. And there were.

When Ranjit eventually returned, my immediate needs were catered for. I was given a supply of biscuits and cold drinks and my 'bath' was brought by one of Ranjit's sons in the form of a large basin and jug of hot water. I had not fancied sharing the bathroom with the wildlife I found there! Towels were produced and curtains for my bedroom window. My breakfast I was to have in Ranjit's home, the midday meal in the college rest-room and dinner at night in the town with the hotel, or the home of a staff member. Plans were rapidly and well made and soon I felt that I belonged.

Teaching All-Comers

How can I express the joy of my teaching here? Without abandoning the main tenets of my programme, I tempered them to the needs of a big happy family. My visit to this place in the middle of nowhere was an event, and all wanted to attend my course. As far as their timetable allowed, I had mathematicians, musicians, geographers etc. along with the English lecturers for whom the seminar was really meant and, very usefully as it turned out, I had the Bahasa staff (mother-tongue department). I had had one or two of these in previous seminars and realised that what we were discussing concerning English could be helpful to them also, but it was here in Rajang where I made more of it and I carried the idea forward to the seminar in Kuching. Whatever the language of the curriculum, and here in Malaysia, English and Bahasa were uneasy bedfellows, all teachers of whatever subject had to be cognisant with the importance of the learning medium.

Whether or not I was able to make this clear to my present students I don't know, but I found myself teaching people from all departments and also some of the trainees who were their students. My materials were pounced upon, my stories, songs and games were enjoyed with great enthusiasm and my demonstration lesson with children who were brought from somewhere, again no doubt with much difficulty, was watched with total amazement. School was never like this. I had experienced these things before and in other countries too, but somehow in this place in the middle of Borneo, where two generations back the people had been head-hunters, I was conscious of bringing about a meeting, I hoped not a clash, of cultures from opposite poles, across time as well as place. Once again my head was full of questions but somehow I felt the answers didn't matter. There was such warmth and joy in just being together. A lasting memory is the sound of padding bare feet (*I* lectured in bare feet!) on the walkway outside the room where I was working, as the man designated to look after the portable generator came to my failed projector. The electricity went off at frequent intervals. And how very dark this could be when it happened at night! But the point I am making is that the running generator man was typical of the ways in which these lovely people helped me. Nothing was too much effort.

A Reluctant Moving On

There is so much more that I could say about the Rajang seminar, but I have to move on. On the way back to Sibu airport, this time by road in the college land cruiser, I was privileged to visit a longhouse. Most of the land Dyaks who were in the area then, lived in these houses and the one we went to was the home of the college driver. He happily agreed to take us (Ranjit and me) to visit his family. The pleasure of this helped to offset the goodbyes at Rajang. I don't know when I felt quite so sad to leave somewhere after such a short stay. It seemed that my hosts were also sad. One of the Chinese lecturers was in tears as she waved me off. Now, not very far from the college, we came to the longhouse and with what warmth and dignity was I received and offered hospitality in spite of a recent bereavement! The longhouse is home to a whole community and can be easily extended at either end. The individual dwellings open on to a common gallery where communal activities and ceremonies take place. After visiting the chief's house we were taken to that of our driver where we were offered rice-wine. Whilst the older ladies wanted to know (through the interpreter) all about the husband and children I don't have and couldn't understand why I didn't, the younger folks, some trying out limited English, discussed my work and were happy to receive my business card. It was so interesting to be with a community showing such marked signs of cultural transition. Tied to the pillars on the verandah were the shrivelled heads of yesterday while on the walls were posters of current football stars and a few pictures of Christ. The entire community had become Roman Catholic. And so, with this amazing experience, I left Rajang and flew on to my next and last place of work on this tour.

Kuching – Last Stop

Kuching is the state capital of Sarawak and the former seat of the Brooks, the famous White Rajahs. Theirs is another story which cannot be told here. May I recommend readers to the book *The White Rajahs of Sarawak* by Robert Payne, published by Oxford University Press. I saw the palace, now being converted to a place of Islam! Batu Luitang College, where I was to work, had been a camp for British and Allied prisoners of war in World War II. I learned that quite a number of Japanese had remained or come back to Malaysia to live and work in spite of their unpopularity during the war. Some had married local girls. Like Miri, this is a very Chinese area. It was here that I met again several of the people I had tutored in England and was delighted to do so. It was so good to see them in situ and to have a better picture of where they were coming from. It seemed to round off my whole Malaysian experience. But for the first few hours, in spite of all the welcome noises from Malaysians, British and other westerners who seemed to be gathered in this place, I missed Rajang sorely and realised I had had a very special time there for which I gave profound thanks to God. It was difficult to come out of yet another 'Shangri La' and face again the normal frenzied living I was used to, the finishing up and the debriefing in Kuala Lumpur.

But first there was the seminar here. It went extremely well, as it should have done after five others. I had learnt much in the passing. I remember this one especially for the ways in which the different groups of participants worked together. Again there were lecturers from different departments. And here too, the young teacher trainees who were their students came to several of my sessions. So there were a good number present when I did my demonstration lesson. I should have said that at all the seminars these lessons were videoed. I only hope the films were useful afterwards. For all I know, I am still teaching in Malaysia, just as I was for a long time in Uganda, on radio. It is quite a responsibility.

As with my other seminars, time was found in Kuching for me to do some sightseeing. There are beautiful Chinese temples in the area and one of the best museums in South East Asia. In the latter I was able to experience a simulation of the great caves near Miri which there had not been time to visit. I can still hear in my mind's ear the mingled shrieks of the bats and the cries of the swiftlets as the one lot go into the caves and the other leaves, just on sunset. And every time I have bird's nest soup in a Chinese restaurant I think of these caves and the courage of the people who climb the high and dangerous poles to acquire the nests. The simulation was exceedingly realistic.

Debriefing

Before long I was back in Kuala Lumpur where I met John Stoddart again and others interested in the training college work. There was a general debriefing and I shared my findings and recommendations, though these were later finalised in the report after time had allowed for more thought. The whole Malaysian 'package' from Broadstairs 1983 to this tour of colleges in 1987 had been a tremendous learning experience for me, however and whatever I had contributed. The Zambian and South African assignments had run alongside, and interestingly the next South African one in 1988 was the training college project. Each gave to the other in my work. And all of this was reflected in my book *Story as Vehicle*, which was published in 1989 and was a kind of summation. After Malaysia I concentrated on the writing, greatly helped by the recollections from the seminars. I felt that my book was a true result of my rich hands-on experience. It was another milestone for me. Just as my first book affected and greatly coloured my work during the early eighties, the second had the same effect in the later eighties and nineties. But to my next adventure.

Story from The Middle East
(1990)

WEST BANK

This was a very short, sharp assignment, sharp in more senses than one. I was there for two weeks, and until the eleventh hour not at all sure that I would be going. It was not long after Saddam Hussein had gone in to Kuwait and the Middle East was seething to boiling point. It seemed to the world that we were on the brink of a regional if not a world war. All that summer I had been expecting the Foreign Office to advise me not to go. On holiday with my friend Jean in the Scottish highlands in August, I had kept in touch with the British Council office, but as far as they were concerned I was still on target for the 16th of September.

And so on the 15th I found myself in the El Al departure lounge at Heathrow, bound for Tel Aviv. The security measures were greater than I had ever known. We had to keep all our luggage until the very last minute and the spot-checking was still going on when the flight was called. The plane was less than full, most of the passengers in the orthodox Jewish dress. There were no tourists and the only others travelling were those with business that couldn't wait. Did I come into that category? In a funny kind of way I persuaded myself that I did. The training of teachers in my view was a fitting issue to put on the scales opposite the issues of war. It might help to redress the balance and the cultural diplomacy of The British Council seemed more urgent than ever.

St George's Hospice

Be that as it may, after a smooth flight and landing, there I was, in the British Council car, making for Jerusalem with the dawn coming up beyond the hills and the cypresses standing stark against its rosy glow. Once again I just could not believe that I was actually here in the Holy Land and that that place over there was the Mount of Olives. In spite of my natural apprehension, my excitement rose and the adrenalin was flowing. As the cocks were crowing, my driver roused the sleepy gateman at the door of the St George's Hospice in Nablus Street which was to be my place of accommodation in East Jerusalem and in no time at all I was shown my room where I slept a little, only to be wakened by the cathedral bell which I assumed rightly was calling people to prayer. I felt moved to go, not realising that this was the service in Arabic. But it was easy to follow and the bilingual priest said the words of the communion to me in English. It seemed right for me to be there and a fitting start to my assignment. I was to find St George's a true haven of peace amid the turmoil. In its quiet cloisters and beautiful garden, in the services of early communion and evensong, in the meals shared at the refectory table with people from many countries and vocations, I felt a wonderful sense of security, which was enhanced when I heard the sound of the muezzin also calling the faithful to prayer. My 'Uganda factor' surged in me once again and I knew the presence of God. St George's was a kind of powerhouse in which strength for the many challenges of the day was generated.

A Wonderful Sharing

Although I was in the 'Occupied Territories' for only two weeks, it seems in retrospect very much longer because of the intensity of the living and the richness and width of the whole experience. For this short period I shared with the Palestinians something of their agony, the indignities of being occupied, the constraints on the quality of life, the almost total abandonment of hope that the rest of the world would ever understand and give constructive help. And even as I write, sixteen years on, I wonder what has changed! Indeed as I continue to write of my mission in 1990 it seems to me that I could be writing the same story today. Except for changes in certain particulars like that from one Bush to another, the human tragedy remains the same, the same bitterness and evil pervading the so-called Holy Land, as one Arab gentleman put it to me, the spirit of anti-Christ. And one of the worst aspects of this tragedy, it seemed to me was the frustration at what was seen as foreign interference. I am not writing a political treatise though I am in great danger of doing so, but I feel that I have to record something which another Palestinian said when discussing Saddam and his actions which Palestinians did not condone. "Nevertheless", he said, "He is our son-of-a-bitch, not yours!" This, for me, said it all. The Palestinians did not like the American President nor had they much time for Mrs Thatcher, the British Prime Minister at the time. As an 'ambassador' for the UK and the 'interfering' West, it was not always easy to know how to play my own role. In the event I was surprised how much I and my story vehicle, songs and language games etc. were welcomed, and given an interested hearing. I felt I had arrived when one teacher from a refugee camp was heard to remark to colleagues that my story methodology would be equally useful in the teaching of Arabic.

Importance of Education and Communication

If there was any hope at all in Palestine it seemed to lie in the education of its children, particularly in the learning of the English language. The language of world communication was seen as a prize to be gained. In this and in so many other respects I saw a parallel with the black people in South Africa during apartheid. My work lay in training the elementary school teachers, those in the schools administered by the United Nations Relief Work Agency (UNRWA). The teachers therefore came from the refugee camps in the West Bank and the Gaza Strip. My tour had been suggested by Shelagh Rixon after *her* visit in 1989. She had seen a particular need for helping the teachers of English to children of 9-11 years. The work would be part of the ongoing training being done locally.

Considering the political situation with its strikes, curfews and roadblocks, and the general intifada or insurrection, it is quite remarkable that my own programme proceeded so smoothly. I was grateful to a great many people whose careful planning made this possible. Perhaps the best way to describe my work experience is to select a few strong memories as cameos on which to hang some thoughts. I think for instance of Nablus, a town north of Jerusalem which has been a hotbed of trouble over the years, and still is. I remember vividly the 'noises off' while I conducted my teachers' seminar in the classroom of a girls' school. Taking my cue from the teachers, I tried not to flinch at the sound of grenades and gunfire. All our eyes had strayed to the windows. Then a quiet, polite voice said, "You were saying, Madam, about the past tense." I turned to face my class again, thinking ironically that any moment it *could* be the past tense! I never ceased to be amazed at the courage and calmness of these remarkable people. At the end of this particular session I was picked up by Issa, my U.N. minder in the West Bank. He was a Christian Arab. As we went to the car he hesitated. "There are many very interesting places here, places mentioned in the Bible." He obviously wanted to show me a few. But an explosion rather too near for comfort sent us scuttling back to Jerusalem.

Then there was the time when I was being driven to another seminar.

Girls at school where Edie talked
to teachers in Nablus

My driver was Helen Hawari, an English lady who had been there for eleven years and was married to an Arab. She was in charge of the English Language Teaching Programme and ran the centre in Jerusalem. Helen understood and spoke Arabic fluently and understood Hebrew also. As we came to one of the many Israeli checkpoints, our copy of the *Jerusalem Post* much in evidence, a soldier asked our business in a threatening way. Helen said very nonchalantly, "British Council". The soldier then disappeared into his sentry box and spoke into his walkie-talkie. We were reluctantly waved on. Once out of earshot, Helen burst out laughing. She had heard and understood the whole proceedings. The message which had gone along the line was "British Consul"! For the nonce, I had become a very important diplomatic figure and the Israelis perhaps were wary of causing an international incident. We did have 'diplomatic' number plates also so that may have helped.

Life Goes on Amid Tension

The English Language Centre in Jerusalem was quite near to where I was staying. I could walk there and I conducted several workshops with Helen and Issa supporting and translating. Issa in particular was most interested in my story methodology and my new book, and intended to pursue this work further after I had gone. Again, I based my training on a collection of materials and had the teachers making their own and using stories from their own culture. But in the midst of my happy busyness,

I was conscious all the time of the tensions in the air. There was one occasion when two of the centre staff were overdue from a mission. They eventually came back but it had been an anxious few hours. This was all part of everyday life.

Issa did manage to take me to the Mount of Olives where I stood amongst the camels and marvelled at the wonderful view of the city's domes and minarets. We even had lunch on the sixth floor of the National Palace Hotel. He also took me to his home in Ramallah, the Palestinian centre of administration and very much in the news today. I met his delightful family and enjoyed lavish hospitality as I sat on the verandah amid the vines. At that time Issa's home was a quiet oasis in the clamour. As of course my 'home' at St George's continued to be. After I had been there for a day I met Sheelagh and Kenneth Mackenzie who came from Musselburgh on

With Issa and teachers in East Jerusalem

the outskirts of Edinburgh. We became friends immediately and they too took me out on the few times when I had some leisure. They knew the city extremely well as they had been coming to the Holy Land for many years and were sponsoring a little girl in a school which I also visited. That girl is now married and the Mackenzies still visit. And I have found another home in Edinburgh. Once again my travels have yielded a lasting friendship. I shall never forget Kenneth's glorious organ playing in the St George's cathedral. He now plays for me in Edinburgh. I even joined his Gaelic choir on one occasion. We are united by our common experience, our music and our Scottishness.

Another vivid memory is my brief visit to Bethlehem en route to work somewhere else. I went into a shop in the deserted 'Manger Square' to buy postcards. The courteous elderly shop keeper enquired if I was a tourist, as well he might with soldiers, guns at the ready, keeping an eye on us from the rooftops all around. "No", I replied, "I am here to train teachers of English." "Oh", he said, "You are Eddie Garvie" (note the two ds). I gasped. "How do you know that?" I asked. "One moment." The gentleman disappeared into the back of the shop and returned with the daily newspaper. There, amongst all the Arabic, was my name. Helen later confessed that the wrong spelling was her fault. This was an advertisement for my ubiquitous public lecture which, in this case, was to be in Jerusalem. I remember it was well attended. Once again I was impressed by the way in which the ordinary things of life went on amongst the extraordinary.

GAZA

To Go or Not to Go

For a time it was doubtful if I would be able to fulfil the second part of my assignment, the week in Gaza. Because of an 'incident', the road to Gaza had been blocked. My predecessor had met the same situation and had had to return to the UK early. Miraculously, the road was suddenly opened again and I was driven into Gaza, not at all sure about getting out again. I stayed in the Manton House Hotel, the only guest actually sleeping there, though a few people came to dine. The lady who ran the establishment was Lebanese, I believe, and in the evening as she watched the television, she knitted a Scandinavian type sweater. I thought of the ladies sitting at the foot of the guillotine during the French revolution! The place was swathed in dustsheets but there were glimpses of fine, solid furniture and expensive drapes; there was an air of past glory. Next door was a hospital with constant comings and goings of ambulances and frequent sounds of screaming and distress. As I sat in the neglected garden of the hotel, waiting for Hussain my U.N. minder in Gaza, I befriended a little cat which behaved and responded like cats everywhere, while my ears were regaled by the noises across the flower-beds, and my thoughts were in tumult. Would I be able to do my work today? Would Hussain have decided that it was not safe to go into the refugee camp designated in my programme?

Working in Refugee Camps

My week in Gaza was like a dream going on nightmare. Every day was an exciting challenge, to put it mildly, and every day had to finish before 8.00pm as that was when the curfew started. This was the context of my work. But, once again, there was 'normality' and joy amongst the fear and sadness. Some more key memories. I can see myself now, a kind of Margaret Rutherford figure, walking briskly in the midst of a group of Arab gentlemen in a refugee camp, clutching my set of pictures for a particular story and making towards a classroom where sixty little boys of ten or so were packed into a small space so that they nearly climbed up the chalkboard. I had insisted that I wanted to teach children. The teachers were sure I would not be understood as these boys had no English. To my joy and the amazement of these good people, the children answered my English questions correctly, but in Arabic. That was a small triumph for my story methodology and soon the teachers in my seminars were developing their own stories, as had the Jerusalem teachers.

In this same camp another memory prevails. The staple basic in the Bedouin menu is lamb. Hussain had informed my teacher hosts that I did not eat lamb. With typical Bedouin hospitality the lamb in the common pot was changed to chicken. That was one problem solved. Another was a little more complex. For some reason, in this particular camp, I dealt only with men teachers. Everywhere else I had a mixed clientele. What to do with me at mealtimes? There seemed to be a strict segregation of the sexes. The womenfolk here were not teachers. They were the wives and other family members of the men teachers and they seemed to be confined to the kitchen area and had no English. I would have to eat with the men. To resolve the problem, I was made an honorary man, just as the South Africans in their apartheid policy made the Chinese honorary whites when they needed their expertise! So I found myself sitting on the floor in the circle of men and dipping with them into the common pot. Later I was taken to a large house on the boundary of the camp which seemed to belong to a family who were surprisingly wealthy. The house had several storeys. Like the longhouses in Borneo, it could be added to as the means were found, but here the additions were vertical rather than horizontal. The view across the windswept desert from the present roof was quite staggering, and kept these delightful Bedouins close to their sandy past.

But this really was a one-off experience. Most of my camp memories relate to poverty and squalor, the streets lined with mounting rubbish as the official refuse wagons did not visit. How the teachers and their pupils could turn out as they did, neatly and cleanly dressed, I just could not understand, and how they could come to my seminars and workshops when their minds were occupied with such terrible things as fear of having their homes bulldozed in collective punishment, or their innocent teenage children arrested. I cherish a small bottle of perfume given to me by a woman who was celebrating her son's release on one occasion. My time in the Holy Land, and particularly in Gaza, showed me the strength and the resilience of which the human spirit is capable.

Hussain invited me home where I met his lovely wife and two teenage children. Again, I was to sample typical Arab hospitality and to share something of their culture, not only in the food and drink but also in the conversation. And the young daughter danced for me. I reciprocated by doing the Highland Fling! How I longed to be able to find a way of getting her and her brother to Britain or somewhere else, a place where they could extend their education and spread their wings. Hussain himself, in his early years, had been able to leave Palestine to study in Europe. It was nigh impossible now for any to leave or, if they did, to be able to return. Yet their hopes were high on that score and they reached out for any chance of learning which came their way. Hence the enthusiasm for my seminars. I longed for more time with them and to be able to teach the children, but I had to accept the restrictions put upon me.

End of Assignment

The return journey to Jerusalem was without incident, though we heard gunfire in the distance and I had to crouch on the floor of the car from time to time when boys threw stones, taking us for Israelis. My driver this time was the Director of The British Council in the area. He had had his windscreen broken by stones on his way to pick me up. All too soon came the usual (or perhaps not so usual in this case) debriefing session and I was off again to Tel Aviv and the airport, where I was virtually frog-marched into a room by two young officials and interrogated. I had been warned about this and guided in how I should react. I must not say I had been in Gaza for instance. But I decided that one *could* be too bland, an attitude that might cause suspicion. So I told them I had been to Ramallah, which brought a strong reaction! I insisted that I was only visiting friends, which was true, in a sense, and not doing anything political. I even mentioned Issa's name, knowing that it is a very common one in the region. It means 'Jesus'. I did not tell them that Issa worked for the U.N. I finished up by saying something to the effect that I sympathised with them (my interrogators) in their work, and appreciated the need for security. We had a general laugh about something and I tried to walk on nonchalantly to the departure gate. It took me some time to unwind. A ship rather than a plane would have helped. The sun sparkling on the snowy peaks of the Alps restored me somewhat and of course I was soon immersed once again in another ploy.

European Kaleidoscope
(1983 – 1991)

Norway 1983

Seminar in the Mountains

Not long after I had started to freelance, and soon after I had written that paper for the University of Graz on my view of multicultural education in Britain, I was invited by The British Council to go to Norway for them. The Council had been collaborating for some time with the Norwegian authorities concerned with the educational and cultural problems of immigrants. I was asked to contribute to a conference, and to express a British point of view. Once again, as in my earlier work on the Continent, I felt hugely responsible and not a little apprehensive. The conference was organised by a Nordic Council and those attending would come from all the Nordic countries. Their aim was to set up a network of information for 'Innovation in Education'.

The seminar, ably chaired by Lars Stølen, was held in a very comfortable hotel, an establishment catering specially for the needs of conferences. It was a little bit out of Oslo and up in the mountains, a luxurious chalet on several levels with verandahs all round. My room was on the lowest level and I had to go up to the dining room and lounges. It was a glorious spot basking in the autumn colours and very soon to be thronged with skiers. This was the in-between time. Almost overnight the weather could turn to winter. But, while I was there, there was a mixture of sunshine, rain and fog, the latter swirling eerily around our hilltop dwelling and making driving to and from Oslo and other places somewhat hazardous.

Wendy Scott, English Adviser to the Ministry, acted as my interpreter and did it extremely well. When she had a break, people from amongst the delegates took over, as most were fluent English speakers. It made for a very tiring day for both the interpreter and myself, as the translation was continuously whispered into my ear. I suppose I could have done without this and had a nice holiday except for the day of my own lecture, but it was much better that I listened to the others and so was more able to understand the context and to contribute to it accordingly.

I did have one reservation. The focus of the seminar was on the 16-19 year old language learner. I felt that there were others in the UK who might have been more suited to this slot. But in the event, my emphasis on the younger learner did seem to be of interest and opened new avenues. I had the impression that more had been done in the adult field of immigrant education in the Nordic countries generally. In fact I was to find this a trend in other European countries too. Yet there were many teachers of children who needed help. Perhaps my own particular interest *would* be of use.

Amongst the many topics covered in the seminar, that of the linguistic support for the needs of the learner was very much to the fore, and ways of assessing those needs. More materials to link language with other studies were called for. This gave a way in for me to speak of 'language across the curriculum', a concept which I had now developed more fully. I talked of language 'in' the curriculum, 'of', 'for' and 'by means of' the curriculum, and 'through' as well as 'across'. I had an acetate sheet of this list for the projector and spoke to each at some length. This school 'language policy' took up the first half of my presentation. After the break (I had two hours in all) I focused more on practicalities and demonstrated techniques. I think that these high-powered Nordic educationists quite enjoyed being children in a classroom for a while. I felt reasonably happy with my input. And I was flattered when the Danish Minister of Education asked if I would now go and work in Denmark.

Further Work in Oslo

At the conclusion of the seminar I moved to a hotel in the centre of Oslo where my next task was to give a talk to teachers from all over the city and then to stay on for a few days to advise generally. The talk was held in a centre for immigrant women. They came there daily to learn Norwegian. I was struck by the caring work going on. It was a real haven of peace and security for them, tastefully furnished and well equipped for its purpose. There was also a crèche. The teachers who came to my talk were both primary and secondary. All had children of immigrant background in their classes. Some of the centre students also attended the talk and even a few of their children. It was an interesting and interested audience. I spent quite a lot of time here on classroom methodology. The question of culture and language maintenance arose in this session and I shared something of the current 'mother-tongue debate' in the UK. One Japanese lady, married to a Swede and settled in Oslo, asked my advice about the language development of her child who was attending the American school whose medium of instruction was English. I tried to persuade her to keep the Japanese tongue alive in the midst of this complicated linguistic scene, suggesting the use of story and song at least.

I was happy also during my stay to meet two people who had approached The British Council in Oslo for advice. One, an Englishman, was to be doing some sociolinguistic research amongst the Sikh community in Smethwick. I was able to give him some contacts which could be useful. The other was a Norwegian wanting suggestions for placements for his teacher-trainees when he took them on a visit to York. This work was in line with a growing part of my freelancing work generally. The Council was sending me more and more visitors who were seeking advice of one kind or another.

And to finish this Norwegian tale on a more personal note, I was able while in Oslo to meet relatives of my cousin's husband. Anne and George lived in Kelso; I speak of them in Book 1. George's sister, Sheila, was married to a Norwegian, Paul, and I met them and their delightful family. They drove through the fog to pick me up from my hilltop hotel and I enjoyed some time off in their lovely homes. There was also time to attend an orchestral concert in Oslo. Even there the cross-cultural interest was maintained. A slow hand-clap seemed to mean approval in that setting and the conductor, a man, was presented with a bouquet of flowers, unusual in Britain at that time. Finally, my Norwegian experience was capped by a lovely party given in my honour in the pleasant flat of Mary Wade, the British Council representative. Mary, who was near to retirement, had once been in the Diplomatic service and had served in Moscow. She had some interesting tales to tell. She introduced me to a colleague, a young man married to a Norwegian. To my delight he had been one of my TEA students in Uganda! (see Book 1). The more I travelled, the more I was convinced of how small the world is! So ended my Scandinavian adventure.

GERMANY 1983

A Depressing 'Climate'

Earlier that same year, I did the first of two lecture tours in Germany. These visits arose from personal contact with René Dirven, a Belgian and professor at the University of Trier and later Duisburg. We had met at a conference of IATEFL and found that our interests, both academic and professional, marched together. Professor Dirven asked me to go to Germany and speak to his students and perhaps to extend my visit and go to other universities and colleges. The organising of the project became too large in the end for my busy professor to take on alone, and The British Council took over. It is difficult to believe, looking back now, that so much was done in the course of two weeks, but so it was, a positive whirl of activity and a marathon of travelling.

It began in Hamburg. I have a very clear memory of the River Elbe in the moonlight and thought of our bomber pilots in World War II using this same river as a guide to their targets. Such thoughts prompt me to say at this point that my two visits (the next in 1990) were in very different contexts. Now, in 1983, I was in the Federal Republic of Germany or West Germany. The East was still a separate state, a satellite of the Soviet Union, and the Cold War was still 'raging'. My next visit took place just after the 'wall' had come down and the two Germanys had become united again, with the Cold War gradually receding. These differing contexts made for differing effects on my work.

My first tour in Germany, 1983, like my work in Norway, was generated by the paper I had written for the University of Graz in 1980. My aim in this paper had been to give an overview of the development in the UK of the multicultural concept in education. The paper had been sent to René Dirven who had distributed copies to his colleagues in other universities. A degree of interest was aroused in one or two places, especially in the north, though I was to find that the whole notion of multiculturalism was foreign to most educationists in Germany at that time and was seldom discussed. The 'Turk', the German equivalent of 'Paki' in Britain, was very much a migrant who would eventually return to his own land, and the quicker the better. A newspaper headline I spotted while travelling to give one of my lectures, "10,500 DM Pramie wenn Gastarbeiter heimkerren" (10,500 DM offered to guest workers to go home), was not very encouraging for my immediate task!

I was conscious the whole time of the depressing political and economic climate in which I was working. This was not helped by the proceedings of the Economic Summit in Stuttgart which took place while I was in that city. It may have been imagination but I felt that I had to work harder after that event. One taxi driver who, I was convinced, saw me as Margaret Thatcher, accused me of using *his* money to pay for ridiculous things like the Falklands War! Matters of financial cutbacks and the high rate of teacher unemployment were also an important talking point at that time and it was quite a battle for me to bring suggestions of educational innovation and change. Nevertheless, in spite of all this, my friend René Dirven was determined that I should go ahead and he certainly worked hard to drum up support for my lectures, The British Council making good the shortfall when universities declared that they could not afford me!

Choice of Three Lectures

I offered three lectures covering the two prongs of my role as I still saw them, help on the one hand with the particular language needs and on the other with general awareness making of diversity. One lecture was entitled *Multicultural/Multiracial Education, A Changing View in Britain* and was directly related to my Graz paper. Another was *Some Educational Strategies for the Multicultural Education of all Children* and was obviously more specifically geared to the school teacher, reflecting my work of recent years in Britain, and the third, which I also used in Norway, was *School Language Policy in Multicultural Education*. The choice of lecture obviously told me much about the establishment I was to speak in, though not necessarily about the audience. My talks were public lectures. I was given the slot of a professor whose students might or might not attend. And in addition there were people from other departments, and members of the general public who had seen the advertising poster. So I never quite knew what kind of audience I would have. In Hamburg, for instance, there were a number of American women, wives of Germans, who were attending the series of language lectures into which I had 'crashed'. I was amused by one who came up to me at the end, declaring that she had never experienced a professor like me before! When I questioned her further she said that I "kinda looked at the students as though they were there"! The German professors seemed to keep their noses buried in their notes and often the students had the impression that they were not very enthusiastic about contacts and preferred the scholarship part of the work. There is an apocryphal story about the professor who put his lecture on tape and placed this in the lecture room. About half way through the allotted time for the lecture he went along to check that his students were still listening and found forty other tape recorders busily in action! Perhaps now (2006) this would not be so surprising.

Tour in Two Parts

How to describe my experience over these two weeks and twelve institutions? Again, some highlights must be selected. First it should be said that the tour divided into two quite distinct parts, north and south, and The British Council had a different person looking after each. Thereby hangs a tale. Cologne was the changing point. I arrived there on a Sunday which could have been difficult as I missed my contact at first. The British Council office would be closed and I had no home telephone number. It all happened because of an over-zealous German helper who took my luggage off the train for me and carried it beyond the platform before I could stop him. I had my usual extra case full of books and equipment. There followed more help while I managed to have a tannoy message put out in English to the British Council Representative to say that I would be on platform so-and-so, the one I had come in on originally. More help to get back there and a somewhat frantic ten minutes or so while I wondered what I should do if he didn't come. This British Council representative had all my tickets and documents for the second half of my tour. I was displaying The British Council identity label, of bright pink and blue. It was one of the few times when I really needed this 'cloak and dagger' strategy. I considered going to the police and then, to my utter relief, I saw a curly head emerging from a staircase on to the platform. I saw a corresponding label and gave a shout of recognition. All was well. We retrieved all my luggage from its helpful carers and went off to the home of my friend for an informal and very pleasant lunch, after which I was sent on my way.

Procedure and Protocol

The informality of my British contacts contrasted quite markedly with the formality of my German hosts. Around each professor there was an interesting group of people and usually, particularly in the south, quite a strict hierarchy of assistant lecturers, lektors, student assistants etc. Depending on how much prestige I was rated, I could be met at the station by anyone from the most junior assistant to the professor her/himself. I wondered how I might compete with Salman Rushdie who was another British Council guest at that time! There was also a special procedure when I arrived at the university where I was to lecture. I was given a seat amongst the numerous plants in the outer, secretary's office and a tray of tea brought, no matter if the train had been late (which. seldom happened) or for some other reason time was pressing. This was the way a guest lecturer had to be dealt with! Something which did startle me a little at first was that the students applauded at the end of my lecture. Somehow I was not expecting this, and I was somewhat concerned when they did it by banging with their fists on the writing desks. It seemed very fierce and disapproving.

Valuable Memories

As always, on my short, sharp assignments, there was such interesting variety of experience, of personnel, degree of concern, environment and scenery. I had been to Germany before, with my friend Mairi and with family, and I renewed old memories. It was lovely to be by the Rhine again and to see the places on the Mosel where Mairi and I had wandered. I remembered mein host at Cochem with his meerschaum pipe standing at the door of his ancient inn, the wooden staircase to our room rising straight out of the taproom and our passage to bed for the night accompanied by the German equivalent of wolf whistles. Something of the very German country life was reflected now in Siegen where my host took me with his rambler friends for a picnic in the forest nearby. In Passau also, a quaint old town standing at the confluence of three rivers, the Inn, the Ils and the Danube, I enjoyed something of Teutonic things past. All of this contrasted with the towns of the industrial north such as Essen and Aachen and also with the very new as in Stuttgart, rebuilt after our bombers had completely flattened it. Perhaps it was appropriate that the summit meeting should be held there.

Out of the twelve institutions where I worked, there were two which were not universities. One was a technical college and the other was a college for teacher training. Interestingly, this last one was working closely with a college in England, in Teesside. There had been exchange visits and discussions on syllabi with a multicultural bias. Gisela Göhrum, the Head of the English Department, was an enlightened and deep-thinking lady with whom I made another of my lasting friendships. She also worked for the Peace Movement and at the time was doing some brave and dangerous things in protest at the siting of nuclear missiles near her home. As I write, we are still in touch. Another poignant memory is of the two young university teachers who took me sightseeing in Nuremberg. The hairs at the back of my neck stood on end as we entered the huge plaza where Hitler had ranted at the crowds on his podium. I felt as though someone had walked over my grave.

There were a few days of worry after Stuttgart when I discovered that I had left a certain green bag behind in that city. It contained the books I needed in particular for showing to my audiences, the ones I had used most and which I had put in this bag so that I could reach them quickly. I remembered the briefcase I had left in Edinburgh when I was going to Uganda and how it was sent on to London after me in the care of the guard of the next train. Could a German guard do the same? Some hectic phoning from various places eventually brought the bag, but by post, which must have cost a bomb. My audience in Augsburg were startled by my shriek of delight when the bag was brought in by an official and laid in front of me. All of a sudden, life was good again.

I flew home from Munich, wondering as always after such assignments, if my efforts had borne any fruit and if I had really contributed to the awareness of multiculturalism and the place of language. I could but pray that some seeds had fallen on good ground. For me personally it had been once again a time of great richness, full of memories I should treasure. I was grateful not only to the Council for its support, but to all my German hosts and in particular to Belgian René who had set everything up. More of him below.

GERMANY 1990

Change of Atmosphere

I visited again and, as I have indicated, the political climate was very different. The Berlin Wall had just come down and I saw, for the first time, adults skateboarding. They were skating in and out of the traffic on the Kurfurstendam, the main street in West Berlin. The excitement and ebullience seemed to be brimming over. And not only were there differences in the world about me, but there was also a difference within myself. My book *Story as Vehicle* had just been published. It had been at the Frankfurt Book Fair and was becoming known and talked about. In it I had firmly nailed my colours to the mast of the young child in my multicultural world, to developing child lingualism and to story as a classroom methodology. I quote from the back-cover of the book:

> "The word 'story' is interpreted in the widest possible sense - the story of life and the lingualism that goes with it - especially interesting and exciting in multicultural situations. It is suggested that the motivated teacher, working from a story bank rich in all manner of tales from a variety of cultures, can produce the kind of learning environment which stimulates and carries learners forward, the different genres and cross-cultural experience offering more and more sets of particulars from which more and more universals of life can be gleaned. It is in this sense that a learning journey is implied, and that story is seen as vehicle."

Three in One

This time I offered only one lecture, though no doubt it reflected the three given in 1983. It was entitled *Story as Vehicle; Teaching English to Young Children.* I offered it with some trepidation, remembering my audiences of seven years previously and the very formal and academic line I had had to take most of the time. To my gratified surprise, I was well received and my ideas accepted as something new and innovative which Germany in its new beginning could readily take on board. I had an exciting and very fulfilling experience. I was also happy to meet old friends from the last tour, and even people who had been with me at the UNESCO round-table in Zurich. There had been much communication amongst us over the years even without the Internet!

Excursion to Belgium

On this occasion my work lasted for just over a week, but it was extended to cover a very pleasant period of festivity in Belgium as I had been invited to the wedding of René's daughter, Greet. René, his wife Lutgard and their family had become good friends. I had now visited their home in Mechelen several times and was beginning to know parts of Belgium very well. I enjoyed meeting René's friends and colleagues and joining in the often high-powered conversations and arguments, in so far as I could manage in this multilingual setting. The whole family and their

194

friends were fluent in several languages. Lutgard, mother of the bride, giving her speech at the wedding for instance, spoke in four languages. The young ones were equally fluent. Belgium is a virtual 'cockpit' of lingualism, sadly sometimes a place of conflict as the Flemish and French-speaking communities stake their claims.

For some years there was much coming and going between the Mechelen family and myself. We arranged exchanges of the young folks, for example. After I had taken my nephew, David, for a holiday there, Werner, René's son, came to Glasgow and stayed with my family. And before Greet married, she came to Peterborough to stay with a colleague of mine and his wife, as

Belgian René and his wife Lutgard in the garden of their home in Mechelen

they had a daughter of the same age. Then there was the time that René brought a party of his students to the UK. I arranged a tour for them of Cambridge and Peterborough which included a hilarious evening at one of our primary schools with a large Italian intake, where the German students learned the tricks of a Beetle Drive from Italian parents and children. The noise and the laughter still ring in my ears.

Belgium too has been the scene of conferences which I would have attended in any case, but which were enriched for me because of my new and valuable connections. I was still doing the conference circuit, BAAL and IATEFL etc. in between British Council and other assignments. I just have to tell one story of my conference going. It concerns my good friend, Father Maguire, the Catholic priest from my Makerere days in Uganda. For some reason he and I found ourselves in the same institution, each attending a different conference. Mine was a BAAL gathering. When Father Maguire spotted me there, and learned that I was part of BAAL, he teased me unmercifully as his religious concept of BAAL came to the fore! From his point of view it was an unfortunate acronym.

Now, on my 1990 tour of German universities, again set up by Belgian René as he taught in Germany, I included lectures in Belgium, starting my tour in Antwerp and finishing it in Leuven. There was time on this occasion for some interesting sightseeing in Trier, the oldest town in Germany I believe, with some well-preserved Roman remains. But perhaps the high-light of my visit was Berlin, the centre of all the political reaction to the coming down of the wall and the birth of the new, united Germany. Berlin would take over again as the capital. I was there for two or three days so there was time for seeing places in both the west and east. Checkpoint Charlie and the Brandenburg Gate were places which evoked special memories and the spot in the east where Hitler had made a bonfire of books. It was painful and sad to see the contrast between the affluent west and the down-at-heel east. It is amazing how the two Germanys eventually came together, not without sweat and tears. But in that immediate aftermath of the cessation of boundaries, I was caught up in the general mood of optimism and joy. It was even reflected in the music of the Philharmonic orchestra which I went to hear. I was staying in a small hotel up a side-street just off the Kurfurstendam. I was amused at the Pakistani receptionist whose German

In front of the opera house in East Berlin

was worse than mine. He produced a miniature door and had me practis-ing the use of the key, which was peculiar to say the least! Many patrons must have had problems.

My reception at the Free University of Berlin was specially warm with an offer of further work. There was talk of a visiting lectureship at one stage. Though this did not in fact take place, I felt greatly encouraged by the way in which this and other academic communities listened to and accepted my suggestions for the teaching of the young child. Once again I had to thank René, himself a wonderful mixture of the academic and the professional, for paving the way for me and The British Council for its support.

HUNGARY 1991

Conference in Pécs

And about eighteen months later I was to experience another interesting follow-up to both the change around me in the form of the end of the Cold War and that within myself as a result of the publication of my book and my now strong identification with the language needs of young children and the use of story. I attended a conference in Pécs, in Hungary, where I met people from eastern Europe just emerging from the Soviet thrall and excitedly talking to the West for the first time. And to my astonishment, I found that my book was known and already in use in their teacher-training work. There was one particular lady who was whipping up support for my talk and I received another offer of future work. One of the good things about freelancing was that one thing led to another and I was never short of exciting things to look forward to.

This gathering in Hungary, the first open to the West for many years, was very significant. There were teachers and teacher educators, as well as researchers of language learning, from all over the world. The central issue of the congress was 'Life-long Language Learning' so the whole range of learning from young children to adults was dealt with. At the same time there was a spotlight on the issue of peace and international understanding, of lifelong language learning turned towards peace, friendship and better understanding among people. The procedures were multilingual. Though the main working languages were English, Finnish, French, German, Hungarian, Italian, Russian, Serbo-Croatian and Spanish, other languages were welcomed both as a topic and as a medium of communication. I was back in Strasbourg in 1979, where other languages were treated as we in Britain might treat dialects of English. I was excited, inspired, but suffering, as before, from a huge linguistic inferiority complex.

About three hundred people from approximately thirty countries attended. There was the usual mixture of plenary happenings, round-tables and symposia, and section meetings arranged in themes and languages. There was also an interesting cultural programme. The four days were extremely full and passed very quickly. I recall with amusement the dilemma of the girls on Reception at my hotel. I couldn't understand why they seemed to have a fit of the giggles. Had I grown an ass's head or something? It turned out that they had assumed 'Edie' to be a man's name and had paired me off with one of my male colleagues. We were sharing rooms. In the end I did well as I was one of the few to have a single room. Considering the fact that the Hungarians were new to the organisation of gatherings where initiative would have to be exercised, used as they were to 'command' government, there were few hiccups. There were the usual grumblers and moaners but on the whole there was great understanding and reaching-out. We formed a kind of microcosm of the world the congress wanted to see.

A New Spirit Abroad

Shall I ever forget attending a concert in the cathedral? I sat next to a Polish lady. As we knelt in prayer before the concert began, I was dismayed to see my neighbour sobbing her heart out. She explained that she had just become so overwhelmed at the thought that once again she could pray in church and that God had never gone away! At a less lofty level, I saw a balloon rise up from the market place carrying an advert for the opening of the new McDonalds-like cafe which I later patronised. The spotless premises, the pristine uniforms of the staff and their zealous care of the customers, were most impressive. I thought of our somewhat jaded McDonalds back home and wondered how long all this 'spotlessness' would last! Both the affairs in the congress and the new spirit abroad around us seemed to offer untold opportunities. Would they be taken up? As I write in 2006, I wonder if they really were, and what has been lost.

It was good to see a little of the elegant city of Budapest, and also something of the surrounding countryside. On excursion day we were taken in buses to the wine-growing area and later to a sculpture park. An old quarry had been utilised and artists allowed to buy a plot. I should have liked longer to study and meditate. It seemed to me that 'the hopes and fears of all the years' as one of our old hymns says, were present in this exhibition of sculpture. I said an arrow prayer for the Hungarian people, that there would never be another '1956' and that their new-found freedom would have them soaring to the heights. As I prayed, a group of women, dressed in the local costume, started to sing in words to match my thoughts. I felt better able to help my Ukrainian neighbour in the bus as we returned to Pécs. She was having great difficulties adjusting and her lack of 'hard cash' did not help. At times it was difficult to keep one's mind on the business of the meeting. There were so many 'human' issues. But I would not have missed this experience for anything. It was very much a part of my pearl of great price.

Short Update

Before I turn to the last years of my freelancing period, it is timely to pause and sum up a little. The 80s had been very traumatic for me. In work I had moved, in line with my second book, to an emphasis on young learners and story, though still keeping my two-pronged approach to multiculturalism in general. In my personal life, as I have said, I had had several bereavements including Mother in 1984. It was wonderful that a few months earlier, Dorothy had brought her to visit me and we had some precious time together, including a short holiday in Broadstairs.

Then, while I was helping Dorothy to move to a flat in Edinburgh when the family home broke up after Mother's death, I became ill with Bell's Palsy, a disease of a facial nerve. The right side of my face twisted and the eye had difficulty opening. I had a short-lived panic, thinking I was having a stroke and that my career was over. Even when I realised that the trouble was local, it was hard to face the thought of meeting people, and especially of speaking to audiences. But I hadn't come to the end of the road. Everyone was most understanding, particularly the large group of twelve-year-olds I spoke to in Stirling just after I became ill, and my colleague Ted Jackson and his wife, Deborah, who looked after me in Middlesbrough when I had to talk to a Heads' conference. Twisted face or not, I was able to go on as though nothing had happened, except that my singing voice was affected and I could no longer sing solo. I still cannot open my right eye fully.

And in the world at large, the Cold War came to an end and South Africa lost its apartheid policy. It seemed to me at the end of the decade that there was a general tide of optimism, and I rose with it. In 1990 I attended a conference in Dublin, a very important staging post in my life, as it heralded the end of my freelancing days. At the same time, it ensured that I went out on a high.

Last 'Waltz' in Vienna
(1990 – 1993)

Dublin 1990

Lest my title confuse the reader, let me try to explain. This is still part of my European kaleidoscope, but because events moved so fast and were all part of one important milestone in these last years of my professional life, they have come together in a special merger and merit a place to themselves. It all started in Dublin 1990, at the IATEFL conference, the last of such conferences which I attended. It was highly significant for me. The organisation had set up several special interest groups or SIGS and I had become the coordinator of the one dealing with Young Learners of language. This linked with a similar working party which The British Council now organised and a number of us were in both. I believe that we shared the aim of keeping Young Learners to the fore in both academic and professional circles. In Dublin, we met formally and informally, cementing friendships internationally and planning new ventures. From this experience there came for me three new ploys in particular, central to which was my work in Vienna, home of the waltz king. As my own 'party' was almost over, the title to this part suggested itself. 'Vienna' makes a very good hub for the wheel of these last happenings and the 'Canary Islands' and 'Malta' especially, two other areas of work generated by 'Dublin' are important spokes.

The Canary Islands – Work with Annie

In Dublin I was approached by personnel from all these places, and there started a correspondence which resulted first in my going to Tenerife in 1990. This was my first contact with the Spanish culture and the glorious siesta. How I loved the latter! We worked intensively from early morning till lunchtime, rested in the shade until late afternoon and worked again until early evening, all very sensible and civilised. We, or some of us, then partied from midnight onwards. It was hard-going and I wished I had been at least ten years younger, but I could not help being swept up in the sheer ebullience and fun of living which seemed to be prevalent. The work involved running the section on Young Learners. Once again, the learning curve for me was to find out as much as possible about *this* culture, the on-going work and teacher-training locally. It was yet another aspect of 'language across the curriculum'. I even managed a little sightseeing on this strange, moon-like island with its black sand. I was struck in particular by the contrast between the banana groves basking in the heat and the snows of the Teide mountain-top above them, a great crater which spouted lava as recently as 1957. I was struck also by the warm hospitality of the people, as our local colleagues introduced us to their relatives and friends who even opened their shops and taverns in the small hours if our party descended on them. I have a keyring with a tavern crest on it still in constant use. It brings back a special night of laughter and fun.

Tenerife led to 'Gran Canaria' the following year. I was flattered that I was one of three lecturers from the first conference to be asked back. So I found myself in Las Palmas and experiencing a little more of the Canary Islands. The important thing for me about this occasion was that I worked closely with Annie Hughes, the lady who wrote the Foreword to my Book 1. Each of us returnees had been asked to bring another in our field (both conferences covered a wide range of interests) and I asked Annie. We had worked together in both the British Council working party and the IATEFL SIG concerned with Young Learners. Though I had not up till then seen Annie in action, as it were, we enjoyed an empathy of ideas and educational philosophy, not only about the teaching of language to young

A happy night out in a shop which opened late especially for Edie's party

children but also about the place of language in culture. Annie also agreed with my story methodology. It is my book, *Story as Vehicle*, she refers to in her Foreword, the copy I gave to her in that taxi.

So Annie came to Las Palmas and brought her mother who was greatly interested in the whole proceedings. I think it was here that I began to see Annie as someone who might carry on my work. I had become known in the language-teaching world for the specialism which had developed in my later years, the work with young learners and in particular, since the publication of my book in 1989, my use of story in the context of Field and Focus. I had become coordinator of bodies which dealt in these matters and now found myself as a kind of international consultant. I had a wide parish. But I was also in my early sixties by now and I was beginning to slow down. I could see an end before very long for myself and I was concerned about my work going on. It was still a fairly tender shoot in the ELT environment. Did God send me Annie? She became my close friend and colleague and there were several other very able people working with her and keeping the flag flying for the little ones and for story and all that went with it. I could begin to wind down, but not quite yet.

Glimpse of Things to Come

The years from 1990 until 1993 were those of my last 'waltz'. Apart from work overseas, there was still much in Britain itself, both academic and professional, and the period also covered a Christmas 1990 visit to Zimbabwe to see Junko and Ian, parents of my godson, Tora. It also covered a world tour when I was away for three months. But perhaps most importantly, from the point of view of my continuing life's journey, I began at this time to look towards a new career in the church. I was accepted for training as a Reader. But there was no abrupt break. It was more of an overlap and a glide from one to the other. More of this in Part 3. But first my professional 'end-piece'.

I had three visits to Malta and two to Vienna in these early nineties, in both of which my English teaching was firmly put into multicultural context. Malta, the George Cross Island, strategically placed in the centre of the Mediterranean Sea and half way between Britain and the Arab lands, is a glorious mixture of culture and language. The native language, Maltese, has a large Arabic content and influence. English and Italian are spoken widely and the television programmes reflect all this. And my time in Vienna, particularly the second visit which was a conference in the International School, put me in the midst of many cultures.

Malta – Hard Work but also Play

My first tour in Malta was on the invitation of the university, a representative of which I had met in Dublin. I lectured to both staff and students and the visit was supported by The British Council. Through Graham Graves, their officer in Malta, I was introduced to school personnel and to the national inspectorate. I also gave my required public lecture. In the three weeks of the visit I was put in the picture of the highly complicated but rich cultural scene and its lingualism. I found myself in a kind of 'Zambian' situation once again, advising on language policy and particularly reading policy in the schools. As I had found so many times in my work, the cultural diplomacy I was supposed to be portraying verged on the political with a small 'p' and often pulled me further in that direction than I felt competent to deal with. It was all very challenging.

Within months I was asked back to Malta and this time my work concentrated on schools. I directed a course for serving teachers which was based in St Anton, a school which was a community-run establishment with parent governors who were fiercely and justifiably proud of their school and its development. They did not suffer fools gladly and were wary of outside advice. I learned such a lot from them. I also found it interesting to work with so many nuns and priests. In this very Catholic island, the church has a large place.

My third visit, in 1992, was a combination of work with the university and the schools, and the inspectorate took a large part too. There was an important local language project going on and we all had our part to play in this. The exciting thing for me was that without realising it I had become very much a part of Malta's educational picture, a kind of general dogsbody, with individuals as well as groups coming to discuss their work, and ask for my opinion. Working-groups of teachers from across the schools had been formed and these were chaired by university staff. I was asked to set tasks. The work was to be on-going after I had left. In fact all this had started during my second visit and much of the third was spent in assessment and setting more work. A further exciting thing was that I worked with Jennifer Jarvis of Leeds University. She had been to Malta on a consultation just before my first visit and her report was an inspirational spur to my work. We came together later. See below.

Special Memories

As always in my experience of 'all this and heaven too', I was privileged to have some time off, and how I enjoyed Malta! People were unsparing with their time and hospitality. I visited some beautiful homes and quaint old farm-houses. I enjoyed wonderful food and drink. I saw the historic places which also spoke of Malta's multi-culture, especially in Gozo, with its lovely golden, mellow stone. I went to something called 'The Malta Experience', and learned more of the heroic stance taken by the place in World War II. This last was filled out for me when I was asked to present the prizes at St Dorothy's Girls School, an ancient institution at the heart of Valletta. Here I met the old nun who had been headmistress during the war. In a quiet, sad voice she described conditions. Examination papers came from Britain by submarine and were returned the same way, to be marked. Malta was British at the time. The little archipelago was bombed to bits, not only by the Germans but also by erstwhile friends, its Italian neighbours, now on the other side in the war. Food was in such short supply that the people were forced to eat bulbs at one stage, and yet they survived. Now a thriving, independent country, Malta is a mecca for tourists who revel in its beautiful scenery and comfortable hotels. I only hope that something of the old fishing communities with their quaintly painted boats is still to be seen.

Other lovely memories for me are visits to the famous Manoel Theatre and that to the Scots Church, the latter on a steep hill near the centre of Valletta, the St Andrew's flag flying bravely from its pole. The church had joined with the Methodists, but these Protestant ventures had a hard time, I felt, competing with the large Catholic influence. Hardly a day passed while I was there without some reminder of this, especially the festivals in the country areas, accompanied by fireworks. The only thing about Malta that I did not like was the sport of bird-shooting. There was a continual slaughter of these lovely song-birds, many of them migrants from Britain. My heart bled for these creatures. I am a member of 'Animals Voice' in the UK and I told them about it. How I hope the practice no longer goes on! Though I did not return to Malta after that third time, I remained in correspondence and still am. Malta was a large part of my 'last waltz'. And my work there was rounded off when I met Jennifer Jarvis not long after my last visit. She was hosting a course for teachers in her department at Leeds University. Annie and I each gave an input, as did many of the people now prominent in the work of Young Learners. It was an important gathering, of teachers and teacher-trainers, of academics and publishers' representatives and an extremely useful meeting for both reflection and further planning. It seemed that the matter of Young Learners was at last being given both the academic and professional recognition it deserved.

Vienna – Centre of it all

The conference in Leeds had come just two months after the one in Vienna which gave me the idea for my title and which was a tremendous booster for Young Learners, no doubt giving some impetus to 'Leeds'. Vienna has a warm spot in my heart in spite of the intense cold of my first visit, which was in January 1991. I had met Franz and Tony in Dublin; they were in charge of EFL work in Vienna and wanted my help. I agreed to take part in their Expo Lingua, a huge operation in the centre of the city. I remember a day of non-stop storytelling in a vast building with what seemed like thousands of people milling round the stalls. There were many school children and their teachers. My own stance was near the cafeteria, and so I had to compete with the clatter of dishes and the shouts of kitchen staff. As one class of children after another was brought to hear an authentic 'English' story from an authentic 'English' speaker, my throat became gradually more and more hoarse and I needed the drinks which sympathetic teachers kept bringing me from next door. I was utterly exhausted by the end of the day and have no idea what I said to the lady from Radio Vienna when I was later accosted and interviewed. But Franz and Tony seemed pleased with their day and with my efforts on their behalf.

I followed this work by running a course for serving teachers whose English had to be good enough to understand my Scots! It was exciting to have some there from Bratislava, the capital of the new Slovakia, only forty miles from Vienna, but until recently very far away politically. One of these teachers came in late and was so embarrassed. Her husband had lost the way in the car. Later in the day she brought me a bouquet of flowers by way of retribution. On that visit I talked with Franz and Tony for long periods about the teaching of English and saw the materials they were producing. I was asked if I would write for them. Sadly I never did get round to this.

There was just so much else to be done, one thing in particular being to try and suss out a suitable venue for an IATEFL Young Learners' conference. This would be the first time that the SIG had organised one outside Britain. It was to be coordinated by Annie who had taken my place as Chair. It had been decided for all kinds of reasons that Vienna should be the venue but an exact place had yet to be established. With all the new-found contacts made in this first visit, I was able to discover the International School and its most cooperative staff. I spent time with both teachers and pupils who came from a great number of different nations. My visit here prompted me later to visit other such schools, and also those called European Schools, not quite the same but with similar aims. At this school in Vienna I had fun sitting next to a little German boy in a class which was learning geography in French. He was a helpful guide.

Franz and Tony and teachers from my previous course also registered for the conference and important truths were reiterated. There were high-powered personnel from many countries present and a fair representation from the UK. I was happy to see friends from Moray House College of Education in Edinburgh, my old alma mater and a place where I had recently lectured. There were also journalists from the various countries. One Italian lady chased me from pillar to post, finally pinning me down in my digs near the school. She interviewed me for her magazine. It was here at the Vienna conference that I suddenly knew it was almost time for me to go. I had reached a kind of peak and I was tired. But I was happy.

Goodbye to All That

What was left? My journal tells of several things, including the Leeds meeting I spoke of above. I continued giving advice to students and others, I carried on with my writing, more and more for a clientele I nicknamed the 'white highlands'. I wrote many chapters in edited books and articles in journals and my reviewing for publishers seemed to accelerate at this time. Then gradually it all slowed down and a new life began to open up for me. But there were two last meetings which, if anything, constituted my goodbye to my freelancing years. The first was at the University of Essex, in Colchester, a seminar of BAAL. My memory is of a leafy, spacious campus, where for some reason the lawns were covered by rabbits, as we moved between the residential quarters and the conference rooms. They seemed not to be disturbed by our constant comings and goings. I was conscious at this meeting of many new beginnings. There seemed to be all kinds of avenues opening up for linguists, including of course the rapidly developing world of technology. Had I been ten years younger I would have been happy to travel along them. But I had done my stint and rejoiced in the issues of yesterday! With a new-found sense of freedom, I listened to my younger colleagues, friends with whom I had shared some of my nomadic days, as they propounded future schemes in the last summing up session. I even raised a few questions which prompted the chairman to run after me as I left, urging me to pursue these thoughts further. He would be in touch. I didn't and he never was!

There was a barn dance on the final evening, one of the best social occasions I can ever remember at a conference. As I was partnered by Chris Brumfitt in one dance, I felt that the circle for me was closing. Chris had been one of my TEA students at Makerere in Uganda. He was now Professor of Linguistics at the University of Southampton and a prominent figure in the field. I basked in reflected glory. As I said my goodbyes the following morning, the same rabbits were sitting peacefully on the lawns and I was strangely comforted. I drove off and never looked back.

The second significant meeting was in The British Council offices in London. This was in the autumn of 1993. It was a meeting of the Young Learners working party where the statutory business was carried out. I had just returned from my three months world tour, more play than work, and I was already training for my new 'career' as a Reader in the church. I felt somewhat remote, though happy to see Annie and the others and to congratulate them on the success of 'Vienna'. They were interested to hear of my change of direction and my official standing-down was accepted. I did of course write an official letter to The British Council Head of Specialist Tours. But, how does a freelancer resign? I never really did that very efficiently. Besides, my British Council work, though a large part of my life, was only one aspect of it. Here at this meeting, however, just as at Vienna and Colchester, I felt that I was really going into the wings as the curtain came down. I left with the voices of the others ringing in my ears and knew a moment of sadness when I heard them sharing plans for new assignments and travel. I walked along Pall Mall towards St James's Street and Over-Seas House, my club and home in London. Like the rabbits at Essex University, the porters and reception staff were still there and so was Green Park as I looked from the window of my room. The last waltz had been played and the party for me seemed to be over, but as I thought of the young people I had just left I knew that my two-pronged role would continue and go on from strength to strength. And for myself, I felt a frisson of anticipatory excitement.

Part 3

Retired?

1993 and beyond

Continuing Life in Peterborough

THE OVERLAP

The early nineties were a strange time of overlap. I was in the process of changing from a cosmopolitan to a local which meant more time spent on home and community matters, at the centre of which for me was the church. However, until 1993 I was still engaged on my 'last waltz' in the Educational world, and was still away from home a good deal. But a piece had appeared in the EFL Gazette about my change of 'career' and after that last meeting at The British Council I began seriously to reorientate.

Many people wondered why I stayed in Peterborough. I could have moved during my freelancing period as it would not really have mattered then where I lived. Some expected me to return to Scotland. For several reasons I decided to stay put. In my busy, travelling years, I just had no time to move and later, it would have been a wrench. With all my flitting about, I had become part of the community and had acquired local friends and neighbours whom I would sorely miss. I liked Peterborough which had become a homely base. It had a lot going for it I felt. As for returning to Scotland, much as I loved and still do love going for holidays, I no longer saw it as home. It was so many years since I had lived there. My friends and even family members in Scotland had moved on, as I had. We no longer had the close intimacy of the earlier years, though I loved them all dearly and was always conscious of their understanding support. At the time of writing these things continue to be. I am still in Peterborough, but who knows what the future may bring?

FINDING A NEW PURPOSE

In 1992, not long after the burglary and just five days before I had to be in Vienna at that important conference, I moved from Orton Malborne to Orton Goldhay where I acquired a pleasant three-bedroomed bungalow with a small garden. I was much helped in the moving by John, a young jack-of-all-trades who sadly died of cancer a short time later. Without his assistance and that of Barbara, my cleaning-lady, who had become a very good friend, I would not have been able to manage. As it was, it was some time before all my boxes were unpacked and I could really call this new place home. Fourteen years later amidst new neighbours and friends and memories of those gone, and with new cleaning-ladies, first Gillian and then Maureen and now Jenny not to mention Ted, my gardener, I am very much at home and greatly blessed. I even acquired another cat, a tabby called Tigger, who became a personality in the neighbourhood. Only last year, 2005, did I have to put him down when he became ill and lost all quality of life.

Back in 1992, as I faced giving up my educational work, I had to decide on a programme to match my diminishing energies. But it would have to be purposeful. Knitting in front of the telly was not for me! In fact as life began to fill up I very soon gave up my television, and I never did acquire another. I still have a love/hate relationship with the media (see Book 1). I had joined a number of groups in the earlier years and had attended spasmodically. I continued now with these, joined others and attended more frequently. There was for instance the Civic Society, the local branch of the National Trust and that of the United Nations Association. I attended the Film Club and supported the Peterborough Symphony Orchestra. For a time I continued as a Soroptomist and even reached the dizzy heights of President but had to stand down as I was still travelling too much to fulfil my duties. Then, to my delight, I discovered the MASK Theatre company and was able once again to take part in dramatic activities in so far as time allowed. But soon, the interest which predominated was the church and I began to see a possible way forward as a lay preacher. Hence the notion of a change of career.

BECOMING A READER IN THE CHURCH OF ENGLAND

I don't quite know why this came about. Perhaps there was a mixture of reasons. The venture would give purpose to my new life, and preaching had much in common, as I saw it, with teaching and lecturing. Even the pastoral side of both had something in common. I remembered a teacher at a workshop I was running in Bristol saying to me at the end, "I feel like a jelly-fish which has just been given a corset"! It was an unusual compliment, to say the least. I wondered now if I would be able to give 'corsets' in my new career. Another reason for this way forward could have been that I was anxious to share that pearl of great price and this might be a good way of doing it. Whatever my motives, I spoke to Michael Soulsby, the rector at Holy Trinity church, and he put the operation in motion. It would mean that I must become an Anglican. I was not too sure about this, but eventually agreed and attended the confirmation classes along with the young and the mature, culminating in the ceremony conducted by the Bishop of Ely. But I have to say that I questioned the procedure a little. I was already a Christian and what I was doing now was surely only a matter of changing denominations, or so it seemed to me. Instead, I was made to feel as though I were coming to the faith for the first time. Also, something deeply Scottish and Presbyterian in me felt some discomfort at the thought of giving allegiance to the Bishop. But I went through with it and saw it as a kind of means to an end, as it turned out to be. I feel that just as 'York' made 'Bradford' possible in my professional journey so Anglicanism and the work of a Reader (the Anglican name for lay preacher) led to the Quakerism which has become so important to my spiritual way. I shall be forever grateful for this step and what it taught me.

Being by this time somewhat past my sell-by date and already a university graduate, I was given special dispensation for a shortened course. The usual three years became eighteen months. I enjoyed the tutoring given by two clergymen in their vicarages and I worked hard to produce the required essays. I became an avid reader of the journal called *Theology* and joined the local Theological Society. It was interesting and very good for me to be a student again. From time to time I had to go to Ely and meet with fellow trainees. I remember these workshops with great warmth. Meanwhile I continued my worship at Christian Presence and Holy Trinity, using both in my preaching debut.

As I had suspected, the preaching was much less of a problem to me than the rest of the service, particularly in Holy Trinity where the Anglican rituals were more strictly kept. But somehow I learned to do what was necessary and gradually I shared the taking of the services more and more with both the vicar and the other Reader, an elderly and very experienced gentleman who gave me much good advice. His wife ran the Tuesday Circle in the village and invited me on a regular basis to give talks to her ladies about my former adventures. I continued to sing in the choir and to write for the church magazine. After I was commissioned at Ely Cathedral and received my Readers' stole, I took more services and sometimes went to other churches in the diocese, and of course I shared the pastoral work and began to conduct christenings and funerals. At this stage I seemed to be more with Holy Trinity than with Christian Presence, which I still went to occasionally. It was quite difficult to be a member of two churches and especially now that I was part of the clergy team in one. Then almost suddenly there came a change.

Not long after I qualified, Michael Scott retired. He and Gretta were greatly missed, not only in the Christian Presence church, but in the wider community of Orton Malborne. They went to live in Dorset where Michael's grandmother had left him a cottage, and some of us visited them there from time to time. They are both gone now and we attended the funerals, as did people from Michael's previous churches. We also organised memorial services here. When they retired it was the end of a fifteen year era and Mick-the-Vic was not replaced, nor did it look as though he would be in the foreseeable future. Ian Cornall, a local Methodist preacher, and a member of the Christian Presence, kept the worship ticking over, bringing in visiting clergy to preside at the Eucharist and to take other services. Ian and I also preached and I tried to do some of the neglected pastoral work. Ian endeavoured to find out why no replacement was made and we were told that the Bishop did not really know what was wanted in Orton Malborne. Michael Soulsby at Holy Trinity, whilst helping with weddings, christenings and funerals, and conducting a service occasionally, found it difficult to take on more than the work of his own church. There was a tenuous link between the two, and it remained just that.

Running a Church

A New Commission

When four years had gone by, and how quickly they can in the life of a church, and the situation remained the same, it was agreed after much discussion in many quarters that I, as a Reader with Holy Trinity, should concentrate my work in Christian Presence and provide the pastoral continuity which was presently lacking. I would be supported by Ian in the preaching but not with the parish visiting as he was still in full-time employment and travelled. He was particularly helpful in another way however. Ian was our representative on the numerous committees which seemed to abound at that time, Churches Together, Local Ecumenical Project, Orton Team etc. and on his computer he produced copies of the minutes which kept us in touch, even if few of us fully understood what all this bureaucracy was about. Our concern was more with our own dwindling numbers and the need to build up the church again. Ian also liased with the Methodists for us while Mick-the-Vic had been here and he had forged a link with this church; we had been put on something called the Methodist Plan. This offered lay-preachers as a further resource. So, with such a pool of preachers to call on, including Ian and myself, and me to visit the homes, we plodded forward.

Sense of a Renewed Empowerment

There followed for me a wonderful time of challenge. I think I saw it as one of my British Council short, sharp assignments! Bearing in mind the main thrusts of the work we had inherited from Mick-the-Vic, concentration on the needs of the neighbourhood and the ecumenicism in which this inevitably resulted, I set about meeting the parishioners, visiting homes and hospitals, taking christenings and funerals, planning special family services and reaching out to the other churches in the Ortons. I started a Songs of Praise which was held on the first Sunday of the month and we joyously welcomed people from all denominations. The various incumbents shared the leading with me and the offering went to Christian Aid. We also began to move out from our own place of worship and conducted a service regularly in a complex for the elderly and another at Gloucester Centre, a home for the handicapped. This had been a favourite haunt of Mick-the-Vic who had become its chaplain and who had had a special kind of empathy with the patients. He even used to bring them and their carers to our Sunday services, himself pushing one of the wheelchairs. And the work at Gloucester Centre eventually became an inter-church venture.

In these ways we tried to carry on Mick-the-Vic's tradition. But perhaps it was the rebuilding of the Sunday School that marked the turning point from a holding operation to a building one. My former neighbour, Liz, came to the fore once again and made this her special work. As the numbers of children grew Liz needed help and we recruited one or two of the mums as assistant teachers. Then we ran a holiday club with the help of a team of young folks sent to us by the Methodist church (our Root Group had stopped a long time before). About eighty children came to the club and so great was the enthusiasm that we had to hold a repeat later in the year. The work was Bible-based but/and seemed to be great fun. It even attracted some wandering teenagers who came to mock and left strangely thoughtful. An important outcome of all this was the Friday club which sprang from it. This weekday activity was well supported. The

Taking a christening at Christian Presence Church

215

children began to attend in large numbers. And a special outcome of a different kind which arose from this club was an experience of my own. I was visiting the home of one of the children and found several of the neighbours sitting round the kitchen table with their mugs of tea and their cigarettes. "We were just wondering" said one "what Nehemiah is going to do next". Thinking this was about some new soap opera I had not heard of, I probed further, and found that the children had been learning about Nehemiah's building of Jerusalem, and had been building it themselves with matchsticks. I began to see that there was more than one way of doing Bible study! I also saw that through the children we might be able to reach the mums.

And speaking of Bible study, this did become a very important part of our programme generally just as it had in the early days of Mick-the-Vic. We met in different homes all over the Ortons, sometimes leaving our cosy Malborne to go to homes in other parts and to mix with people of other churches and denominations. It was a time of expansion and excitement. My own home, the new bungalow in Orton Goldhay, became a kind of extension of the community centre. On one occasion I remember there were twenty five in my living room. Sometimes these meetings took the form of a kiddush, a Jewish word which we hijacked. It was a house Eucharist which we shared ecumenically and rejoiced to be doing so. We included the Roman Catholics, one of whom, Mary Howell, had alerted us to the possibility in the first place. The same Mary became a strong support to Liz in her Friday club where we also had help from Barbara Looby, a Roman Catholic mum. We were doing more and more things ecumenically.

"MATURITY IN FAITH: CONFIDENCE IN MISSION"

For a couple of years or so the building of the worshipping group generally proceeded at a great pace and we really began to feel that we were answering the Bishop's question and showing him what was needed in Orton Malborne. As one Catholic attender said, we seemed to be turning corners which others hadn't even reached. But still no new clergyperson was appointed. And the congregation was increasing. Not that growing numbers are everything of course. And, mind you, there were one or two rather unorthodox happenings. Three that I remember well had to do with pubs. I had conducted a funeral and the 'party' afterwards took place in a Malborne pub. As I sat in the lounge bar, speaking with the mother of the deceased, a very pregnant lady approached and insisted on planning the christening there and then. In another pub I discovered that there was a regular meeting of certain parishioners who were questioning our teaching it seemed. The questions reached me through a spokesperson and my responses went back to the pub by the same means. All this seemed to me to be an interesting new form of church extension! I was delighted later to welcome a barmaid at our service. And still with pubs, I had on one occasion to send a godparent to fetch the other who was in the hostelry opposite and had forgotten the time, so we could get on with the christening!

The sense of new empowerment and the presence of the Holy Spirit were palpable. It even seemed right for us to celebrate the communion without benefit of clergy. In a sense I had become the vicar and people expected it. Let me elaborate a little. Near the start of my pastoral coordination I had been given a kind of induction. This was held in the Leighton Community Centre, our place of worship. It was attended by a large number of both clergy and laity from several denominations, and was simply a recognition of what I was already doing. I felt affirmed. I was humbly happy at being used by God in this way, and threw myself impulsively into what I saw as a kind of pioneering mission. I remembered the words of the Bishop of Southwark in his book, *For Such a Time as This*, "*Maturity in Faith; confidence in Mission*" and suddenly my Uganda pearl of great price became very important again.

People, including the church hierarchy, and the local ecumenical sponsoring body, were only too glad to give me my head. This worrying little church whose identity was somewhat nebulous and nobody seemed to know quite what to do with, now had an incumbent… of sorts! They could all forget about it and let me get on with the job. And had it not been for my old friend, Ian, who constantly advised caution, I should probably have run away faster than I did. He had been a reluctant supporter of my 'induction', not I am sure because he opposed me personally or felt that I could not do the work, but because he saw me as a kind of dog-in-the-manger, blocking the appointment of a 'proper' minister. He was probably right. He was also concerned about my age and about how long I could keep going. In fact, in the proposal of plans which I offered, I gave three years. I would then be seventy, the age when a Reader is meant to retire. And what then, if no appointment had been made? These were valid concerns.

Meanwhile was I not in loco sacerdotis? As the resident 'vicar' was it not my duty to preside at communion? The Christian Presence was used to having the Eucharist every Sunday. If this was to continue, it meant bringing in an ordained clergyperson, as had been happening ever since Mick-the-Vic had left. One of my main reasons for taking up this work was to give some stability to the pastorate. The visitors, whom I had christened the 'hit-and-run brigade', no matter how good their preaching, did not know the people and the whole sense of a church community became lost. So now, if I were not to take the communion myself, we were back to square one. The other thing I could do, according to the rules, was to fetch the reserved communion from a church where it had been blessed by a clergy person. I did this for a while and then found it just too exhausting, rushing from one church to the other. Also, I admit, I did question the rightness of it. Why should the elements blessed in one church be used in another? In the end, we settled for a visiting minister on the first Sunday of the month and I took the rest of the services with Ian helping but not taking the communion, whilst I did. I could not find any Biblical reason why I should not. I also felt that in these particular circumstances, the Church should have given me special dispensation. It seemed to me that the letter was more important to them here than the Spirit. Sadly this was all a bit much for Ian and his wife Linda who began to have feelings of strain. They felt that I had now strayed too far from base. And perhaps I had. Whatever the case, they left Christian Presence at this point and joined a more orthodox church, though we never lost them as friends.

ENTHUSIASM TO EXHAUSTION

And on top of all this hassle I had the problem of what I saw as the Anglican/Methodist axis hovering round us. In the village was Holy Trinity, to which as a Reader I was still officially attached, and because we were also on the Methodist Plan, there was the current Methodist minister into whose area we came. As the incumbent of Christian Presence, I was expected to go to innumerable meetings and attend to a considerable amount of paperwork in connection with both denominations, not to mention that to do with the ecumenical project. I became very weary of all this. I had offered three years and I saw my time slipping away. What

I urgently needed was assurance of a successor so that the mission work of Christian Presence could go on. There was still no move on the part of officialdom. It seemed that we had become a lone entity, exotic to any denomination and I have to confess that the whole notion of denomination had become unimportant to me. I even felt that it could be a hindrance! I eventually retired from my Readership but continued as pastor of the church. This way I got rid of many of the pressures but of course we lost our 'umbrella'. The church had become virtually independent.

UNEXPECTED OFFER OF HELP

For some time I continued, serving the needs as I saw fit. Before Ian left, we had established a Council, elected democratically in a kind of roll-on, roll-off manner. This proved to be a helpful move, especially now. Then, quite suddenly, there was the offer of assistance from an unexpected source. It came from one of the 'hit-and-run' brigade. This clergyman had been coming regularly for some years, even in the days of Mick-the-Vic. All of a sudden he was there at my elbow, offering all kinds of advice and more than that, offering to take over when my three years were up. It seemed just too good to be true. We would work together for a time and gradually I would do less and he would do more. It seemed to me and the Council that here was the answer we had been looking for. If I had not been so tired and desperate, I would have been more cautious. I was to find that it *was* too good to be true.

All was well for a while. I was thankful to share the load and to know that soon I could leave, with the church in safe hands. And then I went off for a much-needed holiday. We made a list of jobs to be done in my absence for both my 'assistant' and Council members. The most important of these for the minister was the parish visiting. In spite of many promises this was not done, nor were other things, too numerous to mention. For instance, we had discussed a new and exciting venture, the setting up of 'satellite' Bible study groups, run by members of our vibrant parent one. The neighbourhood was just right for this. The idea had come to me after I visited those mums of the children in our Friday club. They had asked for such a group and it had seemed to me that this would be a novel way of spreading the work of the church, not only spiritually but also socially. We were all set to launch the project and my assistant was to discuss and plan it with the parent group. Not only was this not done but the whole idea was discouraged. It was a turning-point for me. I began to have second thoughts about my successor and I realised that his agenda, whatever that was, differed from ours. The neighbourhood/ecumenical base of our being would get lost.

DISHARMONY

There came division where there had been harmony. Some of the church members who had only just succumbed to my assistant's charm and ready offers of help, as I had done earlier, could not understand my doubts and even suspected me of wrongful thinking. This was a very hurtful time. The Council was having difficulty relating to two 'vicars' who seemed to be going in different directions. One of us would have to go. As my three years were almost up I decided that it should be me in spite of my fears for the future of the church. I was loath to depart, leaving such an uneasy situation and the Council were unhappy to see me go. They offered my assistant a 'contract' of one year in the first instance, to prove that his agenda *was* the same as that of the church. And then, the scene changed again and things looked more hopeful. Out of the blue, one of the young men who had helped with our holiday club, asked if he might come and work with us for a year or so. Ric was considering going into the Church as a career. This was a great joy and of course his offer was accepted. At least we knew that *his* agenda was in tune with ours. I could go with an easier mind.

The Christian Presence gave me a wonderful farewell party. It was a lovely occasion attended by many members of other churches too and also non-church members in the community. I was quite overwhelmed by such a mark of appreciation. Amongst the presents I received was the 'blue book', my name for the loose-leaf file which had been lovingly filled with letters, photographs and other memorabilia of my three year ministry. It remains a great treasure.

END OF MY MINISTRY

And so I left, and had only just done so when my 'successor' sent a circular letter to every member of the congregation saying he couldn't stay because of my opposition to him! His abrupt action caused shock and great sadness for all of us, though I personally was not too surprised in the light of many other things. Obviously I could not go back. I was all the more grateful for our new young man. I wonder, in retrospect, if *his* coming was also something not on my successor's agenda! The wonderful thing is that, helped by Ric, the Christian Presence laity really came to the fore and began to realise the priesthood of all believers. With occasional help they took charge of their own services, several of them finding a talent for preaching, and those flickering candles began to burn brightly again. Now, a decade on and these sad things well in the past, the candles still burn and the depleted numbers are growing again. I feel that God wills it so and that the Christian Presence will continue to be one of His surviving remnants. In my present role of pulpit supply, I take the service there from time to time myself as does Ian and wish to record here in my memoirs the pleasure this gives me. I have mentioned few of the congregation by name for fear of leaving someone out but I wish to express my continuing love for them all and to say how much I admire them for taking the church into the 21st century with no permanent pastor and for maintaining a Christian presence in the neighbourhood. I do begin to wonder if pastors are really necessary!

I decided while once again on a world tour, unwinding and reflecting, that I had had enough of churchianity. At several points in my life Quakerism had impinged. It did so now and seemed to 'speak to my condition' as the Friends say, loud and clear. I had attended the Peterborough Meeting spasmodically over many years. Now I became a regular attender and was eventually accepted as a member of the Religious Society of Friends in 1998. I knew a peaceful feeling of having come home.

Becoming a Quaker

A Precious Pearl

As I write I have no regrets. My strength of faith as a Christian and sense of commitment have, if anything, increased. I suppose that to some I am a strange kind of Quaker, as part of my present commitment involves conducting services in mainstream churches, something I have been doing since my second 'retirement'. I feel that I do this job better since becoming a Quaker in fact. I wonder why this is so. Am I now more aware of the Christ or the Light within in the George Fox sense. Fox was the founder of our movement. I quote from the Epistle of the Quaker Britain Yearly Meeting held in London in 2004. "At the centre of our Religious Society of Friends, lies a precious pearl, the Truth that we know in our hearts. Let us be confident and not withhold the joy of this continuing discovery from the world. To strengthen our meeting, we need to tell others why we are Friends. We must face our fears of conflict and change, but also express our joy in our faith and community". I began to equate this Quaker pearl with mine. And I found myself agreeing with so much that was Quakerly, and realised that I had done so for a long time.

Out of the deep, meaningful silence of Quaker worship, I retrieved something of an inner peace, or perhaps I gained it for the first time. The 'rules' of denomination and the cacophony of churchianity receded, and in the quiet, broad-minded acceptance of my Quaker friends, I breathed more freely. I am convinced that my coming to the Quakers was not a matter of random choice in my place of worship. I suppose, the way I was feeling then, I could have stayed away from any church, as many do, reckoning that I could find God in the countryside or my garden, which of course I can. But I had, and still have, a strong need to worship regularly with others. I needed to belong to a worshipping community of some kind, and I am sure that it was meant that I should come to the Quakers. I did not hover over the church scene in Peterborough and let my pin descend idly on the Quaker meeting-house. There was a strong sense of inevitability and guidance. I just knew that this was right, and from an initial feeling of 'pick-me-up', there gradually grew in me a new sense of God being nearer than ever before. In retrospect I was able to discern many pointers and now, from the distance of some years, I can see that even my short stay with the Anglicans, and my experience of running a church, may have been an essential part of the lead-up.

DIVERSE LIVERIES

I began to find some answers to questions I had been asking for a long time, one in particular, 'What *is* the church?' I envisaged it now as something very wide indeed, a kind of global community of those who believe in the power of prayer and presumably in an entity to which/whom the prayer is directed. In my case this entity is God, a knowledge of whom I try to arrive at through the Biblical Jesus. But there is much room in my heart for those of different faiths and none. I still hear the voice of Nasma, that girl in my Kampala youth club, who questioned why we did not have prayer at our meetings. When I reminded her that she was Muslim and I a Christian, and that her parents might not like it, this fourteen year-old thought for a moment and said, "But Madam, same God". That certainly made me think, as far back as the sixties. Now when I read in our book, *Quaker Faith and Practice*, the words of William Penn, I find Nasma's innocent statement reflected. Penn said, "*And when death has taken off the mask, they will know one another, though the diverse liveries they wear here make them strangers*".

In some ways I see Quakerism as a dimension which runs through all faith communities. I have known so many who would not call themselves Quakers and yet they seem so. In a very real sense my so-called retirement has been imbued with this dimension, a thing of deep richness. My pearl of great price continues in a new way. Again I quote from *Quaker Faith and Practice*, this time the words of John Woolman, speaking in 1762. "*There is a principal which is pure, placed in the human mind; it is however pure and proceeds from God. It is deep and inward, confined to no form of religion nor excluded from any where the heart stands in perfect sincerity. In whomsoever this takes root and grows, of what nation soever, they become brethren.*"

MARY AND MARTHA

I feel that the various strands of my life, those journeys which I have spoken of so often, are being completed now in this new Light, a word very important to Quakers. As I bring down the curtain on my very active life, and I use the word 'very' to suggest that 'active' still remains, I consider the things that, with God's help, I am still able to do. These include taking services, giving talks, visiting in the community, writing, and continuing to belong to many groups and associations. The writing of this autobiography has been an active, verging on the very active, project. It is the 'Mary' in me which is reflecting, but 'Martha' lingers. I have squared the circle and, as I implied in the Preface to this volume, out of the 'focus' of these reflections, may come yet another bit of 'field'. Out of my mature faith, there may yet come more confidence in mission. The Book of James reminds us about the importance of works as well as faith.

> "What does it profit, my brethren, though a man may have faith, and not have works? Can faith save him?"

Was James also a Quaker?

Edie's 70th birthday, celebrated at
Christian Presence Church

With sister Dorothy, in the living-room
of Edie's bungalow in Orton Goldhay.
The cat in the picture above is Rusty.

Tigger at home

Edie's good neighbour and friend, Mavis
Chambers, in Edie's garden

Epilogue

I end my story as I began it in Book 1, sitting by that open drawer in my sideboard, as I have my Quaker quiet time. The scenes of the distant past have flickered and gone, and those of the present and possible future take over again. I become conscious, once more, of the sounds of Peterborough and the neighbourly noises of Orton Goldhay all around me. I feel greatly blessed in my adopted city of thirty years, and value very highly in my old age, the memories which have accrued here, the sharing of joys and griefs, the fellowship and fun. Not least I am thankful for the support given while I have been writing this book, support both moral and practical, over the five years of the project. It feels as though the work belongs to a great many people. And not only my Peterborough neighbours. I am grateful also to friends elsewhere and to family who have helped me by listening, reading, discussing, and criticising in love. Many had shared parts of my life and some still do. Their memories have both corrected and enhanced my own and I wish to record my sincere thanks. The more distant people also include Susan, Nicholas and Annie in York who gave so much help with Book 1 and continue with their support.

In particular, I am indebted to my brother Alex for his wise advice in so many ways, and to Jane and Margaret, each of whom gave me helpful support. My special thanks also to church and Quaker friends and to those who shared my educational and professional experience in Cambridgeshire and elsewhere, many of whom gave me a lot of time. I am grateful for their backing and for the enjoyment as we travelled down memory lane together. My additional thanks to Robbie for her advice on Traveller Education and for her help in many practical ways. And to Chris and Sue for innumerable useful sessions at their home and mine. I wish to express my appreciation also to Mike whose computer produced the photograph on the back cover and which also checked some of my facts. I take full responsibility for any further discrepancies.

Finally, a very big thank you to Ioan for his generous foreword to this volume and to Judith and Tony, Agnes and others at Little Gilding where I spent two very useful weeks researching and writing while they looked after me. And, seventeenthly and lastly brethren, as the Scottish minister might say in the pulpit, my thanks to Diane for her careful typing and quick understanding of both my ways and my handwriting and to Brendan for his meticulous proofreading. Again, any omissions or wrong commissions are entirely down to me. Finally, finally, my thanks to Able Publishing who made the finished work possible.

Quakers believe that their faith is a journey rather than a point of arrival. I certainly go along with that. If they will forgive my secular interpretation of this for a moment, I should like to make an analogy. As I have indicated, I contemplate more 'field' ahead after the present 'focusing'. For instance, I should like to go on writing and perhaps to try different genres. I should also like to do more travelling. Already in my so-called retirement, I have visited many corners of the world, sometimes places where I had worked like Sri Lanka and Australia, and sometimes places new to me such as the Baltic, the Arctic and China. I have also done two world tours, each of three months duration. I had thought of including something of all this in my present memoirs, but realised that to do so would have required at least one more book. Maybe this will yet come about. I should also like to take up my theatre work again, an interest which might have become full-time at one stage but which remained a contributor to my professional journey. How often in my story I found myself referring to drama and role-play! I might even venture also into the world of technology which I have more or less resisted up to now. At least I may bring comfort to some, in showing that a book can still be written without it!

But the Quaker sense of journey is a more spiritual one, and a large part of me still wants to share the message of this book. I continue to be propelled by that 'Uganda factor', supported now by the exciting presence in Britain of John Sentamu, our Archbishop of York. He is a Ugandan and an alumnus of Makerere College. It is possible that more opportunities will arise as I continue with my preaching and the giving of talks, and also in my input as a Quaker to the ecumenical and interfaith mission in the city. Peterborough is rapidly increasing in its diversity where lies, as one Quaker put it, the creativity of God. We are told by Jesus that our hearts are where our treasure is, mine still that pearl which I gained in Churchill's 'pearl of Africa'. Though the years are passing and my energies and Christmas list diminishing, I refuse to be sad. At the opening of Book 1 and the start of my life story I quote T.S. Eliot when I say, "*In my beginning is my end*". Now, as I bring the story to a close, but look nevertheless towards the possibility of further ploys and excitements, I venture to reverse the quotation, recognising the many fulfilled promises of the first. I finish then with the words of Mary, Queen of Scots, though I hope not in her context!

"In my end is my beginning."

Appendix

In Book 1 I said that I was dedicating my writing to all those who had helped me to find my pearl of great price. As I now complete my life story, this still stands, but I am extending the dedication to the many people who are endeavouring in any way to eradicate the scourge of AIDS and to alert the world about it. The disease is one of the worst threats to humanity in the 21st century. I was made very much aware of it during the later years of my professional travel and particularly when I returned to Uganda in 2002. I was greatly saddened by its effects, for instance, whole villages in Africa run by children as most of the adults had died and babies born already affected.

Any profits from the sale of this autobiography go towards the Church of Scotland Project cited below. Thank you for buying my book and may I ask for your further support. Can you buy more copies for friends or ask those friends to buy for themselves? Or, if you don't want to buy, simply send a donation direct to the following address:-

The Church of Scotland
HIV/AIDS Project
Freepost SCO 7200
Edinburgh
EH2 0BR

Edie Garvie
January 2007